PAUL SELIGSON
CAROL LETHABY
LUIZ OTÁVIO BARROS
TOM ABRAHAM
CRIS GONTOW

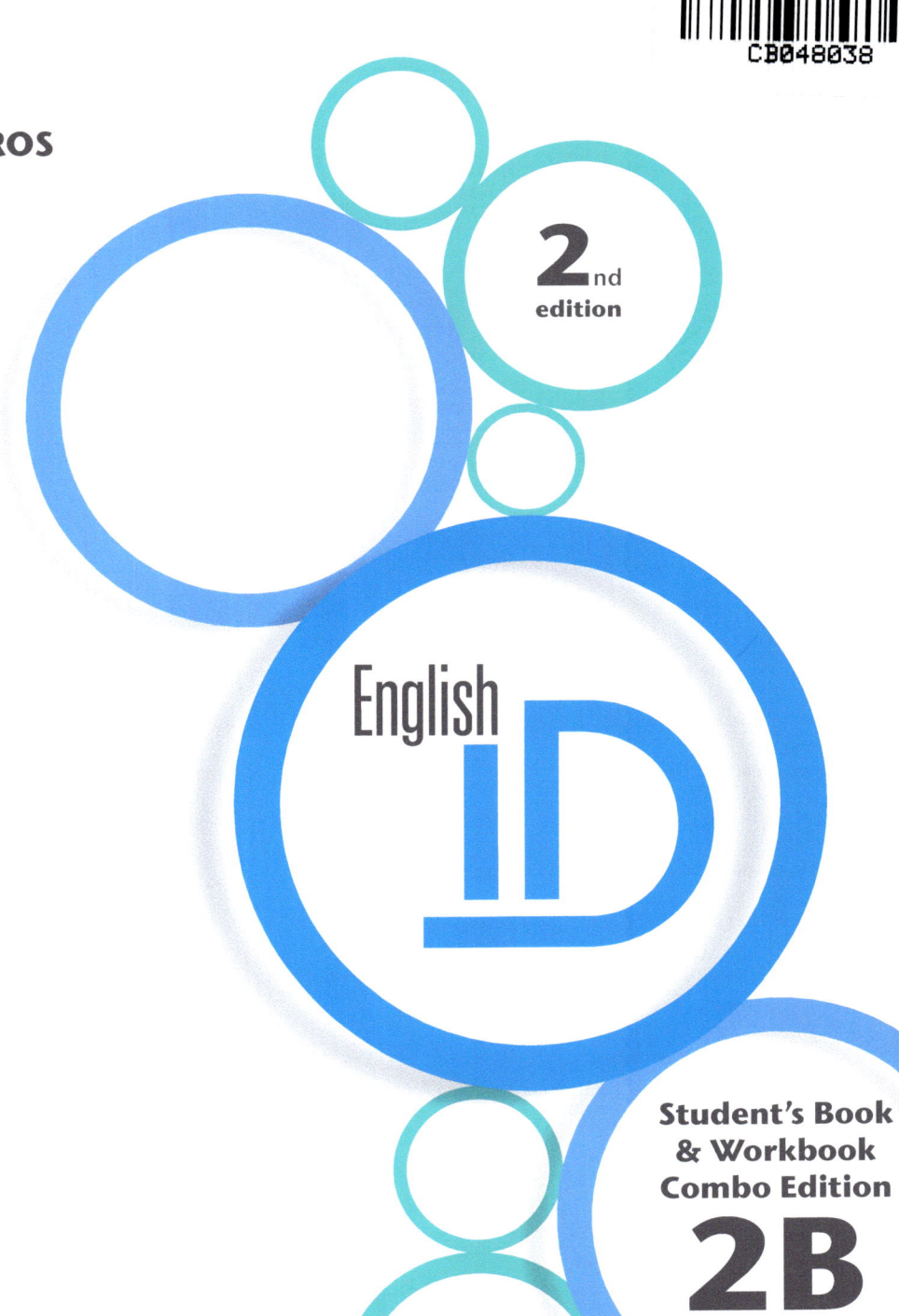

2nd **edition**

English ID

Student's Book & Workbook Combo Edition

2B

ID Language map

ID Language map

Question syllabus		Vocabulary	Grammar	Speaking & Skills
6	**6.1** Have you ever been to Florida?	Leisure time activities	*Go* gerund (verb + *-ing*)	Talk about leisure time activities Talk about a vacation in Florida
	6.2 Would you like to try hang gliding?	Verbs of movement	Prepositions Compound nouns	Talk about how you feel about adventurous sports
	6.3 Do you feel like going out tonight?	Prepositions of movement		Complete two descriptions
	6.4 What do you enjoy doing on your birthday?	Sports vocabulary Phrasal verbs	Verb + infinitive / gerund	Describe how to play a sport
	6.5 Would you rather stay in or go out?	Phrases to express preferences	*would rather*	Make decisions
7	**7.1** How often do you go to the movies?	Movie vocabulary		Write a movie review
	7.2 Are you crazy about music?	Passionate interests	Pronouns *some-, any-, every-, no-*	Describe a birthday
	7.3 What do you have a lot of at home?		*So & such*	Talk about world records Talk about unusual collections
	7.4 Who was Instagram created by?	Numbers	Passive voice – present & past	Talk about movies
	7.5 Are you a good singer?	Agreeing / disagreeing		Give opinions
8	**8.1** Are you into science fiction?	Technology	*At / in / on*	Talk about technology
	8.2 Do you ever switch off from technology?	Phrasal verbs	Phrasal verbs	Give instructions about using an app
	8.3 Will space vacations be popular soon?		Future forms 1	Compare predictions about life in the future
	8.4 Is technology making us more, or less, social?	False cognates	Future forms 2	Talk about the future
	8.5 Who do you talk to when you need help?	Signs of the Zodiac	Reduced sentences	Make fortune-telling predictions
9	**9.1** What do you think of marriage?	Wedding words		Compare weddings Talk about marriage & weddings
	9.2 Do you think romantic movies are entertaining?	Intensifiers	*-ed & -ing* adjectives	Express feelings
	9.3 If you had three wishes, what would they be?		Second conditional	Talk about unreal situations
	9.4 Have you ever performed for an audience?	Performers	*May, might, could, must, can't + be*	Make conclusions
	9.5 How do you get on with your siblings?		Pronouns	Talk about siblings
10	**10.1** Do you often feel stressed?	Causes & symptoms of stress *over / under*		Talk about stress
	10.2 Would you like to change anything in your life?	Lifestyle changes	*less / more / quit* Relative pronouns: *that & who*	Talk about lifestyle changes
	10.3 What's your attitude to money?	Money Alternative lifestyles		Talk about ways to get rich
	10.4 How often do you post on social media?		Questions review *How* + adjective / adverb	Answer a quiz
	10.5 Do you enjoy reading in English?		*one / ones*	Read faster

Audioscript p. 57   Answer Key p. 63   Phrase Bank p. 66   Word List p. 71

English ID

Welcome to English ID!

Finally, an English course you can understand!

Famous **song lines** illustrate language from lessons.

Lesson titles are questions to help you engage with the content.

Word stress in pink on new words.

Contextualized Picture Dictionary to present and review vocabulary.

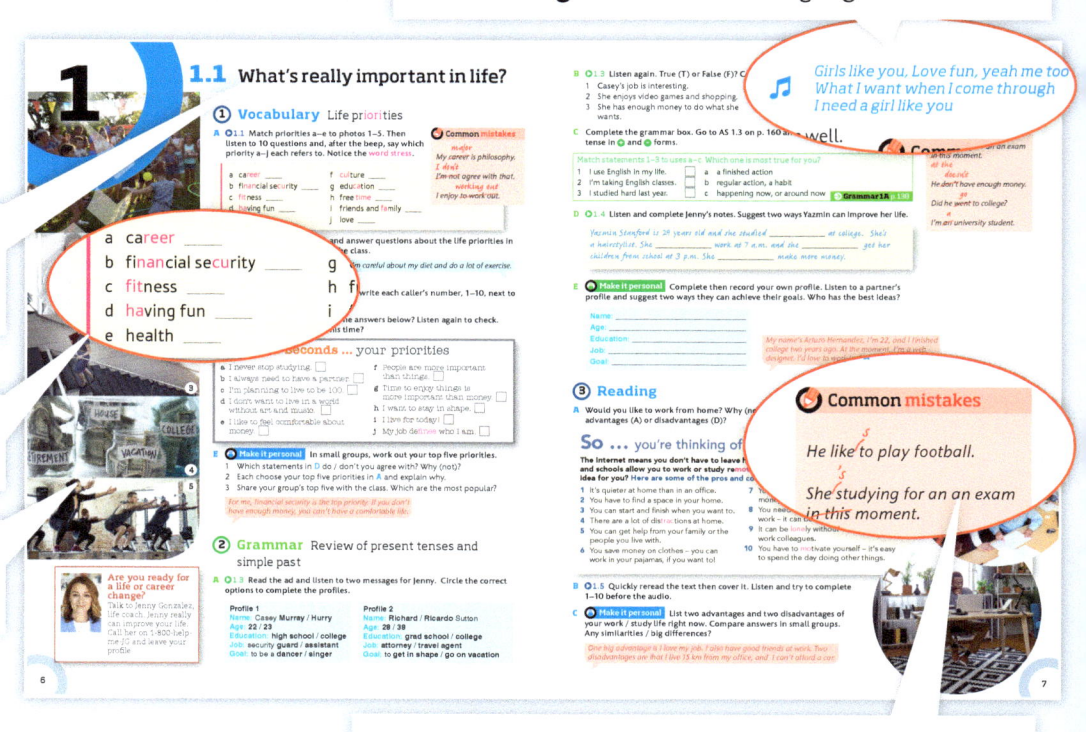

Focus on **Common mistakes** accelerates accuracy.

ID Skills: extra reading and listening practice.

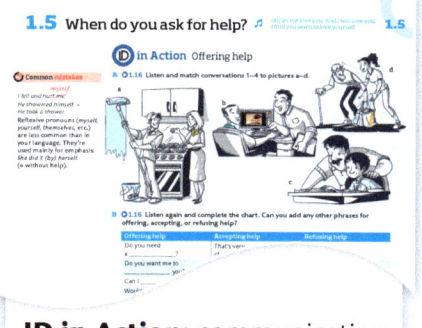

ID in Action: communication in common situations.

Authentic videos present topics in real contexts.

ID Café: sitcom videos to consolidate language.

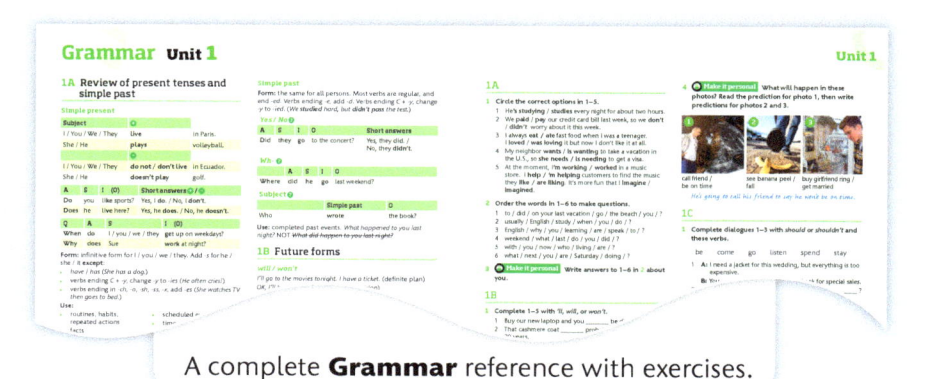

A complete **Grammar** reference with exercises.

Reviews systematically recycle language.

Stimulating **Grammar** practice.

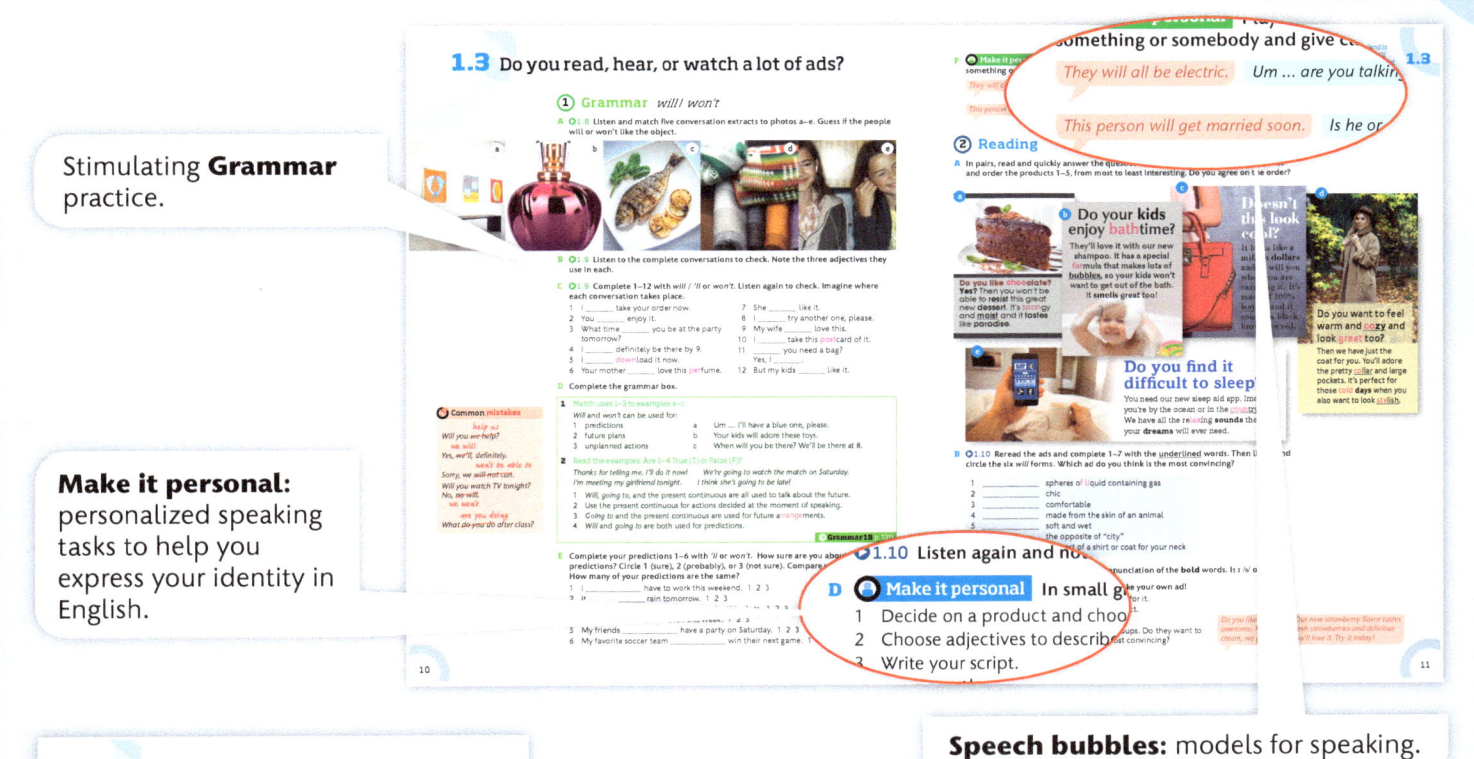

Make it personal: personalized speaking tasks to help you express your identity in English.

Speech bubbles: models for speaking.

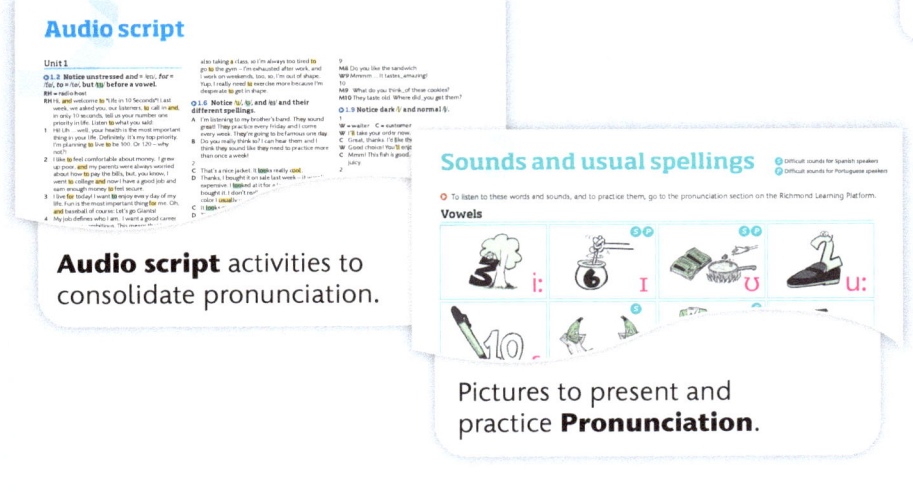

Audio script activities to consolidate pronunciation.

Pictures to present and practice **Pronunciation**.

Richmond *Learning* **Platform**

• Teachers and students can find all their resources in one place.

• **Richmond Test Manager** with interactive and printable tests.

• Activity types including pronunciation, common mistakes and speaking.

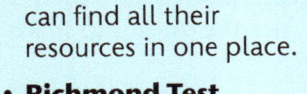

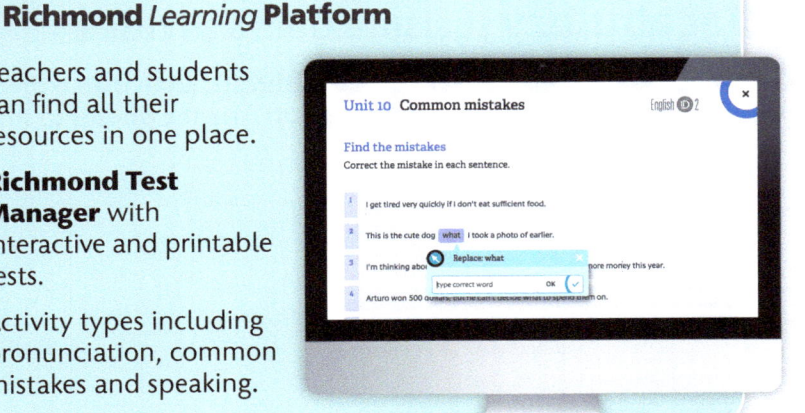

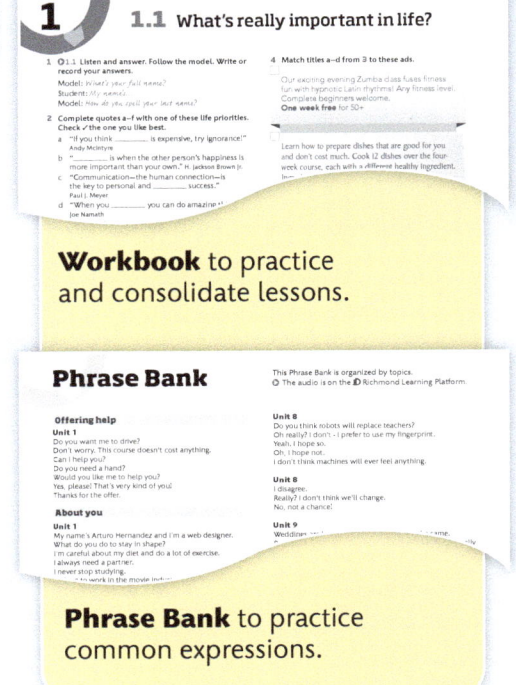

Workbook to practice and consolidate lessons.

Phrase Bank to practice common expressions.

Learn to express your identity in English!

6.1 Have you ever been to Florida?

① **Vocabulary** Leisure time activities

A ▶6.1 Use the clues to complete the verb phrases, then match them to photos 1–9. Listen to an ad to check. In pairs, use the photos to share your experiences. Any surprises?

bowl	camp	climb /klaim/	club	dive
fish	hang out	hike	work out	

- go _ _ _ _ s _ _ _ _ _ _ _
- go h _ _ _ _ _ _ _
- go _ _ _ _ p _ _ _ _
- go _ i _ _ _ _ _ _
- go _ _ _ _ l _ _ _
- go _ _ i _ _ _ _ _ _ _ _
- go _ _ _ _ _ b _ _ _ _
- _ _ _ n _ _ _ _ _ _ with friends
- _ _ _ _ _ _ _ _ _ _ _

I've worked out many times, but never on the beach.

I hang out with friends all the time. A group of us ride our bikes every Sunday.

B ▶6.1 **Listen again and write down the 13 adjectives you hear. Have you been to Florida? Where would you most like to go in the U.S.?**

🎵 *I got my hands up, They're playin' my song, I know I'm gonna be OK, Yeah, it's a party in the USA, Yeah, it's a party in the USA*

I haven't been to Florida, but I'd love to go!

When I was a kid, we went to Orlando. I remember being in a great theme park.

C In pairs, try to divide the activities in **A** into two groups: high risk (H) and low risk (L). Does the whole class agree?

I guess going bowling is usually safe. *Not always! Once, I pulled a muscle bowling.*

D 🔘 **Make it personal** **Read, then do the Florida visitor questionnaire. In pairs, compare and find at least two similarities and two differences between you.**

> 🔴 **Common mistakes**
>
> *Climbing is a high risk activity.*
> ~~*The climbing is an activity of high risk.*~~
> *Skating*
> ~~*To skate*~~ *is fun and good exercise.*
> **Use the verb + -ing as a noun.**

Visitor Feedback

Here in Florida, we want our visitors to have the best possible time, so we'd like to know exactly what you love doing on vacation.

Which are your two favorite:

- outdoor activities?   *going hiking*
- indoor activities?
- cold weather activities?
- warm weather activities?
- exciting or adventurous activities?
- child-friendly activities

My favorite outdoor activities are going hiking and swimming.   *Mine are sunbathing and swimming in a pool.*

② Grammar *Go* + gerund (verb + *-ing*)

A ▶6.2 **Listen and check the activities from 1A that Rosie did in Florida.**

B ▶6.2 **Listen again. True (T) or False (F)? What else did you pick up?**

1 They caught a fish.
2 They saw four different animals.
3 The rain came on the last day of their vacation.
4 They enjoyed the end of the vacation.
5 The tent survived the rain well.
6 Her friend seems very jealous of her holiday.

C **Read the examples and complete the grammar box.**

> *I always go shopping on Friday.* *I'm going skating tonight.*
> *I went skiing last year.* *What are you doing at the moment? I'm sightseeing.*
>
> True (T) or False (F)?
> 1 Verbs like 1–7 in **1A** can be used with or without *go*.
> 2 The *-ing* form after *go* is a noun.
> 3 Two of the examples are in the present continuous.
> 4 *Go + -ing* is often used for routines, completed, and future actions.
> 5 Use *go + -ing* to talk about what someone is doing right now.   ➡ **Grammar 6A** p. 148

D 🟢 **Make it personal** **Which parts of Rosie's vacation sound like fun? What would you do in Florida for a week? In groups, compare. Who has the same ideas as you?**

The first part doesn't sound like fun to me. I hate camping.

Really? It's not so bad if there are showers and a restaurant at the camp site.

6.2 Would you like to try hang gliding?

(1) Vocabulary Verbs of movement

A ▶6.3 Listen to the ad for an extreme sports company. Number the verbs in the order you hear them, 1–12.

- ☐ climb _____
- ☐ dive _____
- ☐ fall _____
- ☐ fly _____
- ☐ *1* get _____
- ☐ get _____
- ☐ hang _____
- ☐☐ jump _____
- ☐ race _____
- ☐ run _____
- ☐ swim _____

B ▶6.3 Match one or two verbs from **A** to each of photos 1–5. Listen to check, and write the preposition you hear after each verb in **A**.

2

3

1

4

5

C 🔒 **Make it personal** **Mime against the clock!** In teams, use the verbs and prepositions in **A** and take turns miming actions for your team to guess. Which team can mime and guess them all the fastest?

Are you getting into the pool?   No.   *I know. Are you getting into the bath?*   Yes!

I came to get down, So get out of your seat and jump around! Jump around! Jump around! Jump around! Jump up, jump up and get down! Jump! Jump! Jump! Jump!

6.2

② **Reading**

A ▶6.4 **Read and complete the website with these extreme sports. Listen to check. Notice which part of each compound word is stressed. Which word is different?**

bungee jumping   **cliff** diving   **hang** gliding
snowboarding   underwater **hock**ey

THIS WEEKEND: Five wild extreme sports!

1 | _____

It's kind of like surfing or skateboarding, but you do it on snow. For those who can't **stand** waiting for the good weather to go surfing again – this is a good option.

2 | _____

Do you like holding your breath? Divers who miss being in the water during the winter months, love this. When the outside water is too cold for diving, you just need a **snor**kel, a stick, and a puck, and you're ready to dive into to the local swimming pool for a game!

3 | _____

How about this? You run off the edge of a cliff or any very high place and hang from a bar with a sail inside a kind of big bag and fly like that. If you feel like flying – without a plane – this may be for you!

4 | _____

A person goes to the top of a steep cliff and dives off into the water below – how about that! Only for those who practice diving a lot! They say it's amazing!

5 | _____

Perhaps you prefer jumping off a bridge, building, or mountain attached to a thick e**las**tic cord that **boun**ces you up and down. Can you imagine doing this? A lot of people love it!

B **Read again and name the sport or sports 1–6 refer to.**
1 People do it when it's cold.
2 It involves flying.
3 It takes place in water.
4 You don't need any special equipment.
5 You need to jump from a great height.
6 It's a game.

C **Read the rule then name the objects in the photos. Does your language have compound nouns?**

Compound words are combinations: two words combine to make a new one, e.g. *boy* + *friend* = *boyfriend*. There's no strict pronunciation rule, but the main stress is usually on the part that describes the word, e.g. *boy*friend.

D 🎧 **Make it personal** **In groups. Which is the most and the least dangerous of the sports? Why? Which activities would you like to do and which would you like to watch? Why? Who is the most adventurous person in your group?**

I think hang gliding is the most dangerous because if you fall, you'll probably die!

I'd like to try cliff diving because I like diving at the pool.

Not me! I'd be too scared. But I'd like to watch it.

6.3 Do you feel like going out tonight?

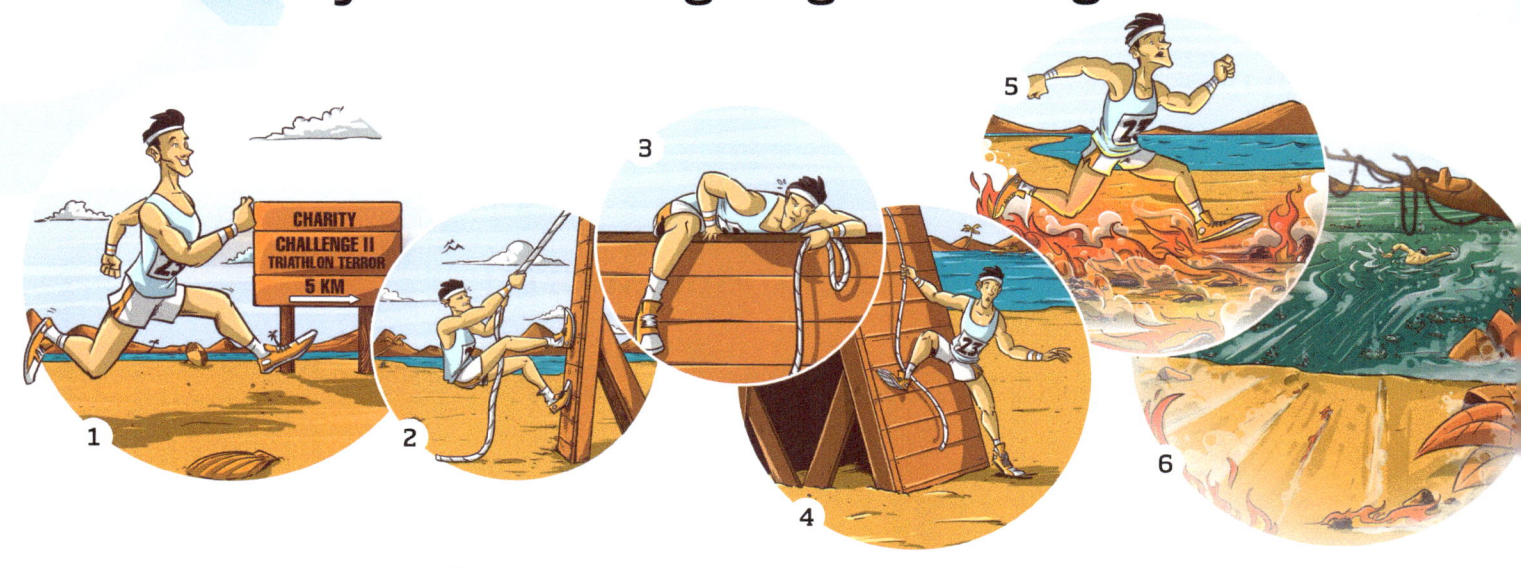

① Vocabulary Prepositions of movement

A ▶6.5 **Match the prepositions to pictures 1–12. Listen to a conversation about the event to check. Which six prepositions are exact opposites?**

a**cross** ☐   a**long** ☐   a**round** ☐   down ☐   **into** ☐   **out** of ☐
over ☐   past ☐   through ☐   to**wards** ☐   **under** ☐   up ☐

B In pairs, retell the story. **A:** as Charlie; **B:** as a TV commentator.

First I ran along the beach …   *And away he goes! Now he's running …*

C 🔘 **Make it personal** In pairs. Which of the race activities can / can't you do?

I can run five kilometers along a beach.   *Really? I don't think I can – it's difficult to run on sand.*

② Listening

A ▶6.6 **Listen to Martin and Jo discussing their plans and note the activities they like (✓) or don't like (✗).**

	Martin	Jo
surfing		
swimming		
bowling		
going to the movies		

B ▶6.6 **Listen again and complete 1–8. Whose weekend plan would you prefer?**

1 I don't feel like _____ hot and tired.
2 I don't really enjoy _____.
3 I really miss _____ to the beach.
4 I adore _____.
5 You keep _____ me that.
6 I can't stand _____.
7 When I met you, you started swimming and _____ with me.
8 I can't imagine _____ onto a surfboard.

⏱ **Common mistakes**

swimming
I can't stand ~~to swim~~.
playing
We adore ~~to play~~ basketball.
cooking
I'm responsible for ~~to cook~~ the dinner.
watching
She enjoys ~~to watch~~ Netflix in the evenings.
See Grammar 6A p. 148 for a list of verbs followed by gerunds.

I know you're really busy and I know you got plans, But are you really too busy for a sun tan? I ain't talking about walking down the high street, I'm talking about laying on a bright white beach

C Complete 1–6 with a gerund. Use your imagination! Then, in pairs, ask and answer. Were any of your questions similar? What was the most interesting answer?

1 Do you enjoy _____?
2 Do you ever feel like _____?
3 When you were a child, what was something you couldn't help _____?
4 What is something you can't stand _____?
5 Can you imagine _____?
6 Would you mind _____?

> *Do you enjoy eating ice cream at the beach?*

D Play *Mad Libs!*

1 Complete 1–10 with nouns and gerunds.

1 the name of a classmate _____
2 an extreme sport _____
3 an indoor activity _____
4 a town / place _____
5 something you often buy _____
6 an outdoor activity _____
7 the name of a friend _____
8 your favorite activity _____
9 an activity you hate _____
10 a bad habit of yours _____

2 Complete the postcard with your words 1–10. In pairs, decide whose postcard is funnier.

Hi (1)_____,

I'm really enjoying (2)_____ here in California.
Yesterday I took a break and I felt like (3)_____, so I went to
(4)_____ and bought (5)_____. Not too many, don't
worry! Tomorrow I'm going (6)_____ with my friend
(7)_____ and we both like (8)_____, so we're going
to do that. I hope we catch something!

The evenings are a little boring. I can't stand (9)_____, but
everyone here loves it, especially The Big Bang Theory. I can't help
(10)_____ when people are watching, so people get mad at me!

See you soon,

Gaby

E ▶6.7 🔵 **Make it personal** Listen and compare your postcards with Gaby's postcard. Did you use any of the same words?

> *I wrote "books" for number 5 because I love reading. How about you?*   *I wrote "bananas", I think I'm addicted to them!*

6.4 What do you enjoy doing on your birthday?

Sports For All
2020–2021 Catalogue

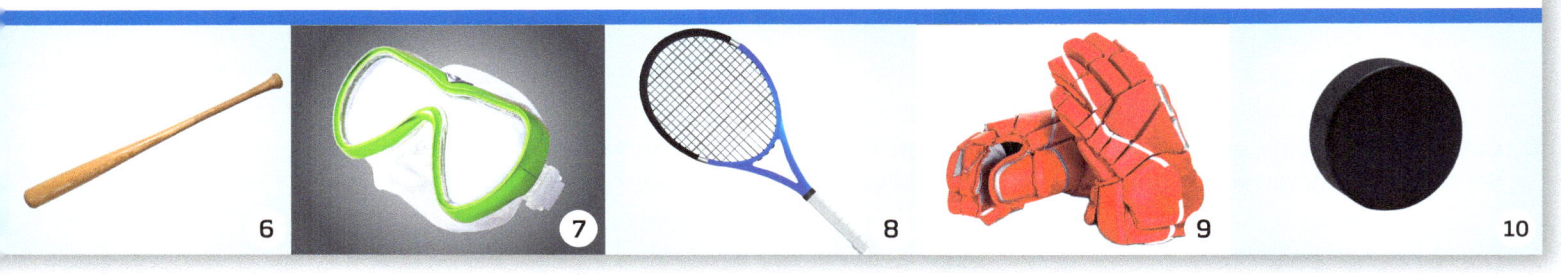

① Listening

A Match the sports equipment to catalog photos 1–10. Name a different sport for each item.

a bat ☐   fins ☐   gloves ☐   a helmet ☐   a mask ☐
a hoop with a net ☐   a puck ☐   a racket ☐   a snorkel ☐   a stick ☐

B ▶6.8 ▶ Watch / Listen and check the six items from **A** you need to play the game.

C ▶6.8 ▶ Watch / Listen again and order the instructions, 1–6.

Jump into the water. ☐   Line up on the wall. ☐
Swim fast to get the puck. ☐   Put your snorkel on. ☐
Put your mask on. ☐   Hold your breath until you score a goal. ☐

D ▶6.9 Listen and guess the sport after the beep.

E 👤 Make it personal   In pairs, write simple instructions explaining to a child how to play a sport. Read them to another pair. What sport is it?

You need a ball and a bat. The batter needs to hit the ball …

⏱ Common mistakes

~~score~~
You make goals by putting the ball in the net.

catch

hit

shoot

kick

♫ *My loneliness is killing me (and I) I must confess, I still believe (still believe), When I'm not with you I lose my mind, Give me a sign, Hit me, baby, one more time*

6.4

② Grammar   Verb + infinitive / verb + gerund

A In pairs, use the photos to brainstorm five facts about Las Vegas.

It's the biggest city in Nevada.

B Read Laura's email. Does she mention all your ideas?

> Dear all,
>
> It's my 30th birthday in April and I've **decided** to do something really different! So, I'm writing to see if any of you **want** to join me on my adventure. You all know how I **adore** driving, especially at high speeds. Well, for the first time ever I'm going to Las Vegas! No, not to drive around the casinos – I hate gambling! I've chosen Vegas because they have an awesome racetrack there. Check it out on the website!
>
> So, who'd like to come with me? There's so much other stuff to do in Vegas too. If you'd **prefer** to catch a show, stay at the hotel and just swim and relax, get a helicopter across the desert to the Grand Canyon, or go to the casinos, whatever, that's fine.
>
> If you prefer watching me drive to driving yourself, that's fine too. But I really hope you all **agree** to come!! Oh, and remember, what happens in Vegas stays in Vegas! 😃 So, don't **forget** to message me soon to let me know if you can make it.
>
> Lots of love, Laura xxx

C ▶6.10 Listen, reread, and repeat the pink-stressed words. Are 1–5 True (T) or False (F)? Which of the activities she suggests would you prefer to do?

1 Laura loves driving, particularly when she can go fast.
2 She chose Las Vegas because there are great hotels and shows.
3 After driving with Laura, her friends can all do what they want.
4 She says she'd prefer her friends to go driving with her than stay at the hotel.
5 She tells her friends to look at the hotel website.

D Complete the grammar box with the **highlighted** words from the email in B.

> Some verbs combine with a gerund (the *-ing* form of the verb), others combine with the infinitive, and some verbs combine with both.
>
> | **Verb + gerund** | **Verb + infinitive** | **Both** |
> |---|---|---|
> | _____, dislike, enjoy, finish, keep, practice, quit | _____, ask, _____, choose, expect, _____, hope, _____ | begin, continue, hate, like, love, _____, start |
>
> ➡ **Grammar 6B** p. 148

Common mistakes

~~to~~
I decided ^to do something.

~~to call~~
Don't forget ~~calling~~ me later.

~~on paying~~
They insisted ~~to pay~~.

E ▶6.11 Complete Jack's reply using these verbs. Listen to check. Notice *to* = /tə/ or /tuː/.

come (x2)   drive (x 2)   gamble   invite   meet   stay

> Hi, Laura!
> It's Jack. What a great idea for your birthday! I really enjoy _____ too, so of course I'd love _____ with you to the racetrack. It looks amazing! I've talked to Margo and she's agreed _____ us in Vegas. She's decided _____ a day later than me as she doesn't want _____. But … she adores _____ – I hope she doesn't lose all our savings! – so she wants _____ at a hotel while we go. So … WE'RE COMING! Yay!
>
> PS As a birthday present, we'd like to _____ you for a helicopter trip. As long as you don't insist on flying it!

F 🔴 **Make it personal** Write a reply to Laura and record it. Compare in pairs. Do you want to do the same things?

You want to gamble, but I don't like to gamble.

79

6.5 What's the highest place you've been to?

ⒹⒾ Skills Guessing meaning

A Read Margee's blog and check how she felt walking 356 m in the air.

	Before the walk	During the walk
confident and excited		
terrified and uncomfortable		
relaxed and thrilled		

Margee's blog

EdgeWalk in Toronto is the CN Tower's most thrilling attraction. It's the world's highest full circle hands-free walk on a 5 ft (1.5 m) wide ledge encircling the top of the Tower, 356 m / 1168 ft (116 stories) above ground.

I remember when I found out about the CN Tower EdgeWalk – I was Googling "terrifying experiences" and it was the first one to pop up. I thought that it would be quite an easy experience that wouldn't be too scary. I've never really been afraid of heights, so I felt confident I'd feel fine hundreds of feet in the air. I was very wrong.

The first thing that impressed me was the very thorough check and preparation for the EdgeWalk. This level of precaution usually means some very scary stuff is about to happen. At this point, I was excited, but not scared.

I was completely unprepared. It was terrifying. I stepped out onto the platform and felt a wave of fear wash over me. I felt like I forgot how to walk for a moment but at the same time I wanted to run away! The guide, Margo, started explaining what we were going to do and I realized I wasn't listening to anything she said. Then I was worried I'd do something wrong.

I had no idea I'd be as scared as I was, and I had a really, really hard time leaning out over that edge. Everything in my body was screaming "THIS IS A BAD IDEA! YOU CANNOT FLY!", even though rationally I knew I was safe and secure. I kept reminding myself that the harnesses are designed to hold hundreds of pounds and that it was impossible to fall. But then you start thinking, "What if THIS TIME the harness breaks?" It's ridiculous to think this – it's just not going to happen. But that's what my body was telling me – DANGER!

Each time I thought about falling, I could feel my entire body start shaking. It was terrifying and uncomfortable, but you have to take a breath, remind yourself you're safe, and relax. After about 10 minutes I leaned out over the edge and the feeling was out of this world!

B ▶6.12 **Listen, reread, and put the events in order, 1–9.**

- ☐ She leaned out over the edge.
- ☐ The guide explained the instructions.
- ☐ She started to relax.
- ☐ She stepped out onto the platform.
- ☐ There was a detailed preparation for the walk.
- ☐ She felt excited.
- ☐ She thought she was going to fall.
- ☐ She started to feel very scared.
- ☐ She Googled the CN Tower EdgeWalk.

C **Use context to circle the correct meaning of 1–8.**

1. to pop up – to appear **suddenly** / **slowly**
2. heights – **high places** / **tall people**
3. a ledge – **narrow** / **wide** surface that projects from a wall or rock
4. to lean out – to **move your body from a vertical position** / **sit down on a chair**
5. a harness – a **part of the body** / **piece of equipment**
6. to shake – to **move uncontrollably** / **stay completely still**
7. stories – number of **floors** / **rooms** in a building
8. fear – **being afraid of** / **enjoy** someone or something

D **Find five words in the blog that you don't use yet, but are similar in your language. Compare in groups and help each other with pronunciation.**

E 🔒 **Make it personal** Would you like to do the EdgeWalk? Why (not)? Are you or any people you know afraid of heights, spiders, snakes, dogs, open or crowded spaces, or thunderstorms?

Yes, I'd definitely do it, because I love feeling scared!

6.5 Would you rather stay in or go out?

ID in Action Expressing **pref**erences

A ▶6.13 **What did they decide to do? Listen and circle the correct picture.**

1 2 3 4

B ▶6.13 **Complete the dialogue with these words. Listen again to check.**

'd rather (x 2)   do (x 4)   feel like   like (x 2)   prefer (x 3)   would

A: What _____¹ you want to do this evening? _____² you want to go out?

B: I think I _____³ stay in.

A: _____⁴ you _____⁵ to cook or order in?

B: You know me, I always _____⁶ someone else's cooking!

A: Mmmm, yes. Well, _____⁷ you _____⁸ pizza or Chinese food?

B: I _____⁹ Chinese food better, but I _____¹⁰ eating pizza.

A: OK. _____¹¹ you _____¹² Alice's or Eric's better?

B: I _____¹³ order from Alice's. They're faster.

A: OK, great. Sounds good to me.

C **Decide if 1–10 refer to a general preference (GP) or a preference on a specific occasion (SO). In pairs, ask and answer 1–7. Then complete the chart.**

1 Do you prefer to read or listen?
2 Did you use to like to read comics?
3 Do you want to learn some new words?
4 Would you rather study at home or at school?
5 Would you like a hot or cold drink?
6 Would you like to see some apps?
7 Do you like speaking English?
8 I'd like to pass the English test.
9 I'd rather study at home.
10 I want to pass the English test.

Asking about general preferences	Asking about preferences on a specific occasion	Expressing general preferences	Expressing preferences on a specific occasion
_____¹ you prefer (to) …?	Would you like (to) …?	I like to + verb	I'd like to + verb
_____² you like (to) …?	Would you rather … ?	I like + _____⁵	I'd prefer to + verb
	_____³ you prefer (to) …?	I prefer to + verb	I'd rather _____⁷
	_____⁴ you want (to) …?	I prefer + _____⁶	I want to + verb
			I want + noun
			I feel like + _____⁸

D **In pairs, use the dialogue in B as a model to talk about options 1 or 2.**

1 watch TV / go to the movies
   see action / comedy
   eat popcorn / candy

2 go running / go for a walk
   in the country / in the city
   go for an hour / two hours

E **Make it personal** **Difficult decisions!** **Think of two options in any situation and ask classmates to decide between them and give a reason. Which is the most difficult decision to make? Who had the best reply and reason?**

Would you rather eat alligator or snake?

I'd prefer to eat snake, because I think it would be more tender than alligator!

Know with all of your heart, you can't shake me, When I am with you, there's no place I'd rather be, N-n-no, no no, no place I'd rather be

Writing 6   An adventure vacation blog

A Look at the photos and read the extracts from Adam's blog. Which activity would you prefer to do, and why?

Day 2: Hiking in the forest

Today we carried backpacks and all our camping equipment. At first it was easy, as we were walking along clear paths through trees. But after a while the path started to go up the side of the mountain. We walked uphill all afternoon – it was really tiring. Finally, we reached the top where we were going to camp. The views across the valley were absolutely magnificent. It was definitely worth the climb. We arrived at the campsite just before 5:00. By then, we were all completely exhausted, so we ate supper and then went straight to bed.

Day 4: On a glacier

What a day! Totally awesome. Before starting, the guides told us always to hold onto the ropes. They explained that during the day, the ice melts a little, so you have to be extremely careful. We actually walked inside the glacier. On the narrow ice paths, you could look down into deep crevasses – that was absolutely terrifying. In the afternoon, we tried ice climbing using ropes and special equipment. My friend Louis slipped and nearly fell, but the guides were amazing. When they saw what was happening, they were instantly there to help. Later, we laughed about it, but it made me realize that glaciers are not only beautiful, but also incredibly dangerous.

B Reread. Are 1–8 True (T) or False (F)?
1. The hike started out difficult but got easier.
2. It took a long time to reach the top of the mountain.
3. When Adam reached the top, he wished he hadn't made the effort.
4. They were already very tired when they got to the campsite.
5. The guides explained the risks of being on a glacier at the beginning of the day.
6. They spent most of the day ice climbing.
7. The guides were slow to react when Louis slipped.
8. Adam and Louis enjoyed most of their experience of being on a glacier.

C Look at the highlighted time expressions in the blog and read **Write it right!** Then reread the blog and find:
1. four more time expressions.
2. six adverb-adjective combinations describing a place or activity.
3. two adverb-adjective combinations describing how someone felt or behaved.

✓ Write it right!

When you're describing an experience:
- use time expressions to help the reader understand exactly when things happened: *at first, after a while, by then, during (the day), in the morning / afternoon, later.*
- use adverbs to intensify adjectives: *absolutely, completely, extremely, incredibly, really, totally.*
  - *absolutely, completely, totally* can be used only with non-gradable adjectives (*absolutely freezing, totally impossible*)
  - *very, extremely, incredibly* can be used with gradable adjectives (*extremely interesting, incredibly high*)
  - *really* can be used with any adjective

D Complete the blog with these expressions.

absolutely fantastic   after a while
at first   before starting   by then
during the morning   extremely useful
really hungry   totally amazing

> **Day 5: Kayaking**
>
> Today we went kayaking. Our guide was Lauren, and [1] she gave us a safety talk which was [2]_____. Then we started paddling. [3]_____ it was quite hard, but [4]_____ things improved. [5]_____ the weather was calm and we saw a lot of seabirds. At 1:00, we stopped for lunch – [6]_____ we were all [7]_____. In the afternoon, the weather got worse and we had to return to the beach. On the way, we met a family of dolphins, which was [8]_____, as they are quite rare here. Later, we all agreed it had been an [9]_____ day.

E Imagine you're on a two-day adventure vacation. Choose two or three experiences and make notes about what you did and how you felt about them.

F 🔵 **Make it personal** Write a blog about your adventure vacation in 150–200 words.

Before	Use your notes in **E**. Look back at the blog in **A** and underline any words or phrases you could use in your own blog.
While	Order your blog using a variety of time expressions. Use adverbs to intensify adjectives correctly.
After	Exchange blogs with another student. Check each other's use of time expressions and adverb-adjective combinations.

6 Brains vs. brawn

 **ID Café**

① Before watching

A Read the definition. Is the example true for you? Do the sports in the chart require more brains or more brawn? Check the correct word for each sport.

brawn ◀ /brɔn/ *n.* Muscular strength. Often used to compare physical strength to intelligence.
"Most people prefer brains over brawn."

	Brains	Brawn
boxing		
chess		
golf		
rock / wall climbing		
skateboarding		
skiing		
soccer		
swimming		
table tennis		
video games		

B ⭕ **Make it personal** Which are "real sports"? Which two do you like best a) to watch b) to do?

I love going swimming, and I love watching soccer.

C Guess which two activities Rory, Daniel, and August are each good at.

② While watching

A Watch up to 3:08 to check. How do August (A), Daniel (D), and Rory (R) feel about these activities? Complete the chart. Some activities have two answers.

	Likes	Is good at	Hates
wall climbing			
playing golf			
playing video games			
playing table tennis			
using muscles / strength			
using speed and precision			
climbing quickly			
winning at games			

B In pairs, try to pronounce these words correctly. Watch again to check. Who's the most competitive? What else did you pick up?

enemy	balanced	courage	pure
battle	precision	honestly	proven
admire	champion	strategy	victory
muscle	require	challenge	

C Guess how the episode ends. Watch with sound off to check. Was your guess close?

Maybe August is too afraid to climb?

D Watch again with sound on, and note the five times you hear.

③ After watching

A True (T) or False (F)? Correct the false ones.

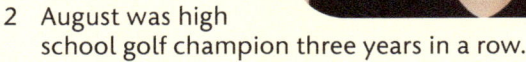

1 August loves defeating his enemies, and his friends.
2 August was high school golf champion three years in a row.
3 Daniel prioritizes balance, and really needed to get out of the house.
4 August challenges the others at two activities.
5 Daniel doesn't think he'll beat August on the wall.
6 Daniel and Rory aren't happy about August's victories.

B Check the correct situation for each phrase.

	Agreeing to participate	Reacting to someone's victory
You're on!		
Not again! I can't believe this.		
It's luck. It's gotta be pure luck.		
I don't know how he does it.		
Great job!		
OK … you win!		

C ⭕ **Make it personal** In pairs, compare "unexpected victory" stories you know. Which was the biggest shock?

I'll never forget the 2018 World Cup, when Germany lost to Japan, two nil.

Yeah! How did that happen?

R3 Grammar and vocabulary

A **Picture dictionary.** Cover the words on these pages and use the pictures to remember:

page	
58	18 school subjects
60	10 classroom tasks
67	a warning and a promise for 3 situations
72	9 leisure time activities
74	5 extreme sports
76/77	the 12 parts of Charlie's triathlon
78	10 items of sports equipment and the sports you use them for
79	5 attractions in Las Vegas
155	the first 8 pairs of picture words for the consonants

B ▶R3.1 Complete the sports club's poster. Listen to check.

Premier Sports Club offers _____ a fabulous variety of activities. You can go _____ on our new 15–meter wall, or maybe you would _____ to go _____ in our heated 25-meter pool. If you want to get in shape, why not _____ out in our fully-equipped _____? For more relaxing activities, we have 12 ten-pin lanes where you can go _____ with your friends, or you can just _____ out in our café and enjoy our delicious, healthy food and _____. All for just $49 a month!

C ▶R3.2 Use the photos to write the five pool rules. Listen to check. Which are good rules and which ones aren't? Change the ones you don't like.

Children have to …   *You can't …*

D Complete 1–4. Make a first conditional chain (minimum five steps) for each. Any funny ones?

1 If the weather's good this weekend, I'll _____.
2 I won't _____ if _____.
3 If I don't pass this class, _____.
4 I'll _____ if I don't _____ .

If the weather's good this weekend, I'll play soccer.

If I play soccer, I'll see my friend Roberto and then if I see Roberto, …

E Match 1–5 to a–e to make facts about the human body.

1 If people eat too many calories,
2 If we don't get enough sleep,
3 If people have too much sugar,
4 When your body is too hot,
5 If we don't eat anything,

a your heart beats faster.
b we can survive for about 50 days.
c we can go crazy.
d they can lose their teeth.
e they get fat.

F ▶R3.3 Listen to the beginning of Clara's presentation and complete the chart.

Name:	Clara _____
Age:	
From:	
Living in:	
Reason:	
Leaving In:	

G ▶R3.4 Listen to the rest of Clara's presentation. After each pause, predict the form of verbs 1–8. Will it be *to* or *-ing*?

1 travel   3 study   5 speak   7 go
2 go   4 pay   6 pass   8 study

H Correct the mistakes. Check your answers in units 5 and 6.

⊘ **Common mistakes**

1 *Do you have a master degree?* (1 mistake)
2 *How many homeworks do we have to make?* (3 mistakes)
3 *You have to assist to class every day.* (2 mistakes)
4 *Kim is too tall. She's enough tall to play basketball.* (2 mistakes)
5 *If you will lose any classes, you'll fail.* (2 mistakes)
6 *We haven't to read that book, but we can if we want to.* (1 mistake)
7 *We want go shop after work.* (2 mistakes)
8 *Before to eat dinner let's go to jog.* (2 mistakes)
9 *Jack can't stand to wait for her daughters.* (2 mistakes)
10 *You prefer stay at home or going out?* (2 mistakes)

Skills practice

A In pairs, play **Promises, promises!** Write an *If you* clause with a favor you want someone to do for you. Exchange papers and complete your partner's sentence with a promise. Read them out and vote for the funniest one in the class.

> *If you wash my car,*   *I'll let you borrow it.*

B ▶R3.5 Complete Ben's directions with the correct prepositions. Listen to check.

> Hi Lena!
>
> So, here's how to get to my house again.
>
> First you go _____ a long street called York Street. Then you go _____ a tunnel. When you come _____ the tunnel you walk _____ a park and you go a footbridge. Then you walk _____ the street and my house is number 25 York Street. It's the purple one ____ the left. Call me if you get lost, OK?
>
> Can't wait _____ see you!
>
> Ben Xx

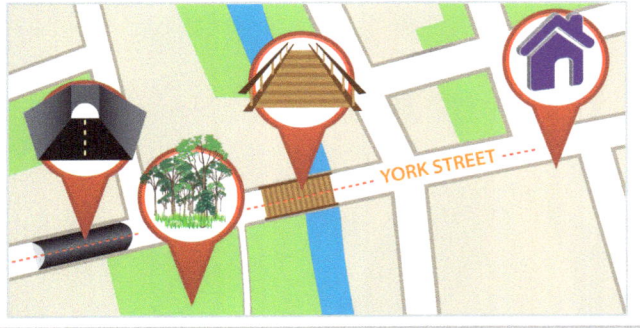

YORK STREET

C Read the ad and answer 1–3.
1. Where's Crocosaurus Cove?
2. Can you touch a crocodile?
3. What other animals can you see there?

Crocosaurus Cove!
Visit Australia's premier crocodile attraction!

An amazing, unique experience and only an hour from downtown Cairns.

- Jump into the "Cage of Death" to swim with saltwater crocodiles (age 15+).
- Hold a baby saltwater croc for a magical selfie.
- Visit our aquarium, full of exotic fish, coral, and sharks!
- See the largest turtle sanctuary in Queensland.

D ▶R3.6 Listen to a conversation about the "Cage of Death." True (T), False (F), or Not mentioned (N)? Correct the false ones.
1. The plastic cage is just one inch thick.
2. The man thinks it's a ridiculous idea.
3. You stay with the crocodiles for 50 minutes.
4. You can give food to the crocodiles.
5. Two people can get in the cage.
6. The crocodiles are very hungry.

E Write five warnings or pieces of advice about the "Cage of Death." Use these words. Compare in groups and choose the best five.

break	calm	feed	get out of	open
take	touch	wear		

> *Don't open the cage to take a selfie!*

F **Mini role-play. A:** You're a visitor to Crocosaurus Cove. Use the ad in **C** and your imagination to interview B. **B:** You've worked there for 20 years and are a local celebrity. Answer and give A safety advice.

G Do the questionnaire. Compare answers. Which are the class favorites?

> ## Would you rather ...
> - stay at home or go out tonight?
> - go clubbing or eat out on your birthday?
> - walk on the beach or in the mountains?
> - do writing exercises at home or in school?
> - be married or single?
>
> ## Do you prefer ...
> - noisy places or quiet places on vacation?
> - Mexican food or Peruvian food?
> - to get up early or stay in bed on weekends?
> - action movies or comedies?
> - brains or brawn?

> *Marta would rather stay at home tonight but I'd rather go out, so we're different.*

> *Most people in class prefer Mexican food, but a lot of them haven't tried Peruvian food before.*

F ▶R3.7 🔵 **Make it personal** **Question time!**
1. Listen to the 12 lesson titles in units 5 and 6.
2. In pairs, practice asking and answering. Use the book map on p. 2–3. Ask at least two follow-up questions. Try to answer in different ways. Can you have a short conversation about all the questions?

CLASSIC MOVIE WEEK

① **Vocabulary** Movies

A ▶7.1 Complete the movie genres with the correct vowels. Match the movies in photos 1–7 to the best genre. Listen to check. Then think of another movie you know for each genre. Check its English title online if necessary.

__cti__n   dr__m__
__dventur__   f__nt__sy
__nimat__d   h__rr__r
c__m__dy   myst__ry
d__cument__ry   thr__ll__r

For action, how about Spiderman: Far From Home?

B ▶7.2 Listen to two friends at the movies and number what they do in order, 1–6.

☐ buy the tickets   ☐ stand in line   ☐ buy the sodas
☐ go into the theater   ☐ buy the popcorn   ☐ choose the seats

C ▶7.2 Listen again and write if Kelly (K) or Jack (J) did each thing.

⚠ Common mistakes

I think the most the men enjoys the adventure movies.

Remember, the suffixes -or, -er, -ure, -ive, -y are never stressed.

D 🔵 **Make it personal** In groups. Which kinds of movies do you like? Use questions 1–8 to talk about the last time you went to the movies. Who had the best experience? Who had the worst experience?

1 What did you see? Who with?
2 Did you have any snacks?
3 What genre was it? One-off or a sequel?
4 Was it dubbed or subtitled?

5 Did it have good reviews?
6 Who were the main characters / actors?
7 What did / didn't you like about it?
8 Would you recommend it?

> *I like drama so we went to see A Star is Born. I went with my two sisters to the movie theater at the mall.*

> *Did you have any snacks?* *Yes, we bought popcorn.*

② Reading

A Brainstorm five things any good movie needs. Then read the blog to find the movie critic's five choices. How many are the same as yours?

> *How about originality? You know, so you don't feel you've seen it before.*

What makes a great movie?

Some people believe it's the director who makes a movie great – or not so great. Just think of all the directors who have made some terrible movies as well as brilliant ones! So making a great movie must involve more than the director.

I think that plot is the most important factor. A high quality movie needs a high quality story. Then there are the characters and the chemistry between them. A satisfying movie includes characters we're interested in, and who we care enough about to want to know what happens to them – even if we don't like them. This is why the actors who bring the script and the characters to life are so important. If the acting is bad, the movie will be bad too. Then, of course, the reason we watch a movie rather than read a book is for the visuals. Is the cinematography beautiful? Are there amazing special effects? And finally, we can probably all think of good movies that have been ruined by poor sound – when you can't hear the dialogue clearly or the sound effects are too loud – so sound quality is also vital to me in a good movie.

Other people may think that the soundtrack is just as important, or the screenplay, locations, action, and stunts, but, for me at least, these are the top five characteristics essential to any great movie.

B ▶7.3 Listen, reread, and repeat the pink-stressed words. Match the highlighted words in **A** to definitions 1–6.

1 the story of the movie _____
2 the people in the story _____
3 the book that contains complete instructions for the actors and cinematographers _____
4 unusual, difficult, or dangerous pieces of physical acting _____
5 the music used in the movie _____
6 the words the actors have to say _____

C 🔵 **Make it personal** Choose the top three characteristics that make a movie great for you. Then, in pairs, analyze your favorite movies based on your criteria.

> *My favorite movie is The Green Book. It has a superb plot and characters and it's based on a true story. It's funny, has lots of surprises, and it makes you think.*

> *Yeah, I've seen it too. It certainly holds your attention from beginning to end.*

7.2 Are you crazy about music?

① Reading

A Quickly read and match quotes a–g about passions to photos 1–7. Then match the photos to the labels.

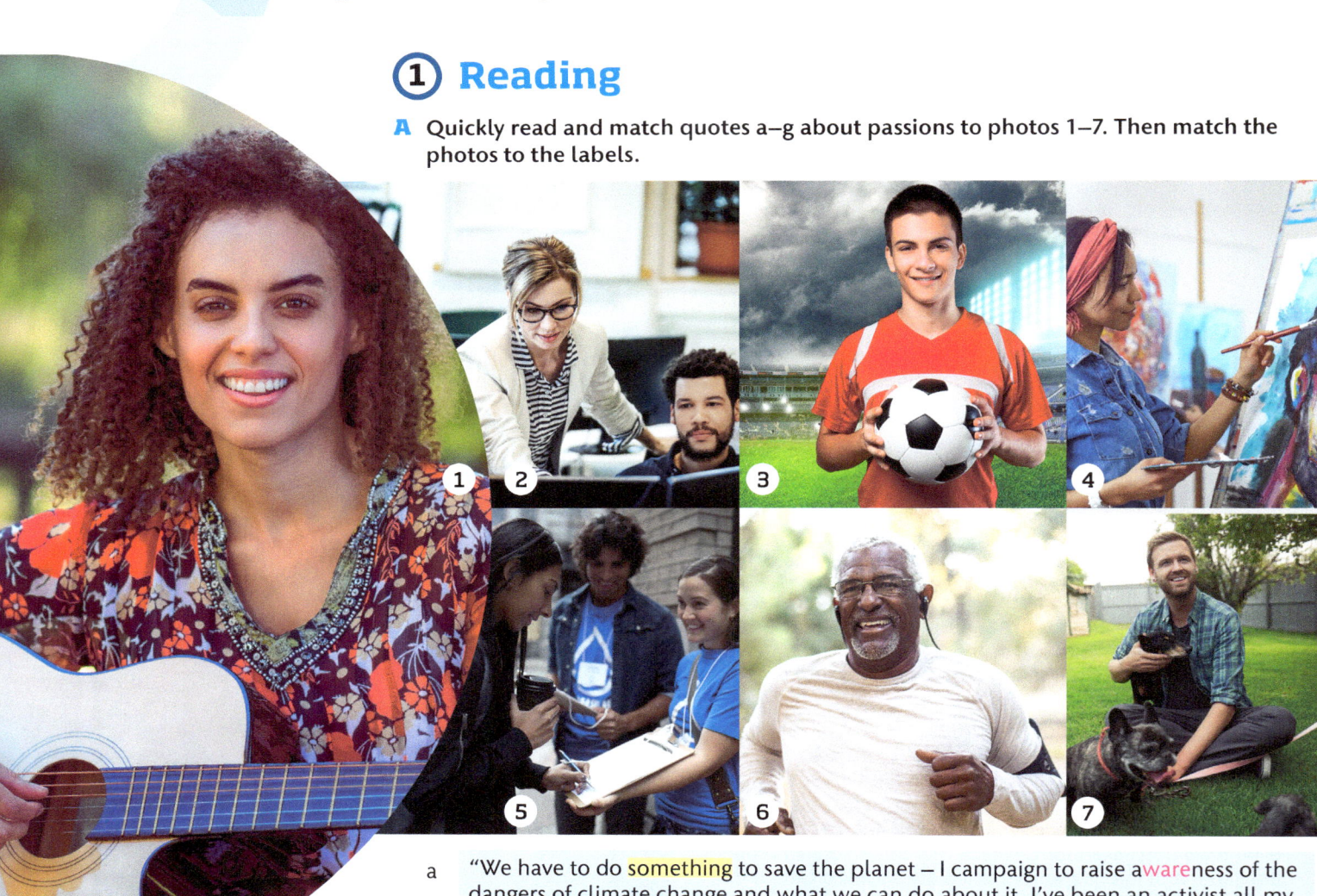

a   "We have to do **something** to save the planet – I campaign to raise awareness of the dangers of climate change and what we can do about it. I've been an activist all my life and I'm a big fan of getting involved." *Leila, Athens*

b   "Manchester United! Does **anyone** love them more than I do? I doubt it – I'm totally into the team and I go to all their games, even though it costs me a fortune. Some say I'm obsessed. I'm ecstatic when they win and I'm devastated when they lose." *Jason, UK*

c   "I play piano, sax, and guitar and practice about five hours a day and perform most evenings too. I rarely get a night off. It's my life – I'm crazy about music." *Marta, Brazil*

d   "I volunteer in a pet hospital and I have five dogs, ten cats, a tortoise, and a rabbit. I love animals and I won't do **anything** to harm them – ever!" *Jurgen, Germany*

e   "There's a great atmosphere at the office – we work as a team on really stimulating projects. Sometimes I work over 80 hours a week! **Everybody** says that's ridiculous and I'm obsessed with work, but I really love what I do and I'm persistent – and I make a lot of money!" *Rachel, the U.S.*

f   "I'm a painter and spend all day looking at art or creating it – it's all I've ever wanted to do and now I'm living that dream – it's so fulfilling to be an artist. I don't make much money, but **nothing** is as important to me as painting." *Claudia, Mexico*

g   "I get up and run about five miles every day, then I go to a spinning class. In the evenings I go to another fitness class and run two miles home – I run **everywhere**. I'm retired so I do all I can to stay in shape." *John, Canada*

an animal lover _____	an instrumentalist _____	a workaholic _____
a committed activist _____	an obsessive sport fan _____	
a fitness fanatic _____	a talented artist _____	

B ▶7.4 **Listen, reread, and name the person(s) who:**

1 spends a lot of time practicing.
2 is probably not paid for what they do.
3 is really into sport.
4 thinks money is not important.
5 goes to classes every day.
6 mentions their work.
7 works with a group of people.

♫ *Blow a kiss, fire a gun, We need someone to lean on, Blow a kiss, fire a gun, All we need is somebody to lean on*

C **In pairs, practice the pink-stressed words and underline the expressions that each person uses to describe their passion.**

⏱ **Common mistakes**

I don't know ~~nobody~~. *anybody*

No one
~~Anyone~~ can help me now.

D 👤 **Make it personal**

1 Do you know anyone like the people in **A**?
2 Imagine you're being interviewed. What are you passionate about? Record your answer. In groups, listen to the recordings and decide who sounds most passionate.

I'm really into plants and I have my own garden.

② Grammar Pronouns *some-, any-, every-, no-*

A **Answer 1–4 about the six phrases with a highlighted pronoun in 1A.**

1 Does the pronoun refer to a thing, a person, or a place?
2 Is the verb positive, negative, or a question?
3 Does the sentence have a positive or negative meaning?
4 Does the pronoun refer to a thing, person, or place that is **unidentified** or **a group** of things, people, or places?

B **Complete the grammar box. Are the ➕ and ➖ forms different in your language too?**

1 Complete the pronouns with *some-, any-, no-, every-*.

➕ sentences	I know _____ one who's just like this. _____ one (= all of us) knows _____ one like that.
❓ questions	Do you know _____ one like this guy?
➖ negative	I don't know _____ one like this.
➕ verb with ➖ meaning:	_____ one wants to be like her at all.

2   -thing   -one   -body   -where

Use _____ or _____ for a person, _____ for a thing, and _____ for a place.

➡ **Grammar 7A** p. 150

C ▶7.5 **Complete 1–6 with the correct pronoun. Listen to check. In pairs, are they true for you? Add details.**

1 I always prefer _____ else's cooking to my own.
2 Radio used to be much better. There's _____ good to listen to these days.
3 You shouldn't go _____ if you have a cold or a cough.
4 There's _____ healthy to eat at fast food restaurants.
5 I don't love _____ or _____ as much as I love my pet.
6 There's _____ I've always wanted to do, but I haven't done it yet.

I definitely prefer my own cooking.   *Are you a good cook?*   *I think so, yeah. I like to try new things.*

D 🔵 **Make it personal** **Search online for a song line you like with *someone, nothing, anywhere*, etc. Share it with the class, and explain the use of the pronoun.**

I like this one by Rita Ora. "Just take me anywhere, Anywhere away with you." She means, it doesn't matter where they go if they are together.

I think there's a Queen song about "somebody."

7.3 What do you have a lot of at home?

① Listening

A ▶7.6 Listen to part one of a show about unusual collections. Match three of photos 1–4 to the people. In pairs, share what else you remember.

Barbara ☐   Percival ☐   David ☐

B ▶7.6 Listen again. Are 1–4 True (T) or False (F)? Correct the false ones.
1 The radio show started with number 1 on the list.
2 All Barbara's chairs are made from wood.
3 Percival 's collection includes over 50,000 toys.
4 David thinks traffic cones are important for safety on roads.

C ▶7.7 Use photos 5 and 6 to try to guess the unusual things Rainer and Nancy collect. Listen to check.

Rainer _____   Nancy _____

Maybe he collects hotel doors?

90

D ▶️7.6 and 7.7 **Match comments 1–5 to Barbara (B), Percival (P), David (D), Rainier (R), or Nancy (N). Listen again to check.**

1 That's such a strange thing to collect!
2 Such a lot of little chairs!
3 They are so important for safety.
4 There are so many better souvenirs.
5 That's so sweet!

E 🔘 **Make it personal** **In pairs. Which is the most unusual collection in the photos? Order them from 1 (most unusual) to 6 (least unusual). Then find another pair with the same order, or persuade a pair to change their order to yours.**

💬 *I don't think the toy collection is very unusual. I know people who collect restaurant toys.*

② Grammar *So* and *such*

A Reread 1–5 in **1D** and study **Common mistakes** and the song line. Then complete the grammar box with *so* or *such a*.

🔘 **Common mistakes**

The hotel had such a̶ wonderful rooms!

Wow! Such a̶ nice weather!

Don't use *such a* with plural or uncountable nouns.

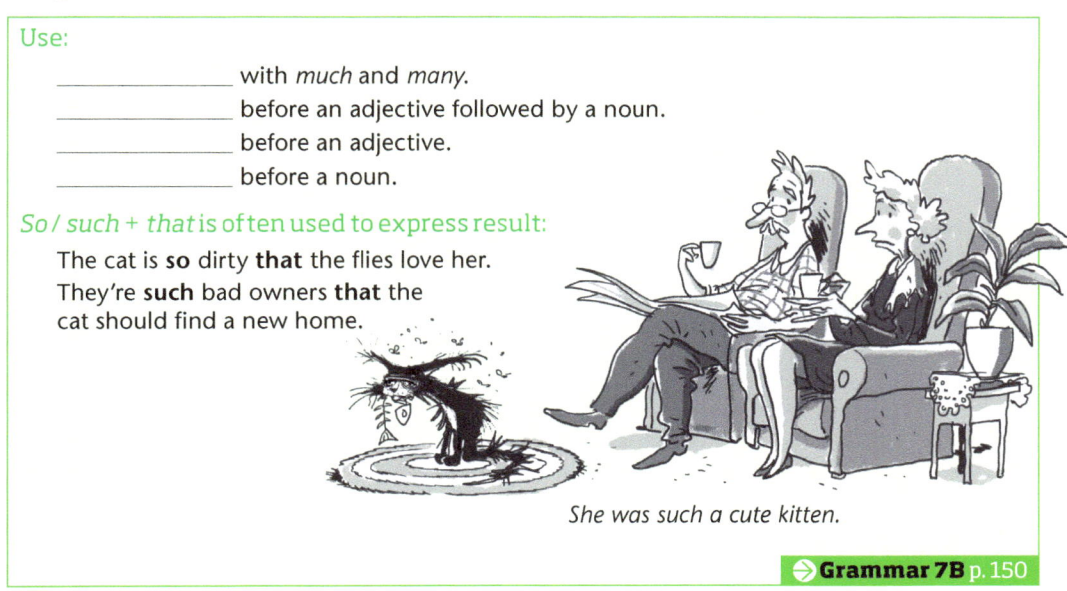

> Use:
>
> _____ with *much* and *many*.
> _____ before an adjective followed by a noun.
> _____ before an adjective.
> _____ before a noun.
>
> *So / such + that* is often used to express result:
>
> The cat is **so** dirty **that** the flies love her.
> They're **such** bad owners **that** the cat should find a new home.
>
> *She was such a cute kitten.*
>
> ➡️ **Grammar 7B** p. 150

B ▶️7.8 **Add *so* or *such* in the correct places in 1–4, then match to endings a–d. Listen to check and repeat, stressing *so* and *such*. In pairs, talk about photos 1–6 on p. 90 using *so* and *such*.**

1 Percival is careful with his toys that ...
2 This man's a passionate traffic cone fan that ...
3 Barbara is a huge fan of miniature chairs that ...
4 She likes them much that ...

a he has a collection of over 500.
b she has collected them from 50 countries in the world.
c he has over 15,000 of them.
d she has her own museum.

C **In pairs, make sentences about the collectors in 1–5 using *so* or *such*.**

1 Carol Vaughn: passionate about soaps / 5,000 bars in her apartment.
  She's so passionate about soaps that she has 5,000 bars in her apartment.
2 Rob Foster: huge fan of *Star Wars* / 3,000 *Star Wars* toys in his bedroom.
3 Leslie Rogers: in love with brown paper bags / names and numbers.
4 Randy Knol: enthusiastic about toy dinosaurs / more than 6,000 in his house.
5 Emeline Duhautoy: fan of toy cows / collected them for more than 10 years.

D 🔘 **Make it personal** **In groups, share stories and ask questions about collectors and their collections. Who's the most obsessive collector? Who has the most unusual story?**

💬 *My cousin used to collect Mexican wrestling masks. He still has about 200.*

💬 *Where does he keep them?   What does his wife think about them?*

7.4 Who was Instagram created by?

"I KNOW IT'S ILLEGAL TO DOWNLOAD MUSIC FROM THE INTERNET... BUT YOU SAID THE STUFF I LISTEN TO ISN'T MUSIC!"

① Reading

A Read / look at the cartoons. Did you find any of them funny? In pairs, answer 1–5.

1 What's the boy doing?
2 Do you think his father ap**proves**?
3 Have you ever had a conversation like this with family or friends?
4 Which do you do more: download or stream?
5 Do you often read or share cartoons or memes? /miːmz/

B Quickly read the infographic. Are you surprised by any of the figures?

3☠0bn

1 Over 300 billion visits were made to **pi**racy websites last year – 106.9 billion to TV piracy websites, 73.9 billion to music piracy sites, and 53.2 billion to movie piracy sites.

71,600

2 Every year, 71,600 jobs are lost in the U.S. because of illegal downloads.

24%

3 About 24% of the global Internet **band**width is used by Internet **pi**rates to illegally download music and other content.

$850

4 An average mobile device contains something like $850 worth of **pi**rated songs.

35%

5 35% of music buyers get at least one song from an illegal source.

87%

6 Mobile devices are used for 87% of all piracy activities and desktop PCs are used in the remaining 13% of cases.

C ▶7.9 Read **Common mistakes**, then in pairs pronounce and write the underlined numbers in **B**. Listen to check, then check your spelling in AS 7.9 on p. 171.

D Circle the correct options in rules 1–3. Then dictate six large numbers to a partner.

1 Use and say **point** / **dot**, not *comma*, in numbers to separate decimal places.
2 In U.S. English, you **can** / **can't** omit *and* between numbers.
3 After numbers, use *hundred*, *thousand*, *million* and *billion* in the **singular** / **plural**.

> *One million five hundred and fifty-two thousand.*

E 🔵 Make it personal What do you think of online piracy? Do you think it's possible to reduce online piracy? Can it be stopped? How?

> *I think if they make downloading cheaper, there will be less piracy.*

⚠ Common mistakes

There are around eight billions of people on the planet Earth.
I have six hundreds friends on Facebook.
1,500 = one thousand and five hundred

Do Spanish and Portuguese speakers make the third mistake?

② **Grammar** Passive voice: present and past

♪ *I'm beautiful in my way, 'Cause God makes no mistakes, I'm on the right track, baby, I was born this way*

A In pairs, try to remember the missing verbs in 1–4. Then complete the grammar box.
1 Over 300 billion visits ... to piracy websites last year.
2 71,600 jobs ... because of illegal downloads.
3 About 24% of the global Internet bandwidth ... by Internet pirates.
4 Mobile devices ... for 87% of all piracy activities.

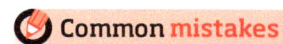 **Common mistakes**

were
Two billion songs ~~was~~
downloaded illegally last year.

are
A lot of movies ~~is~~ shared
illegally every day.

> **1** Circle the correct options in sentences a–c about the passive voice.
>
> a The actions are **more** / **less** important than who did them.
> b *Be (is, are, was, were)* is **always** / **often** used in passive sentences.
> c The main verbs are in the **simple past** / **past participle**.
>
> **2** Look at sentence 3 in **A** and complete the rule.
>
> We use _____ + a _____ to specify who did the action.
>
> → **Grammar 7C** p. 150

B ▶7.10 Complete posts 1–4 on the forum with these verbs in the passive. There's one extra. Listen to check. Which opinion(s) do you disagree with?

create   invent   pay   reduce   share   upload

Downloading = Stealing?

1 Singers and movie stars _____ millions of dollars, anyway. Losing a few thousand dollars makes no difference to them.

2 People were recording TV shows and vinyl albums long before home computers _____ and the Internet _____. Downloading content illegally is basically the same thing.

3 The media industry should lobby to reduce download speeds. If speeds _____ , file sharing will drop too.

4 Every time a file _____ illegally, money is lost. End of discussion.

C ▶7.11 Listen to extracts from the infographic in **1B** and circle the correct option in the rule.

In the passive form, *are*, *was*, and *were* are usually **stressed** / **unstressed**.

D Read questions 1–5 and circle the correct answers. In pairs, ask and answer.
1 When were the first iPhones released?
   a 2006   b 2007   c 2008
2 What were the first words that were spoken on the moon?
   a God bless America.   b That's one small step ...   c Hi, Mom, look where I am!
3 Which music act is considered the best-selling of all time?
   a The Beatles   b Madonna   c Elvis Presley
4 Where's the Wimbledon tennis championship played?
   a New York   b Sydney   c London
5 When was the World Wide Web invented?
   a 1989   b 1990   c 1999

E 🔊 **Make it personal** In pairs, write a five-item trivia quiz to test the class. Ask about music, movies, TV, sports, history – you choose!

> *Where was the video for Luis Fonsi's "Despacito" filmed?*
> *Was it a) Cuba b) Dominican Republic c) Puerto Rico?*

7.5 What do you think about reality TV?

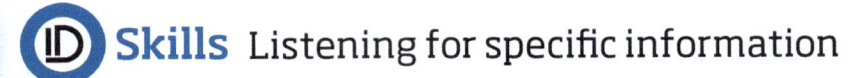 **Skills** Listening for specific information

A In groups, answer 1–9. Who's the biggest fan of reality TV?

Which reality shows ...

1 have you ever watched in English?
2 have adapted versions for your country?
3 have celebrity judges?
4 have you watched at least once?
5 have you contacted to vote?

6 do you like best / least?
7 would you eliminate forever if you could?
8 is the hardest to win?
9 do you think will last the longest?

> *I'd love to eliminate the "Got Talent" show, I can't stand it!*

Tell us about it!

Have you ever auditioned for, or participated in, any of these shows? Call us at **637-8877** and leave a message describing your experience. The best stories will win an extraordinary – and unique – prize you'll never forget!

B ▶ 7.12 Listen to two callers to a radio station. Which shows from **A** are they talking about? Why did they want to be on the show? Did they appear on the show?

C ▶ 7.12 Listen again and complete 1–6 with numbers. Check in pairs.

1 There were _____ people standing in line outside the auditorium.
2 They were only allowed inside the building at _____ a.m.
3 Only _____ contestants perform in front of the celebrity judges.
4 About _____ people read Judy's blog every day.
5 If the woman appeared on the show, her family could be paid _____ dollars.
6 Judy tried to get in touch with the producer of the show at least _____ times.

D Rewrite 1–3 using *such* and 4–6 using the passive voice.

1 The place was so huge! It _____!
2 I was so disappointed! This _____ disappointment!
3 My family is so conventional! I have _____!
4 Someone chose me to be on TV. I _____.
5 They paid families $20,000 to appear on the show. Families _____.
6 They ignored all my calls. All _____.

E Read tips 1–3 and find examples of each in AS 7.12 on p. 171.

To improve fluency in a monologue, you can:

1 pause between ideas, or use phrases like *yeah* or *you know*.
2 repeat words and phrases from time to time for emphasis.
3 use words like *anyway* to help you change subject.

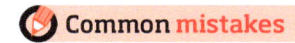

Common mistakes

~~auditioned~~ *auditioned*
I once ~~made an audition~~ for a show.

~~contacted~~ *contacted*
I ~~put myself in contact with~~ the show.

F 🔵 **Make it personal** In pairs, answer 1–3. Can you use the phrases in **D** for any of your experiences? Do you have any similar answers?

1 Who do you feel most sorry for? Why?
2 Why is reality TV so popular?
3 Have you ever or would you ever audition for a show or movie? Which one?

> *I auditioned for a part in my high school play.*

> *I'd audition as an extra in a movie, if I was paid well.*

7.5   Are you a good singer?

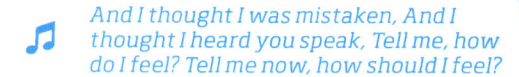

And I thought I was mistaken, And I thought I heard you speak, Tell me, how do I feel? Tell me now, how should I feel?

⑩ in Action   Giving your opinion

A **Look at the picture of Bruce, who's on another talent show. In pairs, answer 1–5.**
1   How confident do you think Bruce looks?
2   Do you think he's a good singer?
3   Has he already sung or is he about to sing?
4   Guess which judge will be more positive about his performance.
5   Guess what each of them is saying.

I'm not sure if he's crying or sweating. What do you think?

B ▶ **7.13** **Listen to check. Were your guesses correct?**

C ▶ **7.13** **Listen again and complete comments 1–5. Will Bruce try again?**
1   You've just _____ my favorite song of all _____.
2   That was _____ an _____ version.
3   You have _____ a lot of _____!
4   You'll need to work very _____. You sounded like you had a _____.
5   Come back again when you're _____.

D ▶ **7.13** **Match beginnings 1–4 to the endings. There are two extra endings. In pairs, listen and, simultaneously, repeat each sentence.**

① I thought …

② I didn't think …

③ It wasn't as good …

④ I have to agree …

☐ … with Simon.
☐ … than I thought.
☐ … it was all that great.
☐ … it was quite good.
☐ … as I expected.
☐ … about Emma.

E ▶ **7.14** 👤 **Make it personal** **In groups of three, imagine you're the judges. Listen to Joe and then Lisa and decide if they should progress to the next round of the show.**

I didn't think Joe was all that great, but he was OK. Maybe we should give him another chance.

Writing 7 A TV series review

A Read the review and decide how many stars the reviewer gives the TV show.

B Which paragraph a–d answers 1–5?

1 Is there anything she doesn't like about the show?
2 Would she recommend the show?
3 What does she particularly like about it?
4 Why is it interesting and enjoyable?
5 What's the name of the TV show, and what is it about?

C Study the highlighted and underlined words in **A**, then complete the rules in **Write it right!**

> ✔ **Write it right!**
>
> Use _____ and _____ to add extra information. _____ can start a sentence, or go before the verb / adjective. _____ goes at the end of a sentence.
> Use _____ and _____ to introduce a contrast.
> Use _____ (*that*) with adjectives.
> Use _____ with uncountable nouns and _____ with countable nouns.

D Complete 1–4 with *also*, *although*, *however*, or *too*. More than one answer may be possible.

1 _____ the visual effects were amazing, the sound was too loud.
2 The leading actor was brilliant. The other actors were _____ very good.
3 The story is very complicated. It keeps you guessing right to the end _____.
4 The violence was graphic. _____, it was important to the story.

E Circle the correct options to complete 1–4.

1 Very few movies get **so** / **such** excellent reviews.
2 The ending was **so** / **such** unexpected – I couldn't believe it!
3 I love Tarantino's movies – I think he's **so** / **such** a great director.
4 The first series was **so** / **such** successful that they decided to make a sequel.

F 👤 **Make it personal** Think of a movie or TV show you really enjoyed and write a review in 200 words.

Before	Brainstorm answers to questions 1–5 in **B** for you. Look back at the review in **A** and underline any words or expressions you want to use in your own review.
While	Follow the structure of the review in **A**. Include four paragraphs and a variety of adjectives. Check you use the connecting words from **Write it Right!** correctly.
After	Exchange reviews with another student. Does their review make you want to see the movie / TV show?

☆☆☆☆☆

a A TV show I've really enjoyed is *Killing Eve*, a spy thriller in eight episodes. It's about a secret service officer, Eve, played by the American actor Sandra Oh. Her mission is to find an international assassin called Villanelle (British actor Jodie Comer), who has killed a number of important people in different countries. As the series develops, both women seem to be looking for each other, which I think is such an original idea.

b I'm a big fan of action movies and TV shows, although the heroes always seem to be men. In *Killing Eve* I particularly like the idea that the two main characters are women. The story is fast-moving, with a lot of drama and excitement. It also has some surprising changes. Eve and Villanelle are both such unusual people that you want to find out more about them. This makes the story very interesting. The audience is meant to sympathize with Eve, however, Villanelle is so mysterious and charismatic that we really like her too.

c *Killing Eve* is quite violent, and I don't like this so much. In places, the violence is so graphic that it's difficult to watch. I think this might upset some viewers. However, it's always connected to the development of the story and isn't just for "entertainment."

d I'd definitely recommend this series to anyone who enjoys great acting and great storytelling. The two leading actors are extremely convincing and the director keeps you guessing what will happen all the way through. Also, the final episode was really unexpected. If you want to know what happens, you'll have to watch it yourself!

Sara T., Portland, USA

7 Sound tracks

1 Before watching

A In pairs, write the name of two movies you've seen (and enjoyed) for each genre, in English. Share and make a class list. Vote for the class favorite.

> action   comedy   horror   romance   science fiction

I used to love those Die Hard films, with Bruce Willis.

B Classify these words. Some can go in both columns in the chart. When you hear the phrase "great soundtrack," what comes to mind?

> to edit   an MP3 file   to record   samples   scenes
> a shot   a song   the soundtrack   that's a wrap

Film	Music

As a kid, I loved the songs in Mamma Mia! I still do!

C Guess what Paolo and Andrea are doing / saying and why.

Maybe he's teaching her some karate moves?

2 While watching

A Watch up to 1:36 to check. Number these phrases, 1–4, in the order you hear them. Then use them to complete the sentences.

> ☐ lifesaver   ☐ no big deal
> ☐ owe you one   ☐ short notice

1 When someone doesn't give you enough time to plan something, it's _____.
2 If you do someone a big favor, they might say you're a _____.
3 After you do someone a favor, you can say it's _____.
4 If someone does you a favor, you can say, "Thanks, I _____."

B Watch the rest and check any movie titles on your class list from **1A** that you hear. Which others does Lucy mention?

C Complete extracts 1–8 with *so, such, so much,* or *so many.* Who said them? Watch again to check. What other phrases did you catch?

1 I'm _____ glad you could do this for me.
2 I know it was _____ short notice.
3 It took _____ longer to edit than I thought.
4 It takes me _____ tries to get one that I think sounds OK.
5 You and I are _____ much alike.
6 The romantic pieces are always _____ easier.
7 That was _____ scary.
8 Thank you _____.

3 After watching

A Order the story, 1–10. If necessary, watch again to check.

> ☐ The movie was edited and sent to Genevieve for the soundtrack.
> ☐ The monster was defeated by Paolo.
> ☐ Genevieve watched the film.
> ☐ Andrea's character screamed.
> 1 The movie was shot in a forest and in an alley.
> ☐ Lucy will tell her professor about Genevieve's music.
> ☐ Genevieve and Lucy listened to music samples.
> ☐ Three exciting music compositions were chosen.
> ☐ Several types of movies were discussed.
> ☐ They talked about the difficult aspects of their work.

B Present or past passive? Complete 1–5 with these verbs.

> finish   match   compose   shoot   write

1 The film _____ in two days.
2 Genevieve says that sometimes a song _____ in half an hour.
3 The scenes _____ up with a few different samples.
4 Action and romantic pieces _____ by Genevieve.
5 When the music _____ Lucy was happy.

C Rewrite 2–5 using the passive.

1 Lucy's movie features Andrea and Paolo.
Andrea and Paolo are featured in Lucy's movie.
2 They chose dramatic and classical music for it.
3 People know John Williams for his great soundtracks.
4 Genevieve created several music samples for it.
5 Lucy wrote the script and shot the movie.

C ⬤ **Make it personal** In groups, choose either:

• a genre, then plan and script a short movie scene.
• a clip you like from a movie, and act it out yourselves.

Let's create a scary scene from a horror movie.

Can we do a scene from La La Land? I love the dance routine between Ryan Gosling and Emma Stone!

8

a b c d e f

① Vocabulary Technology

A Underline the **bold** words you recognize in extracts 1–6 from an audio journal. In pairs, guess their pronunciation. Then match 1–6 to photos a–f.

1 "**The facial recognition device** doesn't know who I am again, so I can't use my **GPS**."
2 "And I can see better too, thanks to the **active contact lenses** that I got at the same time."
3 "It sends this information to the **surveillance camera** in the kitchen, and now the smart refrigerator has locked its doors."
4 "I hope their **smart vending machine**'s not broken again. I'm dying for something to eat."
5 "Why are the **voice-activated speakers** always playing old Justin Bieber songs?"
6 "Oh, I miss the good old days when I could simply press a **button** on the remote and decide what to watch."

B ▶8.1 Listen to check, then cover **A** and test a partner with the photos.

C 🔒 Make it personal Which of the technology items do / don't you use? How many of each do you have at home? Compare in groups. Any surprises?

> *I have facial recognition on my phone.*

> *Oh really? I don't – I prefer to use my fingerprint.*

⚠ Common mistakes

>   *miss*
> I ~~feel a need for~~ my old phone.

Futures made of virtual insanity now, Always seem to, be governed by this love we have, For useless, twisting, our new technology, Oh, now there is no sound for we all live underground

8.1

② Reading

A ▶8.2 **Insert sentences 1–6 from 1A in the journal. Listen, check, and repeat the pink-stressed words.**

9:00 a.m. Thursday's finally here, after a relatively busy working week. So, why on earth did the home entertainment system decide it should wake me up at 9? (a) _____ I specifically requested Mozart!

9:30 a.m. Smart bathroom seems worried about my health. Apparently, I've gained two pounds in the past week. So, here's what it does: (b) _____ No breakfast for me today, thanks to the bathroom-fridge conspiracy. How about that?

10:00 a.m. The kitchen appliances are still refusing to cooperate, so I'm on my way to get a breakfast burrito at the store now. Yes, fast food for breakfast, of all things! (c) _____ I never thought I'd say this, but sometimes I miss human attendants and their inefficiency.

11:00 a.m. I get into the car. (d) _____ That's the third time this week. Could it be the two extra pounds? I guess I have no choice but to answer the same old security questions it asks me.

2:00 p.m. After three hours stuck in the car, trying to prove that I'm not an impostor, I get home, sit down, and tell the TV I want to watch soccer. Guess what, it looks like it has decided that I'm in the mood for classical ballet today. (e) _____

6:00 p.m. I'm having a great time at my brother's birthday party, especially with the sound cancellation ear plugs I bought last week. What a fantastic device! It makes everything sound much nicer. (f) _____

B What do the <u>underlined</u> pronouns refer to? Draw connecting arrows, like the example.

C In pairs, use only the photos in **1A** to reconstruct the main events in the journal.

When he woke up the smart speakers were playing classical music, right?   *No, they were playing Justin Bieber!*

D Which technology items 1–8 are mentioned in the text in **A**? In pairs, talk about the three you would most like to have. Are your choices the same?

1 decision-making devices
2 voice-changing devices
3 identity-checking devices
4 self-driving cars
5 self-locking appliances
6 house-cleaning robots
7 sleep-monitoring cameras
8 conversation-making robots

E In groups, use these verbs (or your own) to create five **innovative** technologies. Use tips 1–3 to help you. Share your lists and choose your two favorite devices.

changing   cleaning   controlling   doing   learning   making   monitoring

1 Use the *-ing* form of verbs to describe what things do: *a money-making scheme; a fitness-tracking watch.*
2 In compound nouns, the stress is usually on the first word.
3 Use *self-* when no one else is involved in operating a machine: *a self-updating program.*

My first one is an English-learning device. I'd love to become fluent automatically!

> ⊘ **Common mistakes**
>
> *money-counting*
> The bank uses ~~money-count~~ machines.
>
> *self-cleaning*
> This oven is ~~self-clean~~.
>
> You don't need to worry, this is a ~~self-updated~~ app.
> *self-updating*

F 🔒 **Make it personal** In pairs, answer 1–3. Do you mainly agree with each other?

1 What are the advantages and disadvantages of the technology in the journal?
2 What problems does technology cause for you and humanity in general?
3 Do you think we will live more and more like this in the future?

I think technology can make life more complicated, not easier.   *No way! Technology is progress!*

8.2 Do you ever switch off from technology?

① Grammar Phrasal verbs

A ▶ 8.3 Listen and match conversations 1–4 to pictures a–d.

B ▶ 8.3 Match a–i to speech bubbles 1–9 in **A**. Listen again to check.

- a I'll get up in five minutes.
- b Let me plug you in.
- c I'm going to switch you off.
- d Please turn the thermostat down! Turn it down!
- e Don't turn on the coffee maker!
- f You know you can't switch me off!
- g I'm going to turn on the coffee maker.
- h I'm going to turn up the thermostat.
- i It's time to wake up.

C Complete the grammar box.

---

1 Match phrasal verbs 1-7 to meanings a-g.

1	get up	a	to decrease
2	wake up	b	to increase
3	plug in	c	to stop (a light or machine)
4	turn up	d	to connect to an electrical outlet
5	turn down	e	to get out of bed
6	turn on / switch on	f	to start (a light or machine)
7	turn off / switch off	g	to stop sleeping

2 Circle the correct options in a-c.

- a The TV is too loud! **Turn down it**. / **Turn it down.**
- b The lights are very bright in here! **Turn them off**. / **Turn off them.**
- c In phrasal verbs, pronouns usually come **after** / **between** the verb and the particle.

➔ **Grammar 8A** p. 152

D ▶ 8.3 Listen again and repeat a–i in **B**. Stress the particle (adverb or preposition), not the verb.

E In pairs, cover a–i in **B**, use the pictures in **A**, and try to remember the sentences.

F 🔊 **Make it personal** Complete 1–5 with phrasal verbs from **C**. Create two more questions using phrasal verbs from the box. Then ask and answer in pairs. Did you learn anything new?

🎵 *Come on, come on, turn the radio on,*
It's Friday night and I won't be long,
Gotta do my hair, I put my make up on,
It's Friday night and I won't be long

1 What time do you usually _____ _____ in the mornings, during the week, and at weekends? How long is it usually before you _____ _____?

What time do you usually wake up at weekends?

2 How often do you _____ _____ your cell phone completely? How long before you _____ it _____ again?

3 When your favorite songs are playing do you usually _____ _____ the volume?

4 Do you have any devices that you _____ _____ and _____ _____ with your voice?

5 How many devices do you have _____ _____ to an outlet now at home?

go out / stay in   pick up / put down   put on / take off   stand up / sit down

Do you normally ask people to take off their shoes at your house?

Do you prefer to stand up or sit down at pop concerts?

② **Pronunciation** Intonation in questions

A ▶8.4 **Listen to more of Michael's conversation with his car computer from 1A. What do 1–5 refer to? Check with a partner.**

1 Huff   2 July   3 Canada   4 a white T-shirt   5 October

B ▶8.5 **Listen and mark if the intonation goes up ↗ or down ↘ at the end of 1–4. Then circle the correct options in the rule.**

1 What's your full name?
2 Are you American?
3 May I ask you a few security questions?
4 Why are you doing this to me?

Intonation usually goes **up** / **down** at the end of *Yes* / *No* questions and **up** / **down** at the end of *Wh-* questions.

C ▶8.6 **Remember the car's questions. Write them using prompts 1–7, then listen, check, and repeat.**

1 what / full name?
2 how / spell "Huff"?
3 American?
4 when / born?
5 how long / have / this **ve**hicle?
6 use / this car / Tuesday?
7 what / wearing?

Good morning surveillance camera. Did you have a busy night? Did you miss me?

D **In pairs, choose a device and role-play a conversation with it. Which pair can create the funniest conversation?**

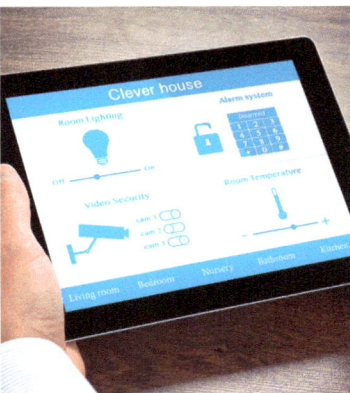

E 🔊 **Make it personal** Share your experiences with technology. What do you think about devices, appliances, and apps that speak? How many in the class like them and how many don't?

I love that I can talk to my phone and ask it questions!   *I don't talk to my phone.*

8.3 Will space vacations be popular soon?

BY THE WAY,
I LOVE THOSE
EARRINGS.

① Reading

A In pairs, answer 1–3 about the cartoon. Give both a "real" answer and a fun one too.

1 Why is the woman surprised?
2 How do you think she should a) react and b) reply?
3 Do you think machines will ever have any human emotions?

> *She should react positively. After all, it's a compliment!*

> *Maybe. Lots of robots in movies get emotional.*

B ▶8.7 Quickly read the article and match three of questions 1–4 to replies a–c. Listen to check.

1 Will we be able to communicate through thought transmission?
2 Will computers have emotions or some sort of consciousness?
3 Are we ever going to travel through time?
4 Are computers going to be more intelligent than us?

Future Perfect?

Penny Duff and Harry Reid

Last week we asked you to tweet us your questions about life in 30 years' time. This is what futurists Penny Duff (PD) and Harry Reid (HR) have to say about the top three questions.

a PD: Probably not. Consciousness is an exclusive attribute of the human brain and we probably won't be able to teach robots how to feel until we know much more about our brain and how it functions.

HR: Probably. We've built robots that can, for example, identify themselves when they look in a mirror or even mimic our emotions according to the quality of our voice, so, yes, I think machines will be able to feel human emotions.

b PD: Maybe. Synthetic telepathy seems like science fiction, I know, but I think it will be possible to establish some form of rudimentary communication through electric signals, not words.

HR: Definitely. Scientists have actually created a computer program that can decode brain activity and put it into words. So it's going to be relatively easy to capture thoughts and transmit them to another brain, I suspect.

c PD: Certainly. Time travel to the future is an essential characteristic of Einstein's theory of relativity, and this has been investigated many times by lots of scientists worldwide, so maybe there will be some form of future time travel. But traveling back to the past is a whole different story. There's no evidence that this is possible. So, who knows?

HR: Possibly. As I've said on a number of occasions, I think computers will probably be as intelligent as humans by 2040 or so. If that happens, I'm pretty sure they're going to help us find a way to travel through time.

C ▶8.7 Try to pronounce the highlighted cognates in the text. Listen again and reread to check. Did any of the pronunciations surprise you?

D Say the first word(s) in each of Penny and Harry's replies in **B**. How confident are their predictions? Complete the Venn diagram with the words.

maybe	definitely
probably	probably not
certainly	possibly

Most confident   Least confident

E 🔘 **Make it personal** In pairs, say which scientist you agree with for each question in **B** and why. Are your opinions the same or different?

🎵 *They will not force us, They will stop degrading us, They will not control us, We will be victorious*

First question ... Who do you agree with?   *Penny Duff. I don't think machines will ever feel anything.*   *I agree, so that's a similarity.*

② **Grammar** Future forms 1

A Study example sentences 1–7. Then decide if a–e in the grammar box are True (T) or False (F). Correct the false ones. Any similarities to your language?

1 Will we be able to communicate through thought transmission?
2 Are computers going to be more intelligent than us?
3 Machines will be able to feel human emotions.
4 We probably won't be able to teach robots how to feel.
5 I think it will be possible.
6 It's going to be relatively easy.
7 There will be some form of future time travel.

⚠️ **Common mistakes**

~~There will be~~
~~Will have~~ no more 4G
technology by 2030.
    be able to
Computers will ~~can~~ read our
minds one day.

> **a** Use both *going to* and *will* to make future predictions.
>
> **b** Word order = *will* + adverb (e.g., *probably, certainly*) + verb; adverb (e.g. *definitely*) + *won't* + verb.
>
> **c** Use *will / won't be able to* for something that will / won't be possible.
>
> **d** *There is / there are* has no future form.
>
> **e** Use verb *be* for questions with *will*.   ➔ **Grammar 8B** p. 152

B Circle the correct options. Check in pairs and say if you agree with the predictions.

1 The Internet **don't** / **won't** change substantially in my lifetime.
2 There will **have** / **be** fewer languages in the world a century from now.
3 Printed newspapers **probably will** / **will probably** disappear before 2040.
4 Ordinary people will **can** / **be able to** travel to the moon very soon.
5 Chinese **is going to be** / **will to be** the official world language at some point.
6 There **won't maybe** / **probably won't** be another outbreak of Ebola in the next five years.

I disagree. There's a good chance it might be much more controlled.

Really? I don't think it'll change, but we'll probably find more uses for it.

C Correct mistakes of word order or form in tweets 1–5. Which of these mistakes have you made?

1  **Gabriel Aguiar** @bielaguiar
Robots will replace teachers?
💬   🔁   ♡   ✉

2 **Lin Jung** @linjung92
Will it be enough food and water in the world?
💬   🔁   ♡   ✉

3 **Javier Blanco** @javiwhite
We gonna to have computers in our brains?
💬   🔁   ♡   ✉

4  **Anna Baum** @cuteanna
People is going to be able to learn languages faster?
💬   🔁   ♡   ✉

5 **Khalef Nassar** @naskhalef
We will ever to find life on other planets? And will survive humans another 1,000 years?
💬   🔁   ♡   ✉

D 🔘 **Make it personal** In small groups, ask and answer questions 1–5 in **C**. Who's the most optimistic person in your group? Who's the most certain?

Will robots replace teachers?   *Possibly for some subjects, but not all of them.*

⚠️ **Common mistakes**

*Will fossil fuels be prohibited
soon?*   *I think ~~that~~, yes.*
        so
        not
*Well, I hope ~~that no~~. We just
bought a new gasoline car!*

8.4 Is technology making us more, or less, social?

① Reading

A **Read the article quickly and choose the best title.**

1 Technology is making us antisocial
2 The art of making bad conversation
3 Here's how to make more friends
4 It's all about you!

Over the last 30 years or so, technology has created a world of instant and fast communication. We're easily accessible and online all the time. Some argue that it's making us less social, while others say it's actually connecting us more and expanding our opportunities. Whichever you believe to be true, here are four sure-fire ways to ruin a face-to-face conversation today. Which ones do you recognize?

1 You get a notification and that's all you need! It doesn't matter if you're in the middle of a very interesting **discussion**, you just have to look at your screen immediately. You make the other person wait while you look at your phone. Good way to lose a friend. 🗨

2 You're just trying to be "helpful" – or perhaps "judgmental" is a better word? If you think the person you're talking to is doing something that you consider wrong – unhealthy, impractical, or immoral – you tell them. And of course, you always **assume** that the other person wants your **sensible** advice. 🗨

3 When your friend is talking, you start talking, too – probably in the middle of the sentence – even if you say something that doesn't make sense. Also, it doesn't matter if you change the subject completely – you're not **actually** listening anyway. 🗨

4 When someone introduces a subject, you find a way to talk about you and your life and experiences. For example, a friend tells you they're going to **attend** an important meeting. You don't ask who, when, or where. Instead, you talk about the last meeting you went to and why it was the most important meeting in the world. You always make it about you! You just need to hear a recording of your conversations. One listen, and you'd be too **embarrassed** ever to speak about yourself again! 🗨

B ▶8.8 **Listen and reread a paragraph at a time. Match each one to ways to ruin a conversation, a–e. There's one extra.**

a keep interrupting
b keep checking your phone
c be the center of the universe
d judge the other person
e break eye contact and slowly turn away

Common mistakes

~~*intends*~~
Marcia ~~pretends~~ to become a doctor.

~~*success*~~
Sue had a lot of ~~exit~~ in her last project.

At the moment
~~Actually,~~ I'm a student, but I'll get a job when I graduate.

kept
She ~~was staying~~ checking her phone all the time.

C Over 90% of Latin-based words are "cognates", with similar meanings in your language. However, there are a few "false cognates", like the **Common mistakes**. In pairs, match definitions 1–6 to the **bold** words in **A**. Do they mean the same in your language?

1 a conversation
2 in reality
3 based on good judgment
4 suppose
5 be present at
6 feel uncomfortable about yourself

D 👤 **Make it personal** In small groups, answer 1–3. Any big differences?

1 Which is the most annoying way to ruin a face-to-face conversation?
2 Are online written "conversation killers" similar or different?
3 Does anyone you know have any of the habits described in the article?

I don't like it when people interrupt ...   *I know what you mean! It really annoys me.*

... me all the time!

② Grammar Future forms 2

A ▶8.9 **Listen to three conversations and identify the "conversation killers" from 1B.**

B ▶8.9 **Listen again. True (T), False (F), or Not mentioned (N)?**

1 Sue's car is brand new.
2 Sue's dad is loyal to a particular car model.
3 Regis has talked to Ann about her health before.
4 Ann sees a doctor regularly.
5 Yuko was about to leave for the airport when Sally called.
6 Yuko has been to New York before.

♫ *All our troubles, We'll lay to rest,*
And we'll wish we could come back
to these days, These days

C ▶8.9 **Complete 1–5 with the verbs in the correct tense. Use your intuition. Listen again to check.**

1 "I _____ to sell mine in October or November." (**try**)
2 "I _____ him right now and tell him." (**call**)
3 "I _____ the doctor on Friday." (**see**)
4 "I _____ a check-up too." (**get**)
5 "The plane _____ at two and I haven't started packing yet." (**leave**)

D **Study the verb forms and uses in C and complete the grammar box.**

> Match verb forms a–d to uses 1–5. Use 4 has two answers.
>
> a simple present   1 prediction based on evidence
> b present continuous 2 quick decision
> c *going to*   3 events on a timetable
> d *will*   4 future arrangement / fixed plan
>   5 intention
>
> → **Grammar 8C** p. 152

E **Match pictures 1–5 to quotes a–e. Circle the best future forms and explain why.**

"DO YOU WANT TO SEE A MOVIE TONIGHT?"

Five irritating types to watch out for …

a ☐ "Yeah, but the movie **starts** / **is starting** in three hours. We've got to leave now!"

b ☐ "Oh, what a pity! I'd love to, but I'm **taking** / **will take** grandma to her karate class tonight. Maybe some other time."

c ☐ "Hmm … I don't know. I mean, look at those clouds. It looks like it's **going to rain** / **raining** tonight … And you know how bad the traffic gets when it rains."

d ☐ "Thanks, but Bob and I are going to **watch** / **will watch** it in Paris next week."

e ☐ "You mean a movie? Tonight? Well, **I'll think** / **I'm thinking** about it and get back to you, OK?"

1 The excuse inventor
2 The punctuality freak
3 The non-decider
4 The pessimist
5 The boaster

F ▶8.10 **Listen to check. Then cover the text and use the pictures to remember each quote.**

G 🔘 **Make it personal** **Irritating types!** **Role-play in pairs. Then change roles.**

A: choose a personality type from **E** and answer **B**'s questions.
B: choose a situation below and ask **A**. Can you guess **A**'s personality type?
  • It's your grandma's birthday on Sunday and all her friends will be there. Invite **A**.
  • You need to borrow **A**'s new car to take your mom to the doctor.
  • You want **A** to help you paint your bedroom.
  • You want **A** to organize a class party with you.

My grandma's turning 90 on Sunday and we're having a party. Would you like to come?

I'd love to, but I'm not sure what I'm doing yet. I'll let you know, OK?

8.5 Who do you talk to when you need help?

 **Skills** Understanding ads

A Scan and match ads a–e to the areas of life below. How many ads offer coaching in more than one area?

- [ ] finances
- [ ] relationships
- [ ] health and diet
- [ ] personal development
- [ ] professional

Coaching Professionals in the Manhattan Area

a Good Life Services

Our health and fitness experts will show you how to stay in good shape and feel healthy and full of life. We'll analyze your diet and lifestyle, and prepare a personalized program for you. Check our website for much more information, or call to speak to one of our personal advisers.

b Money Wizard

Do you have money problems? Credit card bills you can't afford to pay? Need a quick, guaranteed solution? Just send $50 and your details to receive my amazing, exclusive guide to transforming your finances. Millions of dollars already saved for my customers! Get your money back if you're not 100% satisfied.

c Jenny Brook Coaching

Are you trying to get your life back on track? I'll look at you as a whole person and can help with all aspects of your life. I can offer you the benefit of my experience as a grandmother, mother of nine, and someone who has also had a lot of problems in their life. 50% discount on first session.

d Matt Jones

If you need help deciding on a career, or advice about whether to stay in your current job or move on, I can help you to work out the right answer. Specialist in sales and marketing jobs worldwide. See website for references and contact information.

e Heart to Heart Coaching Services

Do you have a history of failed relationships? Are you afraid of love? Do you constantly argue with the people you love most? Don't despair! Understanding how to improve your relationships with loved ones, friends, and colleagues will also help you to understand how to be a better, happier, and more successful person. Call today or make an appointment online.

B ▶8.11 **Listen, read, and, after each ad, repeat the pink-stressed words. Underline words you recognize as cognates.**

C Reread the ads and choose the best coach for the people in 1–5. Would you recommend each coach after reading or listening to their ad? Why (not)?

1 "I can't decide whether to wait for promotion or look for a different job."
2 "My finances are a mess! I owe a lot of money and don't know what to do."
3 "I need to make a lot of changes in my life, but I don't know where to start."
4 "I keep arguing with everyone I know. I feel like everybody hates me."
5 "I always feel tired or sick. How can I lead a healthier life?"

> *I'd recommend Good Life Services. They seem professional and have an informative website.*

D 🗣 **Make it personal** In pairs, answer 1–3.

1 Are you usually more convinced by reading or listening to ads?
2 Which areas of life in **A** do people usually need most help with? Order them 1–5. Any differences?
3 Do you know anyone who pays for coaching? Would you ever pay?

> *My brother pays for a personal fitness trainer at the gym. I don't think it's necessary. It's obvious what to do to keep fit.*

> *But sometimes you need someone to motivate you!*

ID in Action Making predictions

A ▶8.12 Joe's going through a difficult time, so he talked to three coaches from ads a–e on p. 106. Listen and match the coaches to their ads.

coach 1 _____   coach 2 _____   coach 3 _____

B ▶8.12 Listen again and check what you think Joe will do. Give reasons.

Joe's future	Yes	No	Maybe
1 get a promotion			
2 move to a new job			
3 sleep better			
4 check social media at night			
5 tell Emma how he feels			
6 marry Emma			

I think he'll get a promotion. He deserves one beacuse he's been with the company a long time.

I disagree! He needs to look for a new job. He's already waited too long for a promotion.

⏺ Common mistakes

Did your boss talk to you?
~~*You will get a promotion?*~~
w

C ▶8.12 **Test your memory!** Circle the five words / expressions the coaches use. Then listen again to check.

yes	Definitely. / For sure. / Absolutely.
	Probably. / There's a good chance.
fifty-fifty	Maybe. / Perhaps. / Possibly. / That depends.
	Probably not. / I doubt it.
no	Definitely not. / No way. / Not a chance.

D 👤 **Make it personal** **Fortune Telling!** In pairs.

A: Write three questions about your future (money, love, family, travel, career, studies ...) and give each question a **ran**dom number between 1 and 6. Ask B your questions.

B: You're an inex**per**ienced fortune-teller. Listen to A's question and number and make a prediction based on the photo on the corresponding card. Use your imagination and expressions from **C**.

Am I going to marry my boyfriend? Number 4.

No, not a chance! He's going to get a great job abroad and you'll meet someone better.

1 — I THE WARRIOR
2 — II THE TRAVELLER
3 — III THE UNLUCKY
4 — IV THE LUCKY
5 — V THE SUN
6 — VI THE CLOWN

Writing 8 A formal inquiry email

A Read ads 1 and 2 and the email. Which ad is the email responding to?

B In which paragraphs, a–d, does Kiera:
1. ☐ express interest in talking to the coach
2. ☐ make an inquiry about the coach's work
3. ☐ explain why she needs help
4. ☐ thank the coach and request a response
5. ☐ say where she saw the ad
6. ☐ give details about exactly what she wants to know

C Look at the highlighted examples in the email and read **Write it right!** Then correct the mistakes in 2–5.

✔ Write it right!

In a formal inquiry, you need to sound very polite to build a good relationship. Use indirect forms to request information.

Add *if* in *Yes / No* questions and remove the auxiliary *do*. Notice that the word order sometimes changes.

Direct (less polite)	Indirect (more polite)
Do you work in the evenings?	Can / Could you tell me if you work in the evenings?
Where do you work?	Can / Could you tell me where you work?
Can you see me next week?	Do you think you could see me next week?
What are your fees?	I'd appreciate it if you could tell me your fees.
Can I meet you to discuss this?	I'd be interested in meeting you to discuss this.

1. I'd appreciate *it* if you could explain what your work involves.
2. Do you think could you recommend someone to help me?
3. Can you tell me when do you open?
4. I'd be interested to knowing more about your plans.
5. Could you tell me what are your fees?

D Rewrite direct questions 1–5 using more polite, indirect forms.
1. Can I have your phone number?
   Do _____ ?
2. Do you have an office in Boston?
   Could _____ ?
3. Who are your clients?
   I'd _____ .
4. Do you have any clients in Brazil?
   Could _____ ?
5. Can you get back to me by tomorrow?
   I'd _____ .

1
Get the career you want

Becky Smith, professional careers coach. Experience of working with students from all backgrounds. Specialist in the financial and business sectors. 95% success rate. Contact me for a confidential consultation.

2
Change your life for good

Do you want to improve your employment prospects, become more socially confident, or take control or your life? Lifestyle coach **Toby Wilde** can help you succeed in all aspects of your life. Call or email today.

Dear _____,

I saw your ad on the university website. I'd be interested in talking to you about my situation.

a

b I'm 19 years old and studying law. My parents want me to work in a big city law firm. The problem is, I don't want to be a lawyer, but I feel that I'm trapped in my situation. I'm really interested in science, and I'd like to work in research. I'm ambitious, but there are very few job opportunities for someone without a science degree. I know the pay and benefits for lawyers are very good. I want to develop my career, but I'm worried that if I do what my parents want, I'll be unhappy.

c I'd like to know more about the work you do. Firstly, you say in your ad that you specialize in the financial and business sectors. Can you tell me if you also have experience of working with scientific research? You also said you have a very high success rate. Do you think you could give me the names of some people you have helped? Finally, could you tell me what the cost is for a consultation?

d Thank you in advance for taking the time to answer my questions. I'd appreciate it if you could reply to my questions as soon as convenient. I look forward to hearing from you.

Sincerely,

Kiera Jones

E 🔊 **Make it personal** Choose an ad from **A** or p. 106. Write an email in 150–200 words inquiring about the services of the coach.

Before	Decide why you need to hire the coach and what exactly you need to know.
While	Write an inquiry following the structure of the email in **A**. Include four paragraphs and at least three questions using indirect forms.
After	Exchange emails with another student. Check each other's emails, paying attention to the requests for information. Is the email polite?

8 Back to your future

 **Café**

1 Before watching

A Match 1–6 with definitions a–f. Which words do you already know and use? Give examples.

1 a fair   a make someone afraid
2 make stuff up   b a (superior) level of thought, e.g., spiritual
3 a (higher) plane   c a large exhibition, full of fun things to do
     d go somewhere with someone
4 scare   e an action designed to deceive (someone)
5 tag along
6 a trick   f invent things / stories

> *I have a friend who's always making stuff up.*

> *I was tricked into paying too much for my car!*

B Check what each character will be interested in at the fair.

	August	Andrea	Daniel	Lucy
futuristic science exhibits				
being with Daniel				
going somewhere with Lucy				
seeing horses				
the pie-eating contest				

2 While watching

A Watch up to 0:50 to check your answers in 1B. When are they all meeting up again?

B Listen without image up to 1:36. Number these items in the order you hear them, 1–8.

- [ ] coming back
- [ ] environmental reporter
- [ ] experience at least
- [ ] getting people lattes
- [ ] internship in Washington
- [ ] Los Angeles
- [ ] pretty impressive
- [ ] this summer

C Watch to check. What else did you hear and notice?

> *I think they held hands at the end!*

D Watch the rest. True (T) or False (F)?

1 They're both keen to hear their futures.
2 The fortune teller surprises them.
3 Both of them have doubts and ask questions.
4 Daniel shows her his hand then gets angry.
5 He thinks it's some kind of trick.
6 She knows where they're both going.
7 She predicts they'll go far away and never meet again.
8 Neither of them believe anything she says.

E Complete 1–9 with *will* or *be going to* according to the video. Who said each sentence?

1 I _____ go see the horses.
2 What _____ you guys _____ see?
3 I _____ tag along with you if you don't mind my company.
4 So we _____ all _____ meet back here in an hour or so.
5 You _____ be a wonderful environmental reporter.
6 I think you _____ be a fabulous filmmaker!
7 I _____ be running around and trying to find organic chocolate for some crazy actress.
8 You _____ go very far. And you _____ be on many planes, both spiritual and physical.
9 But in the end, you _____ come back together.

3 After watching

A Complete 1–6 with the verbs in the simple present or present continuous.

come back   go (x2)   think   try   wait

1 August _____ to the science exhibits.
2 August _____ all year for the pie-eating contest.
3 What _____ Lucy _____ about doing this summer?
4 Lucy says, "You know I _____ to L.A., right?"
5 Lucy wants to know if Daniel _____.
6 What _____ you _____ to do? Scare us?

B Watch again to check. As you do, whenever your teacher pauses the video, tell your partner the next thing the character is going to say.

C ● **Make it personal** Are you good at predicting (results, weather, etc.)? Any experience of fortune telling, or being tricked?

> *I guess soccer scores every week, but I'm hardly ever right!*

> *My grandmother used to read coffee cups. I loved it!*

> *I was given false money once. I didn't know what to do.*

D ● **Make it personal** In groups of three, role-play Lucy, Daniel, and the fortune teller.

1 Role-play the video as closely as you can.
2 Change roles and do it again. But this time, believe everything she says.

> *Show me your hands, my dears. Oooooh! I see many things, good and bad.*

R4 Grammar and vocabulary

A **Picture dictionary.** Cover the words on these pages and use the pictures to remember:

page	
86	7 movie genres
87	6 key aspects of movies
88	7 labels for passionate people
90	6 unusual collections
95	4 phrases for giving your opinion
98	6 technological items
100	7 phrasal verbs
155	the 8 pairs of picture words in lines 3 and 4 of the consonants chart

B ▶R4.1 **Complete the quiz with these verbs in the passive, then circle the correct answers. Listen to check.**

call   consider   find   sell   write

1 "Imagine" _____ by **John Lennon / Paul McCartney** in 1971.
2 About 1.5 billion **smartphones / iPhones** _____ around the globe every year.
3 Beyoncé's first solo album _____ *Dangerously in Love / Irreplaceable*.
4 Amy Winehouse was only **27 / 31** when she _____ dead in her apartment.
5 **Canadian / American** singer Ariana Grande _____ to be one of the world's best vocalists.

C In small groups, write a five-question quiz using passive sentences. Use the verbs in **B** or choose your own. Give two answer options for each question. Exchange with another group. Any "killer" questions?

> *Love in the Time of Cholera was written by Gabriel García Márquez / Isabel Allende.*

> *Machu Picchu was constructed by the Aztecs / Incas.*

D Complete 1–3 with *so*, *such* or *such a / an*. Choose the best (✓) and worst (✗) line each time. Compare in pairs.

E 🔵 Make it personal Circle the correct options in 1–5. Do you agree with the predictions? In pairs, compare and give reasons.

Life in the Future

1 CDs and DVDs _____ disappear before 2030.
   a probably won't   b won't probably
2 People will _____ travel in self-driving cars soon.
   a can   b be able to
3 _____ less online piracy by 2030.
   a There will have   b There will be
4 Apple _____ disappear in the next 20 years.
   a will   b is going
5 In 100 years, there won't be _____ to live on dry land.
   a anywhere   b nowhere

> *I think CDs and DVDs are going to disappear before 2025.*

> *Right! They've already disappeared in my house.*

F Correct the mistakes. Check your answers in units 7 and 8.

🔴 Common **mistakes**

1 *I'm really into watch horror movies.* (1 mistake)
2 *We didn't do nothing on the weekend.* (1 mistake)
3 *I'm lucky to have so intelligents parents.* (2 mistakes)
4 *Thousands of songs is downloaded illegal every day.* (2 mistakes)
5 *I thought the latest Shawn Mendes album great.* (1 mistake)
6 *"Where did you born?" "On 1988."* (3 mistakes)
7 *How long do you study here?* (2 mistakes)
8 *"Do you go to the party tonight?" "I think yes."* (2 mistakes)
9 *Will have less pollution 100 years from now.* (2 mistakes)
10 *I will ever find true love?* (1 mistake)

Meeting someone for the first time? The right and wrong things to say!

1 A blind date
- [ ] I'm _____ happy to finally get a chance to meet you.
- [ ] Wow! It feels like we've known each other for _____ long time.
- [ ] Hmm … You didn't look _____ short in the photos.

2 Your girl / boyfriend's parents
- [ ] It's _____ honor to meet you.
- [ ] I've heard _____ great things about you.
- [ ] I've heard _____ many great things about your food that I have to try it myself.

3 Your boss
- [ ] It's _____ privilege to work with someone like you.
- [ ] You look _____ much younger in person.
- [ ] It's _____ great to finally meet you.

> *I think the worst one for a blind date is …*

Skills practice

♪ *And I've missed your ginger hair, And the way you like to dress. Won't you come on over, Stop making a fool out of me. Why don't you come on over Valerie?*

R4

A ►**R4.2** **Listen to conversations 1–4. After the beep, you have four seconds to write the number next to the correct sentence. There are three extra sentences.**

I'll turn it down. _____
I'll turn it up. _____
I'll plug it in. _____
I'm going to get up at 5 a.m. _____
I'm going to wake up at 5 a.m. _____
I'm going to turn it on. _____
I'm going to turn it off. _____

B ►**R4.3** **Listen to the news stories and circle the correct options in 1–4.**

1 **More / Fewer** people are out of work.
2 This news item is about **a power outage / politics**.
3 Pineapple is probably a **computer / car** company.
4 This news item is about **a natural disaster / alien life**.

C ►**R4.3** **Listen again and write the numbers in 1–4. Practice saying the sentences. Don't stress the gray words.**

1 Unemployment **has** increased by _____.
2 _____ cities **were** affected.
3 _____ of all iTabs produced in May **were** considered defective.
4 The town, with a population of only _____, **was** visited by UFOs in the past.

D ►**R4.4** **Listen, read, and match review extracts 1–3 to the correct genre. There's one extra genre.**

action ☐   mystery ☐   documentary ☐   drama ☐

E **Reread. Which review is about a movie with ...**

a a lot of emotional conversations?
b very few words?
c a story we've all seen many times?

F 🎧 **Make it personal** **In groups, play *Guess the movie!* Take turns thinking of a movie or TV series plot you can describe in one sentence, like Review 1. The others ask *Yes / No* questions to try to guess the movie / TV series.**

A rich girl meets a poor boy on a boat, they fall in love, the boat hits an iceberg, he dies, but she survives.

Did it win an Oscar?   *Is it an American movie?*

G ►**R4.5** 🎧 **Make it personal** **Question time!**

1 Listen to the 12 lesson titles in units 7 and 8.
2 In pairs, practice asking and answering. Use the book map on p. 2–3. Ask at least two follow-up questions. Try to answer in different ways. Can you have a short conversation about all the questions?

Review 1 ★☆☆☆☆

The plot is so unintelligent that it can be described in a sentence: Girl falls in love with boy, boy dies, girl gets depressed. Think of all the Hollywood clichés you've ever heard. They're in this movie. But it's guaranteed to be a box office success in the U.S. and abroad.

Review 2 ★★★★★

This movie is truly spectacular. If you think a silent movie about an unsolved murder in 1870 is a recipe for disaster, think again. The main character (Lucy Barnes) is played by Jennifer Lawrence with such skill that, honestly, you don't miss hearing her voice. *The Trap* is a classic example of images speaking louder than words, which perhaps explains why subtitles are used only five times in this movie.

Review 3 ★★★★☆

What do you expect from a movie starring Mark Wahlberg? Lots of action scenes, right? Well, wrong. In *Gone*, Wahlberg reconstructs the events leading to the Boston Marathon bombing in 2013 with such sensitivity, precision, and attention to detail that you instantly forget who he is. The interviews with paramedics alone are worth the price of admission. *Gone* is a masterpiece of factual movie-making and it truly deserves to win an Oscar.

9

9.1 What do you think of marriage?

How to plan the perfect wedding

- plan the **enga**gement party ☐
- plan the **ho**neymoon ☐
- book a place for the wedding **ce**remony ☐
- make the guest list and send wedding **invi**tations ☐
- create a **gift** registry ☐
- choose clothes for the **bride**, **groom**, and **brides**maids ☐ ☐ ☐
- plan the **re**ception ☐
- choose the **flow**ers and **deco**rations ☐ ☐

🔔 Common **mistakes**

George got married ~~with~~ Amal in 2012. *to*

We need a ~~local~~ for the wedding. *place / venue*

They ~~compromised themselves~~. *got engaged*

Use *get* for all the stages in a relationship: *get together, get engaged, get (re)married, get divorced!*

① **Vocabulary** Weddings

A ▶9.1 Which **bold** words in the wedding checklist do you recognize? Guess the pronunciation. Then match them to a–k in the photos. Listen to a wedding planner and number them in the order you hear them, 1–11.

B ▶9.1 Listen again. Which two things on the checklist doesn't the planner do? Which three things do you think are the most difficult to organize?

For me, one of the hardest would be choosing …

C 👥 Make it personal In small groups.

1 Would / Did you / your parents use a wedding planner? Why (not)?
2 Search online for a quote you like about weddings and marriage. How does it reflect your opinion?

Here's a good one: "Six words for a successful marriage: I'm sorry, it's my fault!". I totally agree!

♫ *My head's under water, But I'm breathing fine, You're crazy and I'm out of my mind 'Cause all of me, Loves all of you*

9.1

② Listening

A ▶9.2 **Listen to Michaela and her wedding planner. Does the photo show the wedding she wants or the one the wedding planner wants?**

B ▶9.2 **Listen again and complete the chart with what each of them wants.**

		Wedding planner	Michaela
1	color of invitations		
2	ceremony at …		
3	reception in a …		
4	number of bridesmaids		
5	number of wedding guests		
6	type of rings		
7	place for honeymoon		

C 🔘 **Make it personal** **In pairs, answer 1 and 2 then share your best ideas in groups.**
1 Which wedding in **A** would you prefer? Agree three things that are essential for a good wedding. Does the class agree?
2 Describe the best wedding you've been to. Why was it so special?

My sister's wedding was amazing. They got married in a beautiful church and I was a bridesmaid.

③ Reading

A **Read the website and identify three things that are different from a traditional wedding. Compare in pairs. Did you identify the same three things?**

A wedding that is up in the air!

Are you looking for a way to make your wedding more interesting and memorable? Last Saturday, a crane lifted Helen Gomez and James Brandon up onto a platform in the air for their wedding ceremony. They got married up there, 160 feet (50 meters) in the air with the officiant, who conducted the ceremony, and 20 of their friends and family. There was even a platform for musicians to play the music the couple wanted. After they shared their marriage vows, Helen and James did an exciting bungee jump over the side of the platform.

After the ceremony, the wedding party all went back down to earth, but then they all went back up again for the reception. At the reception, guests ate a three-course meal wearing seatbelts so they were safe and couldn't fall. The idea of this kind of wedding is to create an experience that really will be unforgettable. You're probably asking yourself, "is this safe?" Marriage in the Sky, the company who organized the wedding, insist that it is. They operate in more than 40 countries, including ones that have strict rules about safety, such as the U.S., Canada, and Australia.

B ▶9.3 **Listen and reread. Are 1–7 True (T) or False (F)? Correct the false ones.**
1 A large elevator took the bride and groom up in the air.
2 The other people at the ceremony were strangers.
3 The couple chose their own music.
4 They made their marriage promises while they did a bungee jump.
5 The guests stayed up in the air after the ceremony, then did a bungee jump at the end.
6 When the guests ate, they couldn't walk around.
7 The company operates only in Europe and Asia.

C 🔘 **Make it personal** **In pairs. What's similar / different in your culture about weddings and the weddings described in this lesson? Do other pairs agree? Who in class has been to the most unusual wedding?**

Here, most people get married in a church.

Yes, that's true, but not everyone does that anymore.

9.2 Do you think romantic movies are entertaining?

① Vocabulary Romance

A ▶9.4 Listen to two conversations and match them to photos a and b.

1 I met Abby about two years ago and immediately **had a crush on her**. We **dated** for about a year and then we **broke up**. She's seeing someone else now, but I'm still in love with her. I'm really worried that I'm going to lose her forever. What should I do?

2 I found out that my partner **cheated on me** in the past. He says that he fell in love with someone else, but that it's over now, it was a mistake, and he wants to stay with me. Now we **argue** all the time. It's absolutely exhausting! Should I **dump him**? Or try again?

B ▶9.4 Read problems 1 and 2 and match the **bold** phrases to meanings 1–6. Which ones are more informal? Listen to check their pronunciation and remember the listener's responses.

1 _____ = stopped seeing each other
2 _____ = saw each other
3 _____ = was unfaithful to me
4 _____ = was very attracted to her
5 _____ = end the relationship
6 _____ = express different opinions, often angrily

C 🔵 **Make it personal** **Giving advice** In pairs, take turns role-playing the situations in **A**. What's the best advice you can think of?

A: Explain what has happened.
B: Listen sympathetically and give advice.

You have to tell her how you feel. Maybe she'll respond positively.

> ✅ **Common mistakes**
>
> ~~fell~~ *fell*
> She ~~felt~~ in love.
> *felt* = past tense of *feel*;
>
> ~~broke up~~ *broke up*
> They ~~terminated~~.
> She likes *me*. (*I like her.*)
> You like *me*. (*I like you.*)
> **Subject** + *like* + **object**

② **Grammar** -ed and -ing adjectives

♫ *Seasons change and our love went cold, Feed the flame 'cause we can't let go, Run away, but we're running in circles, Run away, run away*

A ▶9.5 **Match sentences 1 and 2 to photos a and b. Listen to the conversations to check.**

1   The man is bored.   2   The man is boring.

B **Circle the correct options in examples 1 and 2 and the rules in the grammar box.**

1   They were **amazed / amazing** by the **amazed / amazing** fireworks.
2   Sci-fi movies often include **frightened / frightening** monsters. As a child, I was really **frightened / frightening** by The Xenomorph in the movie *Alien*.

Adjectives ending in:
   -ed / -ing are used for a feeling.
   -ed / -ing are used for something that causes the feeling.

→ **Grammar 9A** p. 154

C ▶9.6 **Complete 1–8 with the correct form of the words. Listen to check. In pairs, which sentences are true for you? Explain why.**

1   Watching TV alone is _____. (**depress**)
2   I usually find English classes _____. (**interest**)
3   My family is _____ (**surprise**) when I get good grades.
4   The last movie I saw was _____. (**confuse**)
5   I get _____ (**tire**) after I've eaten.
6   Horror movies aren't usually very _____. (**frighten**)
7   I get _____ (**embarrass**) when people talk about me.
8   Falling in love is always _____ (**excite**) , but it can be _____ (**terrify**), too!

Number 1 is true for me. I like to have company when I'm watching TV.

D 🔘 **Make it personal** **Intense experiences! In groups, answer 1–3.**

1   Choose the two adjectives from **C** or below that best describe your opinion of 1) work 2) school 3) weekends 4) going on a first date 5) learning English.

   amazing   boring   entertaining   exhausting   relaxing   stressful

2   Find someone who chose the same adjectives as you. Are your reasons similar?

My work is exciting, because I travel a lot.

Lucky you! My work is boring, because I do the same thing every day.

3   Describe and compare the last time you had these feelings. Who has the best example for each?
   •   very irritated
   •   really bored
   •   extremely excited
   •   absolutely exhausted
   •   completely relaxed
   •   totally terrified

The last time I was absolutely exhausted was after going clubbing on Saturday. I danced nonstop all night!

9.3 If you had three wishes, what would they be?

1 Grammar Second conditional

A ▶9.7 **Listen to the first part of a conversation.**
1 What do you think the relationship is between:
   a Sarah and Max?   b Sarah and Tony?   c Tony and Max?
2 What do you think Max is going to ask Sarah?

B ▶9.8 **Listen to part two to check. What else did you pick up?**

C ▶9.8 **Listen again and circle the correct options in 1–6. In pairs, do you think Tony is cheating on her? Why (not)?**
1 What **would** / **will** you do if Tony **cheats** / **cheated** on you?
2 If I **see** / **saw** him with another person, I'**ll** / '**d** confront him.
3 What if a friend **tells** / **told** you, what **will** / **would** you do?
4 If I **didn't** / **don't** know for sure, I'**d** / '**ll** ask Tony first.
5 **Would** / **Will** you follow him, if you **think** / **thought** he liked someone else?
6 I'**ll** / '**d** trust him to tell me the truth, if he **wants** / **wanted** to date someone else.

D **Complete the grammar box. Are both form and use similar in your language?**

> *I'd be an architect.*

---

1 Match *if* clauses 1–3 to result clauses a–c. In pairs, ask and answer the questions.

If clause		Result clause
1 If you were a bird (but you're not),	a	what would it be?
2 If the Internet didn't exist (but it does),	b	where would you fly to?
3 If you could choose any job (but you can't),	c	how would your life change?

2 Circle the correct options. Use the second conditional for:
– future situations that are **possible** / **impossible** but **not very** / **very** likely to happen.
– imaginary present situations: If we **were** / **are** rich, we'd buy a yacht. But we're not …

→ **Grammar 9B** p. 154

E **Complete second conditional questions 1–6 with the correct form of the verbs.**
1 If your parents _____ (**not like**) your partner, _____ you _____ (**dump**) him / her?
2 If you _____ (**be**) president, what _____ you _____ (**change**) first?
3 If you _____ (**have**) a superpower, which one _____ you _____ (**choose**)?
4 What three items _____ you _____ (**take**) if you _____ (**be**) exiled to a desert island?
5 If you _____ (**have**) a time machine, _____ you _____ (**travel**) back to the past or into the future?
6 If you _____ (**see**) that the person next to you _____ (**have**) a gun in their belt, what _____ you _____ (**do**)?

F 🔘 **Make it personal** **Ice breakers! In groups, ask and answer 1–6 in E and give reasons. Then decide on one answer for each question. Do other groups have similar answers?**

> *I'd choose to be invisible when I want. Then I'd be able to go anywhere!*

> *I'd be Superspeed and do everything faster.*

② Reading

A Take the questionnaire and read about your score. Is it a fair **ver**dict on you?   *Well, yes and no. I'm a bit like that but …*

Are you the jealous kind?

1 **Your friend wants to talk about her latest success. Would you …**

a) listen enthusi**as**tically?
b) listen, but try to change the subject?
c) avoid your friend for a few days?

2 **You're supposed to visit a friend who has a new house. Would you …**

a) go immediately – you'd be very happy for your friend?
b) go soon, but don't say much about the house?
c) try to meet your friend in another place?

3 **If you had some really great news, would you …**

a) not tell anyone, because you wouldn't want them to feel **en**vious?
b) tell your closest friends, but you'd be very modest?
c) tell all your friends, because you want them to feel envious?

4 **Your best friend wants you to go out with their new friend. Would you …**

a) go along happily? You'd love to meet your friend's friend.
b) go, but you'd feel jealous of your friend's friend?
c) make an excuse and not go?

5 **If you saw your partner talking and laughing with someone else, would you …**

a) do nothing? You'd be happy that your partner was having a good time.
b) go and interrupt and join them?
c) in**ter**rogate him / her later at home.

6 **If you and your friend ap**plied** for the same job (or the same school) and your friend was ac**cepted** and you weren't, would you feel …**

a) happy for your friend?
b) disa**ppoint**ed, but still happy for your friend?
c) very unhappy and you wouldn't want to see your friend?

How many
As? _____
Bs? _____
Cs? _____

Mostly As – You're never jealous and tend to trust others and feel genuinely happy for their success.

Mostly Bs – You have a tendency to get jealous and envious of others, but you're not always this way.

Mostly Cs – You definitely have a jealous nature. You feel jealous of others and you want others to be envious of you.

B ▶9.9 **Listen, reread, and repeat the pink-stressed words. In pairs, compare your answers. Any big differences? Do you usually enjoy questionnaires like this?**

The quiz says that I'm a jealous person.   *Do you think that's true?*

Yes, sometimes. For example, if my boyfriend wants to go out with his friend and not me, I get jealous.   *Maybe the quiz is right then!*

⊘ Common mistakes

jealous / envious
He's ~~with envy~~ of her.

C 🔒 **Make it personal** **In pairs, complete 1–6. Which pair has the most original answers?**

1 If my partner were jealous, I'd …
2 If I could be any famous person, I'd be …
3 If I could live anywhere in the world, …
4 If I could invite any three people to dinner, …
5 If I had $50,000 to spend in 24 hours, …
6 If I could change one thing about my life, …

If my partner were jealous, I'd tell her not to worry.   *If I could be any famous person, I'd be Lionel Messi because …*

9.4 Have you ever performed for an audience?

① Vocabulary Performers

A ▶9.10 Listen to two friends fantasizing and count the different types of performers they mention. Which ones would they like to be?

B ▶9.10 Complete the names of the performers. Listen to check, match them to photos 1–10, then add to the correct place in the chart. Add two or more words to each column.

an act___ ___   a gymn___ ___ ___   a danc___ ___   a comed___ ___ ___
a music___ ___ ___   a sing___ ___   a skat___ ___
a magic___ ___ ___   an athl___ ___ ___   a clo___ ___

-or	-er	-ian	other
actor			

C ▶9.10 Listen again. True (T) or False (F)?

1 He thinks she's a good singer.
2 Maybe she has musical talents.
3 She thinks he's athletic.
4 She thinks he's amusing.

D 🔘 **Make it personal** Who are your favorite performers? If you were a performer, what would you like to be? Do your classmates agree?

My favorite actor is Wagner Moura.

I love soccer, so I'd like to be a famous soccer player.   *Really? You're good at telling jokes, so maybe you should be a comedian!*

② Grammar *May, might, could, must, can't + be*

A ▶9.11 Listen to two people speculating about the blond man in the picture. Then match deductions 1–6 to reasons a–f.

Deduction	Reason
1 He's a celebrity.	a He's graceful.
2 He's an athlete.	b He's handsome.
3 He's not an athlete.	c He's wearing a sport shirt.
4 He's a dancer.	d He's thin.
5 He's not a dancer.	e He's making his date laugh.
6 He's a comedian.	f His legs are thin.

B ▶9.11 Listen again and notice the modal verb in each deduction, 1–6. Reconstruct the sentences. Listen again to check.

1 *Must. He must be a celebrity.*   4 _____
2 _____   5 _____
3 _____   6 _____

C Complete the grammar box.

⚠ **Common mistakes**

could / might / may
He ~~can~~ be tired.

Do you think they're
~~Can they be~~ German?

Modal verbs express different degrees of certainty.

She must be tired – she just ran a marathon.   *She might be tired – she was working all day.*
She can't be tired – she slept all day.

Complete 1-3 with *must, could / may /might, can't / must not.*

If you feel: 1 very sure, use _____.
              2 unsure, use _____.
              3 something is definitely not true, use _____.

To ask for a deduction, *must* and *can't* are rarely used. Ask: *Do you think ...?*
Do you think it will rain tomorrow? It might – there are a lot of gray clouds today.

➡ **Grammar 9C** p. 154

D ▶9.11 Listen again and mark the stress in 1–6 in 2B. Practice in pairs, saying the sentences with the same stress and intonation.

♪ *I could be brown, I could be blue, I could be violet sky, I could be hurtful, I could be purple, I could be anything you like*

9.4

E ▶9.12 **In pairs. What do you think the items in photos 1–4 are? Listen for more clues. Compare with other pairs. How many pairs got all four correct first time?**

> *Number 1 might be a kiwi, because of the color.*

> *No, it can't be a kiwi, because of the texture. It could be a …*

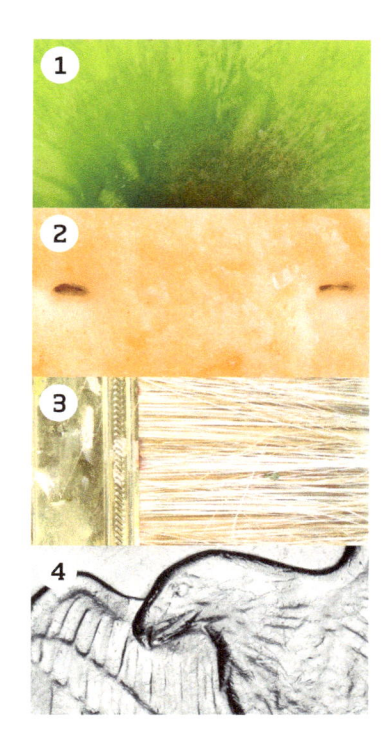

F 🔘 Make it personal **Make a conclusion about situations 1–5. Try to find someone with the same conclusions. Who has the most matches?**

1 You see a handsome man eating alone in a restaurant.
2 Jorge, a good student, has suddenly missed a lot of classes.
3 An old friend doesn't answer your messages.
4 You see a couple holding hands and laughing.
5 One of your neighbors has 14 cats, 10 dogs, and 6 rabbits.

> *What conclusion do you have for situation 1?*   *He must be waiting for someone.*

> *My conclusion is that he might be away from home on a business trip.*

③ Reading

A Why do people jump to conclusions? Choose the option you think is most likely to be true. Then read quickly to check.

1 Because we know we are right.
2 Because experience makes us sure.
3 Because it satisfies the brain.
4 Because it reduces anxiety.

Why we jump to conclusions

You call and text your friend to invite her to a special concert and she doesn't respond. You immediately conclude, "She must be mad, for some reason." We've all done it before – something happens and you jump to a conclusion without any evidence. Psychologists argue that jumping to conclusions is common in many situations, but did you know that there is a reason why we do this? Thanks to what we now know about the brain, we understand why we make these as**sump**tions when we have no evidence.

Neu**rol**ogists say that when we assume something that we don't know and it feels logical to us, our brain feels satisfied. We don't have to be right to feel satisfaction, we just need to believe we're right. In this case, certainty is more important than accuracy. Being sure gives us a feeling of satisfaction, although it also makes us feel anxious and sad. It is much healthier to live in uncertainty than to jump to a conclusion, but uncertainty doesn't come with the same feeling of satisfaction from the brain. 😕

B ▶9.13 **Listen, reread, and circle the best answers.**

1 It is **normal** / **unusual** to make an assumption.
2 The science of the brain **can** / **cannot** explain why we make assumptions.
3 We **don't want to** / **want to** make sense of things.
4 It is **not necessary** / **necessary** to be completely correct to feel satisfaction.
5 It is better for us to be **sure** / **unsure** about something.

C 🔘 Make it personal **Oops, I did it again!** In pairs, share stories about times when you or someone you know jumped to the wrong conclusion. Who has the best example?

> *Once I called my girlfriend and she didn't call me back for two days, so I thought she was angry about something, but she was actually in the hospital!*

ID Skills Identifying reasons

A Where are you in the birth order in your family? First, in the middle, youngest, or are you an only child? Has this had an effect on your life and personality?

I'm an only child, so I like being by myself. And I guess I was spoiled as a child.

B Read the article and match headings 1–6 to paragraphs a–e. There's one extra.

1 The baby of the family
2 The flexible ones
3 The self-sufficient ones
4 The effect of birth order
5 The bossy ones
6 The best of all

Birth order and you

a Your siblings, you love them, you hate them, you need them, you don't need them. Birth order, that is whether you are the oldest, the youngest, or in the middle in your family, can have an effect on your personality and your family dynamics. Are you similar to or completely different than your brothers and sisters? Birth order can help to explain why. According to Alfred Adler, an Austrian psychiatrist, birth order has a profound effect on how you see the world. Here are a few of the observations that Adler makes.

b First-born children are natural leaders – they are more responsible and mature and are more accustomed to adult company. They are often more intelligent than their later born siblings and they can be aggressive, because they are used to being in charge. They like being alone.

c Middle children, on the other hand, are often the opposite of first-born children. They feel they don't have any particular role in their family, so their friends are often more important to them than their family. They are good at negotiating and sociable, and people see them as adaptable and relaxed. At the same time, they often keep secrets and don't open up much about their emotions.

d As for the youngest in the family, they tend to be friendly and sociable. They like to be with other people and are often charming. They like to be the center of attention. They are not good at being alone and they get bored easily, but they have a lot of self-confidence and are not afraid to take risks. They tend to be more

irresponsible, because they know that someone will always help them if they have any kind of problem.

e What about if you are an only child? Well, it seems that one of the main issues for only children is that they have to work harder to make friends, because they don't immediately have them in the family. They are often more independent and are used to spending time alone and entertaining themselves.

C ▶9.14 Listen, reread, and complete the chart. Find the number of adjectives indicated in each column in the text in **B**.

First born (3+)	Middle children (3)	Youngest children (3+)	Only children (1)

D ▶9.15 Listen and note Michael and David's birth order. What's the matter with Michael?

I'd tell Michael to buy a new car with credit!

E ▶9.15 Listen again. In pairs, what would you say to Michael, David, and Jane?

F 🔵 Make it personal Form groups by birth order. Do you agree with what the article says about your position? Then form mixed groups and compare. Any surprises?

I agree that the oldest child is the most intelligent!   *Are you the oldest child?*   *Yes, of course!*

ⓘ in Action Giving advice

A ▶9.16 **Match problems 1–5 to suggestions a–f. There's one extra. Listen to check.**

1 I've lost my phone.
2 My boyfriend works on weekends.
3 I have a headache.
4 I'm bored at my job.
5 I'm failing math.

a Go home and lie down.
b Look in your room.
c Get a new one.
d Work harder.
e Talk to him.
f Why don't you run away?

B ▶9.16 **Listen again and complete dialogues 1–5. Do each of A's lines sound like suggestions or orders?**

1 **A:** _____ go upstairs and look in your room?
   B: That's a good _____.
2 **A:** If I _____ you, I'd _____ to him and explain that it's not fair.
   B: _____ for the suggestion, but you don't know my boyfriend.
3 **A:** You _____ go home and lie down. You _____ be at a party.
   B: You're _____.
4 **A:** _____ looking for a new job?
   B: _____ for the tip.
5 **A:** You _____ start working harder or you won't get into college.
   B: I _____.

C In pairs, think of suggestions for Noah, Harper, or Claudia. Find a new partner who chose a different person and role-play both situations.

I have a cold and a headache, but I have an important meeting with my boss later.

Noah

If I were you, I'd cancel the meeting.

I took a test but I didn't pass because I forgot about it and didn't study.

Harper

Why don't you talk to your teacher?

I've got a promotion in my company's Canadian office, but my boyfriend Juan hasn't finished college.

Claudia

I'd find out how Juan feels.

D 🔒 **Make it personal** Think of real problems people have. In groups of four, role-play giving advice.

A: Explain your problem. **B, C, D:** Give **A** advice.

My sister doesn't like her job because she has to work long hours and they don't pay her very well. *If I were your sister, I'd change my job!*

Writing 9 Giving advice

A Read Ben's post on an online advice forum and the two responses. Which response is from:

a a friend of Ben's?

b a professional counselor?

From: Ben

Can anyone help, please? I'm worried about my brother. His girlfriend broke up with him and now she's dating his best friend. He's lost his job at the restaurant where he was working, and I think he owes money to some of his friends. His school grades are going down too. What do you think I should do? I need some advice.

¹Dear Ben,

You're in a difficult situation, but here are a few ideas and suggestions for you. First of all, try not to panic. You need to stay calm. ² You have to talk to your brother. Why don't you invite him for lunch or coffee? If I were you, I'd tell him how worried I was about him. Then you should give him the opportunity to talk, and let him explain how he's feeling. Ask him if he understands why ³ his girlfriend ended their relationship and let him know that you are there to support him. Try to make him see how important school is for his future, even if it's difficult to see that now. Maybe you could offer to help him with his school work. ⁴ My advice is, ⁵ don't lend him any money: this won't help him. He has to take responsibility for himself and you need to help him with this.

⁶With sincere good wishes,

Marlena Duncan

What's up, dude?

Sounds like yr bro is in a mess, sorry 2 hear bout that – stay cool and talk to him, man, like, ask him for a drink, etc, find out why his gf dumped him – IF he wants to talk about it ;-) best advice? – tell him youll help, not $$ so don't give him nada, call me if you need to talk, ok?

Hang in there man, you hear me?

Joe ☺

B Reread the responses. Who gives advice 1–8: Marlena (M), Joe (J), or both (B)?

1 Ben should stay calm and not panic.

2 He should arrange to meet his brother.

3 He needs to tell his brother he's worried about him.

4 He should find out why his brother's girlfriend left him.

5 He needs to be clear that he will help his brother.

6 He could help his brother with his school work.

7 He shouldn't give his brother money.

8 He should phone to talk more about his problem.

C Match the highlighted expressions in Marlena's response to the corresponding expressions in Joe's.

D Read **Write it right!** then rewrite 1–4 in the opposite style.

✔ Write it right!

To give advice, use a style appropriate to the subject.

	Formal style	Informal style
Start / End	*Dear X; With best wishes / Sincerely*	*Hi / What's up?; Bye*
Sentences	complete sentences	can be incomplete sentences
Directness	less direct: *If I were you, I'd share your worries with him.*	more direct: *Tell him you're worried!*
Idioms, slang, abbreviations, emoticons	do not use	OK to use
Punctuation	use capital letters, periods, and commas correctly	use fewer capitals, commas, and OK to use dashes

1 v sorry 2 hear bout yr prob

2 First, you need to talk to your brother before it is too late.

3 best advice? – stay cool, man & dump her, ok? understand?

4 If I were you, I'd try to persuade your friend to discuss the situation.

E 🔵 **Make it personal** Read the problem and choose to write a formal or informal reply in 80–150 words.

From: Alicia K

Help!

My brother and sister are in the middle of a big fight and I'm caught between them. My brother has started dating my sister's best friend, and my sister is really angry. He's 22 and my sister's friend is only 17. My brother and sister are not speaking, but they call me every day and ask me to do something. What do you think I should do?

With thanks, Alicia

Before	Think of five suggestions and the order you want to say them.
While	Use features of the style you have chosen. Vary the expressions you use to give advice. Refer to the tips in **Write it right!**
After	Exchange responses with a classmate. Is your advice similar?

9 Green-eyed monsters

1 Before watching

A Match 1–10 to definitions a–j.

1	a **back**bone	a	spine, **spi**nal column
2	a beast	b	stupid
3	a chicken	c	take no notice of
4	dumb	d	a scary animal
5	faults	e	a person (usually a man) who helps another (usually a woman)
6	fear		
7	ignore		
8	jealous	f	envious, green-eyed
9	a knight in shining **ar**mor	g	a **cow**ard
		h	be afraid of
10	surrounded by	i	on all sides
		j	**de**fects

B In pairs, with sound off. **A:** Watch up to 0:35 and tell B what you see. **B:** Don't watch! Listen to A. Guess what they actually say. Then change roles.

> **A:** August's in the café, and he's unhappy. He's on his computer, talking to somebody.

> **B:** I think Daniel says, "Look at Paolo and Andrea."

2 While watching

A Watch up to 2:21. True (T) or False (F)?

1 Rory wants to challenge Paolo too.
2 Daniel says he's too nice to be so negative.
3 Daniel tells them to be nice to their friend Paolo.
4 Rory's pleased about how he's feeling.
5 Daniel warns Rory **jea**lousy is changing him.
6 August admits he's jealous too.
7 Rory de**nies** being jealous.
8 August decides to do something to challenge Paolo.

B Who says 1–10, August (A), Rory (R), or Daniel (D)? Watch to check.

1 But you're all just making excuses.
2 I know my faults.
3 That guy is serious competition. In everything.
4 If you really want something, you will do whatever it takes.
5 No more excuses. Use your personality.
6 Dude, you're only physically strong! You have no courage.
7 She only pays attention to me when she wants something.
8 Both of you, grow some backbone.
9 Why didn't Lucy ask me to be her star?
10 Um, I gotta work on my writing.

C ● **Make it personal** Have you (or people close to you) ever been really jealous? What or who of? Did it work out OK in the end?

> Yes, me! I was jealous of all my friends who had the first iPhone. In the end, I did some jobs for neighbors and made enough money to buy one.

3 After watching

A Check the advice Daniel gives August and Rory.

☐ Stop making excuses.
☐ Join the competition.
☐ If you really want something, do whatever it takes.
☐ Don't be like Steve Jobs.
☐ Use your genius brain!
☐ If you want to build muscles, go to the gym.
☐ Get some confidence.
☐ Grow some backbone.
☐ Stop using Paolo as an excuse.

B Complete 1–9 with these expressions.

a knight in shining armor		Chicken! Tell me the truth
Grow some backbone	I bet	Join the club
Mind if I join you	one of the worst	
Tell me if I'm crazy, but	You're all heart	

1 _____! Get more confidence and don't be afraid.
2 He's like _____. He'll help anyone in trouble.
3 _____? I'm on a break.
4 _____. You're a great person!
5 _____ doesn't that girl look just like Liv Tyler?
6 **A:** I'm so tired from that long flight! **B:** _____, so am I.
7 _____ I'm smarter and a better journalist.
8 This is probably _____ feelings in the world
9 _____. Have you ever asked her out again?

C ● **Make it personal** **Role-play!** In groups, create a role-play using as many expressions from **B** as possible. Perform it for the class.

> Tell me if I'm crazy but ... isn't that Zac Efron talking to our teacher?

> No way. You're kidding!

10.1 Do you often feel stressed?

a ☐ b ☐

c ☐ d ☐ e ☐

f ☐ g ☐ h ☐

Institute For
MEDITATION & RELAXATION

Stressed out? Not again!

What's the biggest stressor for you in your daily life?

☐ poor diet
☐ multitasking
☐ financial problems
☐ pressure to succeed
☐ deadlines
☐ caring for a child
☐ a lack of sleep
☐ a lack of exercise
☐ peer pressure

① Vocabulary Causes and symptoms of stress

A ▶10.1 Match the causes of stress to photos a–h. There's one extra cause. Then find six /k/ and five /ʃ/ sounds in the survey. Listen to check.

B ▶10.2 Listen to the survey. Number the photos in **A** in the order you hear them, 1–8.

C ▶10.2 Listen again and write the number of the speaker who:

☐ has no energy in the evenings.
☐ has to finish a piece of work today.
☐ gets sick when she's stressed out.
☐ never has any time off.
☐ makes the problem worse by worrying.
☐ has to pass a lot of exams.
☐ uses credit to buy things.
☐ has to do many things at the same time.

D Read examples 1–5, then match 1–3 below to uses a–c. Which of the examples are true for you?

1 I'm under**paid**. = I don't earn enough money.
2 I'm over**worked**. = I have too much work.
3 I over**slept** this morning. = I didn't wake up when I was supposed to.
4 I undera**chieved** in the test. = I didn't do as well as I could have.
5 I show a lack of interest in my studies. = I'm not motivated enough at school.

1 under-   a goes before a noun and means "not enough"
2 over-   b combines with a verb and means "not enough"
3 (a) lack of c combines with a verb and means "too much"

⏱ Common mistakes

I have ~~lack~~ *a* of money at the moment.
I feel depressed when I don't get ~~sufficient~~ exercise.
enough

E Complete 1–6 with *under-*, *over-*, or *lack of*. Then, in pairs, ask and answer the questions. Any big differences?

1 Is your diet very healthy or is there a _____ fresh fruit and vegetables?
2 Is the salary for teachers fair or are they _____ paid?
3 Do you know anyone who often _____ spends and then has a _____ money the following month?
4 Are you generally calm or do you sometimes _____ react?
5 When was the last time you _____ slept and woke up late?
6 Do you feel you've _____ achieved at anything in your life, when you could have done better?

I'm happy enough with my diet. I rarely overeat.

F 🔊 **Make it personal** Which problems in **A** have you / your friends had? In groups, choose the four most serious problems. Compare your list with another group and try to persuade them that your list is better.

For me, number 1 is financial problems, because if you have problems with money, you'll have other problems too.

Yes, but if you don't sleep enough, you'll get sick, so that's the most serious problem.

② Listening

A ▶10.3 Which of the 12 options do you think are good ways to relieve stress? Listen. Which three does the woman do? Why doesn't she do the others?

B ▶10.3 Listen again. True (T) or False (F)?
1 She's taking a yoga class.
2 She wakes him up in the middle of the night.
3 She has one cup of tea when she's stressed.
4 She discusses her deadlines with her boss.
5 She plans to take a class to help with her stress level.

C What would you do if you were: a) the woman? b) the man?

If I was her, I certainly wouldn't …

D 🔊 **Make it personal** How do you cope with stress? List six things you do. Find someone whose list is the same or almost the same.

I usually stay up all night if I have an exam. I drink coffee and energy drinks all night. After the exam, I sleep for a day!

I play loud music and dance for 10 minutes.

Institute For
MEDITATION & RELAXATION

Relieving stress:
How do you do it?

☐ take a break
☐ medi**ta**te
☐ exercise
☐ eat well
☐ plan your time
☐ have realistic deadlines
☐ relax
☐ spend time with friends
☐ sleep well
☐ breathe **dee**ply
☐ take medicines
☐ go clubbing

① **Vocabulary** Lifestyle changes

A What lifestyle changes do the people in pictures 1 and 2 need to make in their lives? Use these ideas plus your own.

drink less soda   eat better   eat less salt   exercise more   get a new job

get more sleep   lose weight   organize and plan time   spend less time online

spend more time with friends / family   watch less TV   work from home   work less

It looks like the woman should watch less TV.   *Yeah, and look at the bags under her eyes. She needs to …*

B Read and match testimonials a and b to the pictures. Circle and share all the clues you found.

Do you need to "turn your life around"?

a I had a terrific day today, thanks to you. I went to bed early last night, so got up early and went to the gym for an hour, then had an omelet for breakfast back at home. Much better than the donut I usually eat at the office! Got to work on time and made a plan of what I needed to do all day. I also had a chat with my boss about my schedule and she agreed to let me work from home two days a week. Result! I finished everything I had to do today and then shared a home-cooked dinner with my family. I'm back on track and finally taking control of my life. Thank you!
By MyVeryBest

b Man! What a day! Started my new job today – seems like it's gonna be fun. I talked to a guy who travels a lot for work – that's exactly what I want to do. Was so busy that I didn't even have time to look at my phone! When I finally got home I had a late dinner with my sister. We had lasagne which was delicious (it was my nephew who cooked it!) – and I only watched TV for an hour! Wow! I feel so much better. Thank you – it's all thanks to the "Turn Your Life Around" seminar.
By BeginAgain

C ▶10.4 Listen, reread, and check the lifestyle changes in **A** that each person made.

D 🎤 Make it personal Choose two lifestyle changes in **A** or your own ideas. In groups, find out about each other's changes by asking and answering 1–3. Which change do most people want to make? Whose change is the most unusual?

1 What are the advantages / disadvantages of making the change?
2 How easy / difficult is it to make the change?
3 What will happen if you do / don't succeed?

First, I want to stop buying things wrapped in plastic because it's better for the environment. But it's difficult to do because so many products are sold in plastic.

② Grammar Relative pronouns: *that* & *who*

♫ *You know I'm the one who put you up there, Name in the sky, Does it ever get lonely? Thinking you could live without me*

A ▶10.5 **Listen and number the photos in the order Patrick describes them, 1–6.**

a

b

c

d

e

f

B ▶10.5 **Listen again and complete 1–5 by adding the missing words. Then match 1–5 to five of the photos. What might he say about the sixth photo?**

1 This is the hotel was on the website.

2 You can see the swimming pool was right outside our room.

3 This is the lifeguard told us to get out of the water.

4 This is the bar was next to the pool.

5 These are some of the birds were flying around outside.

He might say, "This is the ..."

C **Read the examples in the grammar box and complete the rules. Does your language make a similar distinction?**

> Use **relative pronouns** to join two clauses.
>
> *This is my brother* **who** *lives in Paris. This is my brother* **that** *lives in Paris.*
> *He's the man* **who** *sold me my car. He's the man* **that** *sold me my car.*
> *There's the café* **that** *sells the delicious French pastries.*
> *She's the lady I met yesterday. (lady is the object of the clause).*
> But *She's the lady who (that) lives next door. (lady is the subject of the clause).*
>
> **1** Use _____ and _____ for people. Use _____ for things.
>
> **2** You **can / can't** omit the relative pronoun when it refers to the object of the clause..
>
> → **Grammar 10A** p. 156

⟳ Common mistakes

that
This is the computer ~~what~~
I bought today.

D **Complete 1–6 with *that* or *who*. Ask your classmates the questions and try to be the first to find positive answers to all of them!**

1 Do you know someone _____ speaks three languages?

2 Do you have any friends _____ speak really good English?

3 Have you been to a place near here _____ sells good coffee and snacks?

4 Was there a star _____ you used to idolize when you were young?

5 What's the food _____ you most enjoy eating?

6 Is there anyone in your family _____ has had an accident recently?

Do you know someone who speaks three langauges?

No, but maybe you should ask Milton. I know he speaks Quechua.

E **⬤ Make it personal** **Let me introduce ...** In pairs, take turns showing photos. Identify and explain the main people / things in them. Ask follow-up questions too. Share any unusual stories or interesting information with the class.

This is a selfie that my sister Jane sent me. She's the one who studies in L.A.

Cool. When did she go there?

10.3 What's your attitude to money?

① Reading

A In pairs, use this photo from a documentary movie, the lesson title, and the song line on p. 129 to guess what the documentary is about.

> *It could be about an old woman who decides to go on an expensive vacation.*

B Read the review and choose the best title. In pairs, share what you remember.

The Influence of Money   Living without Money   A Weird Woman

_____ tells the amazing story of Heidemarie Schwermer, a German psychotherapist who decided to start living a very different kind of life in 1996. That year, she left her apartment and gave away all of her things except a suitcase full of clothes. This was a decision that changed her life dramatically. She had no possessions, no place to live, and no way to buy the things she needed. The documentary followed Heidemarie in her day-to-day life and showed what it was like to live an alternative lifestyle.

Heidemarie was constantly on the move, meeting new people, and staying with old and new friends for a few nights. In addition to showing the daily problems she faced, the movie explores Heidemarie's philosophy and why she chose to live this way. We see that it wasn't easy for her to have no money in a society where everything is based on money. People often had strong opinions about how she lived. Some called her a "parasite" while others saw her as an "inspiration."

She managed to survive like this for 20 years, until she died in Kassel, Germany. She lived a very independent life and traveled all around Germany, and also often visited Austria, Switzerland, and Italy. She told people about her experiences and tried to convey the message that a simpler way of life was possible. This is a fascinating documentary for people who are interested in the themes of materialism and consumerism, and how money influences our way of thinking and living.

C ▶10.6 Listen and reread. True (T) or False (F)? Correct the false ones.

1 Heidemarie abandoned everything she owned.
2 She kept some money for emergencies.
3 She sometimes stayed with people she didn't know well.
4 It wasn't too difficult for her to live with no money.
5 She traveled to three continents.
6 The reviewer thinks people of all ages will be interested in the movie.

> *I'd like to see it, because I want to know how she lived without money.*

> *I don't think she's a parasite because ...*

D 🔵 **Make it personal** Would you like to see this documentary? Why (not)? Is Heidemarie a parasite or an inspiration? Do you know any similar stories?

② Vocabulary Money

A ▶10.7 Complete the dialogue between two students with the correct form of these verbs. Listen to check and add the two extra words you hear in each line.

afford   cost   earn   pay for   save   spend   waste   win

Amy: I need a new phone, but I can't _____ one.
Mark: Why don't you enter the raffle? It's only $20 and the first prize is a new iPhone. You might _____.
Amy: That's too much! I don't _____ much money at my job and I have to _____ all my school books. I don't want to _____ my money on raffle tickets.
Mark: Just trying to help! I know that it _____ a lot being a student nowadays. Come on! Let's go out and get a pizza. I just found $20 – let's _____ it!
Amy: You should _____ the money! ... Or give it to me!

B Give two pieces of advice to Amy. What would you do if you found $20?

> *She should definitely buy a raffle ticket.*   *I don't think so. That's a waste of money.*

> *I'd buy some games and have hours of fun!*

⚠ Common mistakes

If I get another job, I can ~~win~~ more money. earn

I have 50 dollars, but I won't spend ~~them already~~. it yet

C **Make it personal** In groups, do the questionnaire. Find the people who are most similar to / different than you.

♫ *Money, it's a crime, Share it fairly but don't take a slice of my pie, Money, so they say, Is the root of all evil today* **10.3**

What's Your Attitude To
MONEY?

1 When you have extra money, do you spend it or save it?
2 Have you ever won anything in a raffle?
3 Do you think gambling is a good idea or a waste of money?
4 Is it better to earn money or to win money?
5 If there's something you want to buy but can't afford, do you buy it on credit or save for it?
6 Do you usually try to bargain when you buy things?
7 Have you ever found any money in the street? Did you keep it?
8 Do you agree with the song that money "is the root of all evil today"?

I'm not very lucky. I never win anything.   *I won a laptop once.*

③ Listening

A ▶10.8 ▶ **What's a "freegan"? Listen to / Watch part one of the video and circle the correct answer.**
A "freegan" is a person who:
1 likes to steal expensive things.
2 tries not to buy things.
3 doesn't care about the environment.

B ▶10.8 ▶ **Listen / Watch again and number these words / phrases in the order you hear them, 1–6.**

☐ alternative living strategies   ☐ freeganism
☐ anti-consumerist lifestyle   ☐ limited participation
☐ conventional economy   ☐ minimal consumption of resources

C ▶10.9 ▶ **Listen to / Watch part two. Circle the correct options in 1–4.**
1 She **often** / **rarely** takes furniture from **stores** / **the trash**.
2 She **works** / **lives** in **New York** / **Mexico** City.
3 She **has** / **hasn't** got **a little** / **a lot** of furniture in her house that's come from the street.
4 People from **the city** / **other towns** think recycling is a **good** / **bad** idea.

D ▶10.10 ▶ **Listen to / Watch part three and check the items she'll take.**
things for her bed ☐   furniture ☐
things that need some cleaning ☐   lost property ☐

E 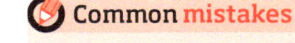 **Make it personal** How much do you recycle? In pairs, ask and answer 1–3 with reasons and follow-up questions.
1 What do you throw in the trash that others recycle?
2 How far would you go yourself? Which of these items have you bought or would you buy second hand?
   bedding   soft / wooden furniture   paintings
   clothes   fresh fruit and vegetables   toys
   jewelry   packaged food   electrical items
3 Are there more and more second-hand and charity shops in your city? Do you use them?

Common mistakes

I've started to buy some ~~items of second hand~~.
second hand items

I'd never take anything out of someone's garbage, but if it's on the street, maybe.

Have you ever found anything useful?

10.4 How often do you post on social media?

① Listening

A Do you ever have reunions with your old school or work friends? How often do you meet and what do you usually do?

> *I still see my friends from middle school.*
> *How often do you get together?*
> *Once or twice a year. We usually go out for a meal.*

B ▶10.11 Dictation. Listen to a message and write as much of it as you can. Check in pairs, then listen again. Did you get it all?

C Identify all the verb tenses in the message. Do you think your English grammar is getting better?

D **Make it personal** In groups. Are reunions, family get-togethers, or surprise parties usually a good idea? Can they ever go wrong? Give examples.

> *I think reunions are usually a terrible idea.*
> *I don't want to see people from my past!*
> *But it's great seeing old friends, and remembering funny stories.*

② Grammar Asking questions: review

A ▶10.12 Listen to the conversation and complete the chart. Is Kyle going to go to the reunion? Why (not)?

Name: Status: Children:	Kyle	Nicki	Mindy

Common mistakes

How ~~much~~ *many* people were there?

How often *do* you eat pizza?

Where *did* you ~~went~~ *go*?

~~You~~ *Do you* like pop music?

How ~~many years do you live~~ *long have you lived* here?

B ▶10.12 Add an auxiliary or main verb and order the words in 1–6 to make questions from the conversation. Listen again to check. In pairs, ask and answer, plus follow-up questions.

1 last see / we / each other / when / ?
2 yet / married / you / ?
3 have / you / kids / any / ?
4 high school / still see / how many / from / you / people / ?
5 restaurant / it / which / at / ?
6 often / the / how / reunions / ?

C Complete the grammar box. Which patterns do you find the easiest?

1 Put examples a–f in the correct places in the chart.

a Where did you go on vacation?
b How was the flight?
c Are you tired?
d How tall are you?
e Did you see that car?
f How many times have you been to France?

To make:	*Yes / No* questions	*Wh-* (subject) questions	*How* + adj / adv questions
Verb *be*:	1 Invert S and V	2 Q + *be* + S	3 *How* + adj / adv + *be* + S
Example:	*c Are you tired?*	_____	_____
Other verbs:	4 Use an A	5 Q + A + S	6 *How* + adj / adv + A
Example:	_____	_____	_____

2 *What* or *which*? Read the examples and complete the rules.

Which apple would you like? The red one or the green one? The red one, please.
What fruit do you like? I like apple, pineapple, and watermelon.

Use _____ to ask a general question.
Use _____ to ask about a restricted group.

→ Grammar 10B p. 156

D 🔘 **Make it personal** Complete and answer 1–6. Compare in small groups. Ask follow-up questions too. Who has the best attitude?

🎵 *How deep is your love?, Is it like the ocean?, What devotion are you?, How deep is your love?, Is it like Nirvana?, Hit me harder again, How deep is your love?* **10.4**

Language learning is more than just coming to class …

1 _____ did you **re**gister for this English class?
  early   on time   late

2 _____ have you missed this semester?
  never   once or twice   more than twice

3 _____ you enjoyed taking English this year?
  yes   more or less   no

4 _____ did you practice English outside of class?
  never   sometimes   often

5 _____ you going to take English again?
  definitely   maybe   no

6 _____ English do you know now?
  more than before   same as before   less than before

I think Lina has the best attitude. She registered for class early and she hasn't missed any classes at all.

③ Pronunciation *How* + adj / adv question stress

A Match these words to emojis a–g. Are you an emoji user?

people   see   home   Facebook
time   English   happy

I love them. I use a lot.

 a
 b
 c
 d
 e
 f
 g

B ▶10.13 Listen to Mickey's messages. Which word has the main stress in each *How* question?

C In pairs, practice the questions using the correct stress. Then share your answers.

D 🔘 **Make it personal** In pairs, imagine you're long-lost friends who have just found each other on social media. Create a chat and include emojis. Then act out the best part of your chat as a conversation.

Mickey
Hey! I'm so 😊 to 👁 you! What's new?

Mickey
How much 🕐 do you spend studying or working?

Mickey
How often do you check f?

Mickey
How long have you lived in your current 🏡?

Mickey
How long ago did you start learning 🇺🇸?

Mickey
How many 👨‍👩‍👧 have you met online?

⏱ **Common mistakes**

How big
~~What size~~ is your apartment?
How far (away)
~~At what distance~~ is it?

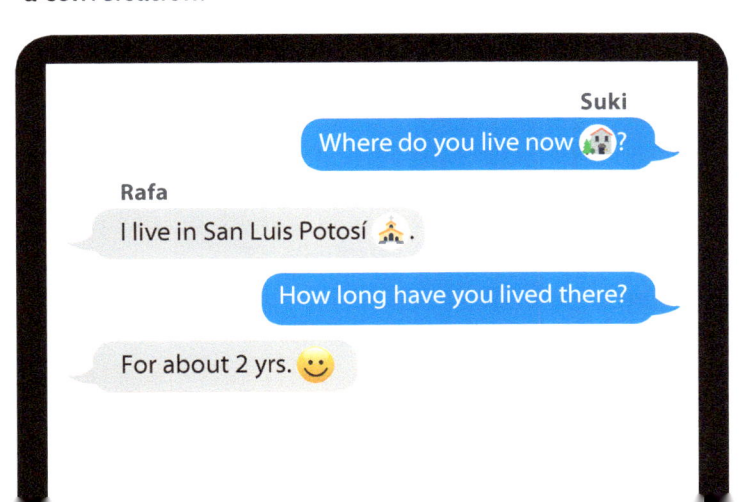

Suki
Where do you live now 🏡?

Rafa
I live in San Luis Potosí ⛪.

How long have you lived there?

For about 2 yrs. 😊

131

10.5 Do you enjoy reading in English?

ID Skills Identifying reasons

A What's different when you read in your language compared to reading in English? Answer in pairs.

> *It's hard for me to read for long in English.*

> *True. I don't read many long texts anyway. I usually just read short things on my phone.*

B Read the article as fast as you comfortably can. How long did you need to read 196 words? In pairs, compare what you remember, then complete the chart.

How to be a better reader

By Dr. Samuel Marshall

The key is to read faster. Here's why it's important. The average reading speed of a child in elementary school is around 200 words per minute (wpm). For adults, it's about 250–300 wpm. Contestants at the World Championship speed reading competitions can reach 1,000–1,200 wpm!

To be an excellent reader, a goal of 500-800 wpm is ideal. This will allow you to read a lot of information in a short time and still understand most of what you are reading. Reading in a second language is different, because, of course, you won't immediately understand a lot of the words that you read. This means that you don't understand what you read, you read slower, and so you don't enjoy reading, which then means you don't read much. It's a vicious circle, one which makes it difficult to improve your reading speed, because you need to practice more to read faster and you also need to read faster to understand more. Many second language readers read at 100 wpm or less. You really need to read at a speed of at least 200 wpm.

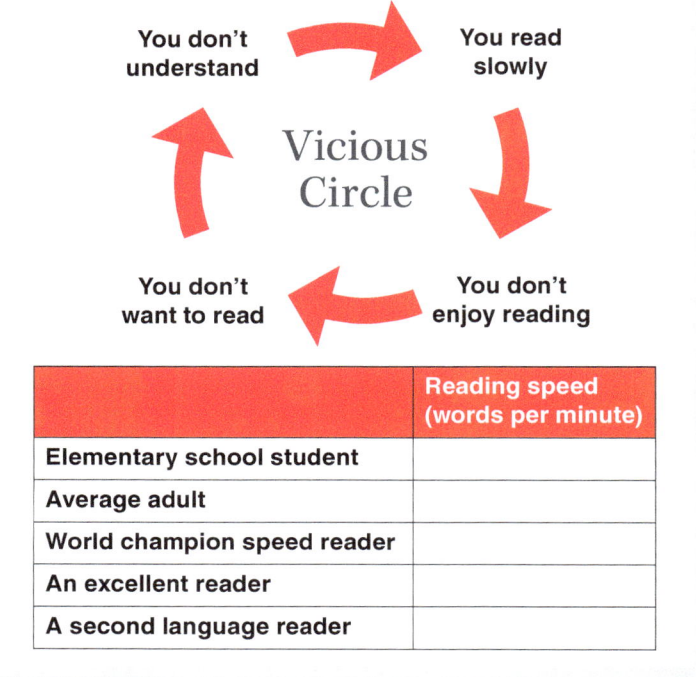

	Reading speed (words per minute)
Elementary school student	
Average adult	
World champion speed reader	
An excellent reader	
A second language reader	

Here are a few tips to help you to read in English.

1 Try to read things you're interested in and already know something about. If you don't enjoy reading, you won't do it.

2 Read something in your language and then try to read it in English.

3 Make sure longer texts aren't too difficult. If you don't understand more than about eight words per paragraph, choose another text before you get frustrated.

4 Use English subtitles when you watch movies in English. This helps your listening, pronunciation, and spelling.

C Do you enjoy reading in a) your first language? b) English? Why (not)? If not, is the reason the vicious circle in **B**?

> *I like catching up with the news online in my language, but when I read it in English there's a lot I don't understand, so I get frustrated quickly.*

D Read tips 1–4 in one minute. Do you do any of these things?

E ▶10.14 Listen and complete Dr. Marshall's other tips, 1–4. Which have you tried?

1 Give yourself _____ minute to read an article. Get as far as you can. Do this _____ times, and try to read _____ each time.

2 Read the same _____-word article as many times as you can in _____ minutes.

3 Read at the same speed as your class. Read an article of _____ words in only _____ seconds.

4 Use an alarm to help you. If you want to read at _____ words per minute, the alarm will go off every _____. See where you are in the text.

F 🔵 Make it personal Find a text of about 400 words. Read it using one of the tips in **E**. Compare in groups. Did it help you to read faster?

> *I read something I'm interested in but the first time I only read half of it in a minute.*

10.5 How would you describe your best friend? 10.5

ID in Action Describing and identifying

A ▶10.15 Listen and circle the items that are referred to in each photo.

B ▶10.15 Study **Common mistakes** and circle the best options in 1–3. Listen to check.

1 A: Pass me my phone, please.
　B: Sure. Which **phone** / **one** is it? The black **phone** / **one**?
　A: No, the silver **phone** / **one**.
　B: This **phone** / **one**?
　A: No, mine is the silver **phone** / **one** in a white case.

2 A: Oh look, there's Rich.
　B: Who's Rich?
　A: You know. He's the guy **who** / **which** Jody's dating.
　B: Oh yeah. Which **guy** / **one** is he? The guy **with** / **without** glasses?
　A: Yeah, the one **with** / **without** a beard. The one **who's** / **which is** wearing a hat.

3 A: Have you seen my glasses?
　B: Are they the **glasses** /**ones** on the table?
　A: No, those are **his** / **Jake's**. Mine are the big **glasses** / **ones**.
　B: There are two big **pairs** / **glasses**.
　A: Well, mine are the black **pairs** / **ones**.

Common mistakes

Which sweater do you want?
The black. ~~/~~ *one*
I don't like the ~~grays~~. *gray ones*
Which ~~book is the~~ your book? *one is*
That ~~is the~~ mine. *one*
What lovely flowers! Do you
like the ~~reds~~? *red ones*

C In pairs, take turns describing one of these people without saying their name. Your partner guesses who it is.

She's the one with curly hair.
　　　Is it Judy?
No, the younger one.
　　　Is it Maria?
　　　Yes.

Ray　Judy　Sam　Carlos　Vicky　Martin　Maria

D In groups, put all your personal items (phones, keys, books, pens …) on a table and mix them up. Describe which one is yours until everybody knows whose everything is.

Mine is the one in the embarrassing gold case.　Mine are the ones with a red key ring.

♫ You say I'm crazy, 'Cause you don't think I know what you've done, But when you call me baby, I know I'm not the only one

E 👤 **Make it personal** In pairs, take turns showing photos with at least two people in each. Answer questions about the people until your partner can identify each one.

Are they the same age?　No, Louise is a year older.　Is Louise the one with red hair?　No, that's Allie.

Writing 10 A narrative

My sister Ella and I were going on vacation on the same day, but traveling to different places at different times. Surprisingly, we had both been very organized and had packed our bags the night before and put our travel documents on the kitchen table.

I left the house first, at 7:30. I had allowed plenty of time to get to the airport, but there was little traffic and I arrived very early, just after 8:00. Until then, everything was going well. But then I checked my travel documents and the awful truth hit me. Stupidly, I had picked up my sister's passport instead of my own! As soon as I realized, I called my sister, but her phone went straight to voicemail. For the next 10 minutes, I kept phoning but she didn't answer. Eventually, I decided there was no option but to drive home. Luckily, there was just enough time before my flight.

I had just arrived home when my phone rang. It was my sister and she had my passport. Unfortunately, she was now at the airport, looking for me! She had realized the mistake a few minutes after I left. Obviously, if I had her passport, neither of us could go on vacation. So she had jumped in her car and driven straight to the airport. She arrived just before I got back home again!

In the end, we met up in the airport car park. I caught my flight with a few minutes to spare. But since then, I've always checked my passport before I leave home!

A Read Tom's story and number the events 1–9 in the order they occurred.

- ☐ Tom arrived at the airport.
- ☐ Ella phoned Tom.
- ☐ Tom and Ella left their passports on the table.
- ☐ Tom tried to phone Ella.
- ☐ Ella drove to the airport.
- ☐ Tom met Ella and got his passport back.
- ☐ Ella realized Tom had the wrong passport.
- ☐ Tom picked up the wrong passport.
- ☐ Tom drove home.

B Match time expressions 1–6 to the underlined expressions in **A**.

1 For a short while
2 Finally
3 After some time
4 Right after
5 So far
6 A little earlier than

C Study **Write it right!**, then find five comment adverbs in the text in **A**.

> ✔ **Write it right!**
>
> In a narrative, you can use comment adverbs to show the reader your attitude or feelings. These include: *clearly, fortunately, hopefully, luckily, obviously, stupidly, surprisingly, unbelievably, unfortunately.*

D Replace the words in *italics* with one of the comment adverbs from **A**.

1 *Like an idiot*, I left my keys at work so couldn't get into my apartment.
2 *It was really lucky that* my neighbor had some extra keys.
3 *As everyone knows and understands*, you can't travel without a passport.
4 *Although I didn't expect it at all*, I got an A in my last project.
5 *I'm very sorry to say that* I can't come to your party — I'll be away on vacation.

E 🔘 **Make it personal** Think of an unusual or lucky story that happened to you or someone you know. Write a narrative in 150–200 words.

Before	Look back at the time expressions in **B** and comment adverbs in **C**. Think about the key moments in your story in the order you want to tell them.
While	Use a variety of past tense forms and time expressions to explain what happened and when. Include comment adverbs to show your attitude or feelings.
After	Exchange narratives with another student. Ask two follow-up questions about their story.

10 The dog days of August

① Before watching

A In pairs, look back at the ID Café lesson titles and photos and remember all you can. Who are your favorite / least favorite characters? Why? How do you think ID Café is going to end?

B Match 1–8 to definitions a–h.

1	improved	a	disorganized, untidy
2	a joke	b	better
3	a makeover	c	a complete change of look
4	a mess	d	a financial prize, usually academic
5	a scholarship	e	intelligent or well-dressed
6	to share	f	have complete confidence in
7	smart	g	the opposite of *serious*
8	to trust	h	each having an equal part

C Guess how August is feeling and why.

② While watching

A In pairs. **A:** Watch but cover your ears. **B:** Listen but cover your eyes, up to 1:58. Compare what you understood.

B Now both listen and watch to check. What else did you pick up? How will Lucy react?

C Watch up to 3:05. True (T) or False (F)?

1 Lucy thinks a tomato has hit his apartment.
2 The house is a mess because Rory's away.
3 Andrea describes August as a disaster.
4 August's mess is self-inflicted.
5 The $35,000 scholarship decision is this afternoon.

D Try to complete the extracts. Watch again to check. Guess what they decide to do.

Andrea: Lucy. Boy, am I _____ you're here.
Lucy: What happened here? It's like a _____ came through here …
Andrea: This is what _____ when Daniel's not here.
Lucy: Who could _____ like this? Not me.
Andrea: Me either. Here is our _____.
Lucy: Is this a _____? What has he done to himself?
Andrea: Yeah. I asked that too. My brother, he's _____ about an interview.

E Watch from 3:10 to 3:32. In pairs, role-play a dialogue for what Andrea and Lucy are thinking.

> *What do you think of his sweater?*
> *I don't like it … He looks like my dad!*

F Listen from 3:48 to the end. Number the words in the order you hear them, 1–10. How does Lucy feel about herself? Will August get the scholarship?

artificial	hand	passion
confidence	improved	special
the first step	intelligence	
foundation	makeover	

③ After watching

A Circle the correct options and complete with the correct form of -*self*.

1 August **has / hasn't** spilled food on _____self.
2 He **does / doesn't** know how to take care of _____self.
3 Andrea can't get him organized by _____self.
4 August has a really **high / low** opinion of _____self.
5 Andrea and Lucy give _____**selves / August** a drum roll as he walks in.
6 Lucy is extremely **fond of / doubtful about** _____self.
7 They encourage August to believe **in / on** _____self.

B Complete 1–8 with these words and phrases.

a little	almost	as smart as	first	for success
more	real	so	whatever	

1 He looked _____ cute.
2 I could _____ date him myself.
3 To do well in that interview, you have to dress _____.
4 You needed a _____ change, August, but this is just the _____ step.
5 You need to have _____ confidence in yourself!
6 Why not look _____ you are?
7 You just needed _____ something special. You know?
8 Artificial automatic intelligence people, or _____ you call them.

C ● **Make it personal** In groups of three, answer 1–4. Any surprises?

1 Are you generally tidy / untidy / good at taking care of yourself? Have you ever lived alone? Did (or would) that change anything?
2 Do you dress / behave very differently at home compared to when you're out? Do your clothes affect how you feel?
3 Would you say you're generally self-confident?
4 Do you like your English-speaking self?

> *I rarely look in a mirror, except when I'm about to go out.*

> *I do get shy if I have to speak in public or in front of a camera.*

R5 Grammar and vocabulary

A Picture dictionary. Cover the words on these pages and use the pictures to remember:

page	
112	11 wedding words
114	5 relationship words and expressions
118	10 types of performers
119	4 mystery objects
124	8 causes of stress
126	13 lifestyle changes
127	descriptions of 6 vacation photos
155	8 pairs of picture words in lines 5 and 6 of the consonants chart

B In pairs, decide which adjective combinations apply to photos 1–3. Do you agree on each?

The teacher is ...   bored / interested

The students are ...   boring / interesting

C 🔵 Make it personal In groups, give at least two answers to each option in 1–3.

1 What makes a teacher interesting / boring?
2 When was the last time you were confused / terrified?
3 What do you find irritating / exhausting?

When teachers just talk about grammar, I think they're ...

D 🔵 Make it personal In groups, make a conditional chain like the model. Use the sentence starters or your own ideas. Which group can make the longest chain?

If I lived in Germany, I'd speak German.

If I spoke German, I could get a better job.

If I got a better job, ...

Sentence starters:

If I spoke English well ...   If I were a superhero ...
If I won the lottery ...   If it were ...

E ▶ R5.1 In pairs, match 1–5 to a–e. Listen to check.

1 Look! They're holding hands.
2 Zara's very late.
3 What's in this package?
4 Who's that guy?
5 Look, the money's gone!

a It could be Kim's son. He looks like Kim.
b It can't be a pair of socks. It's too heavy.
c They must be dating now.
d There must be a thief in the room.
e She might be stuck on the bus.

F 🔵 Make it personal Complete 1–5, then compare in pairs. Do your answers reflect your attitude towards money?

1 A bank is a place ...
2 A lottery is a thing ...
3 Credit cards are things ...
4 Shopping is an activity ...
5 A financial advisor is a person ...

For me a bank is a place you use to save money.

G In pairs, play **Describe it, don't say it!** A: Describe five words / phrases from this book. Use English, mime, drawings, sounds, or rhyme, but don't say the words. B: Listen and say the words / phrases A describes.

It's a phrase for someone who's really jealous!

H Correct the mistakes. Check your answers in units 9 and 10.

⏱ Common mistakes

1 At first, I wasn't interesting in the movie, but the final part was very excited. (2 mistakes)
2 If I would know John, I would talk to him. (1 mistake)
3 What would you do if you see your best friend with your ex-girlfriend? (1 mistake)
4 She can be hungry, because she didn't eat something today. (2 mistakes)
5 You better make your homework. (2 mistakes)
6 My boss made me to stay late in work. (2 mistakes)
7 That's the car who I bought the last week. (2 mistakes)
8 People which play sports have a lot of pression to win. (2 mistakes)
9 My brother wins a lot of money, but he loses it on ridiculous things. (2 mistakes)
10 Could you pass me my coat? No, not that, the blue. (2 mistakes)

Skills practice

♪ *Last Christmas, I gave you my heart, But the very next day you gave it away. This year, to save me from tears, I'll give it to someone special.*

R5

A Read the article about siblings. Are 1–5 True (T) or False (F)? Are sibling relationships good in your family?

1 Brothers and sisters fight more when they're children.

2 It's unusual for siblings to change their opinions of each other.

3 Rivalry always starts when the second child is born.

4 Parents don't like to see competition between their children.

5 The Jacksons had a better relationship when they were younger.

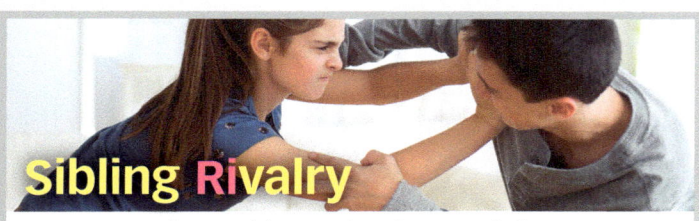

Sibling Rivalry

Do you get along with your brothers and sisters? Are they your best friends or do you never see them? It's really common for siblings to fight, especially when they're young. And don't be surprised if one minute you love your brother or sister and the next minute you can't stand that same sibling.

Competition between brothers and sisters can start before the second child arrives and it continues as children get older and they have to share toys, food, and, most importantly, attention from their parents. It can be hard for parents to watch, but it's very normal and, as children get older, the rivalry hopefully changes into a warm friendship – but not for everyone! Look at the Jacksons and Noel and Liam Gallagher. They used to make music together but now they fight all the time!

My sister's kids fight all the time!

B ▶R5.2 **Listen to part one of a radio show. Complete with Carla (C), Dr. Brayman (DB), or Jack (J).**

1 _____ is nervous.

2 _____ and _____ are in a relationship.

3 _____ calls all the time.

4 _____ asks for advice.

5 _____ gives advice.

6 _____ gets jealous easily.

C ▶R5.3 **Guess the correct options you will hear in 1–6. Then listen to check. All correct? Do you agree with Dr. Brayman's advice?**

1 **She / He** is starting to ignore **his / her** phone calls at work.

2 **She / He** is starting to have secrets and tell lies.

3 **She / He** is becoming more jealous.

4 **She / He** needs to talk to **him / her** and discuss **his / her** emotions.

5 **She / He** needs to make **her / his** partner feel more confident about their relationship.

6 Dr. Brayman thinks this **will / won't** change their situation quickly and **she / he / they** should talk to a counselor.

D In pairs, play *Problems!* Flip a coin. Heads = one space; tails = two spaces. Role-play each situation.

A: Child. You don't want to go to school.
B: Parent. Make your child go to school.

A: Broken heart. Your bf / gf broke up with you.
B: Friend. Support him / her and give advice.

A: Student. Your course is boring.
B: Friend. Give advice.

A: Teenager. You don't have any money. Ask for some.
B: Friend. Give / refuse money. Give advice.

A: Lonely. Your bf / gf travels all the time.
B: Friend. Listen and give advice.

A: Nervous. You have to speak at a friend's wedding.
B: Friend. Make suggestions.

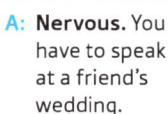

A: Husband. You left your cell phone in a taxi.
B: Wife. Make a suggestion.

A: Tired. You can't sleep at night.
B: Doctor. Give some advice or some medicine.

E In groups, do the quiz then look back to check. Score two points for each correct answer. Which group got the most points?

How much do you remember?

1 Which U.S. state is visited in lesson 6.1?

2 What does Barbara Hartsfield collect in lesson 7.3?

3 What did Penny and Harry talk about in Unit 8?

4 What happened to the two people in lesson 9.2?

5 Who are BeginAgain and MyVeryBest in Unit 10?

I think the state in lesson 6.1 is …

F ▶R5.4 🔵 **Make it personal** **Question time!**

1 Listen to the 12 lesson titles in units 9 and 10.

2 In pairs, practice asking and answering. Use the book map on p. 2–3. Ask at least two follow-up questions. Can you have a short conversation about all the questions?

What do you think about marriage?

I don't think about it at all!

137

Grammar Unit 6

6A Verb + gerund (verb + -ing)

I don't feel like dancing.

Some verb phrases and verbs are followed by a gerund:
- ▸ *I try to **avoid** driving in the rush hour.*
- ▸ *My friend always does funny things at school. I **can't help** laughing in class.*
- ▸ *Do you **enjoy** working here?*
- ▸ *My mom **keeps** losing her glasses, she does it every day.*

Verbs followed by a gerund

adore	dislike	keep	recommend
allow	don't mind	mention	regret
advise	enjoy	mind	risk
avoid	feel like	miss	stop
can't help	finish	practice	suggest
can't stand	hate	propose	understand
consider	imagine	quit	

Go + gerund

Use *go* + gerund to talk about fun activities and hobbies:
- ▸ *I go running every day.*
- ▸ *We went shopping at the mall last week.*

Most verbs can also be used without *go* to mean the same:
- ▸ *I run every day.*
- ▸ *We shopped at the mall last week.*
- ▸ *I went swimming yesterday.* NOT ~~I go to swimming yesterday.~~

In the present perfect, the verb *be* can also be used for activities:
- ▸ *I've gone / been camping many times.*

Gerunds

Use the *-ing* form (gerund) after prepositions and as the subject of a sentence:
- ▸ *I'm interested in snowboarding.*
- ▸ *Skiing is a popular winter sport.*

6B Verb + infinitive / verb + gerund

Verb + infinitive

Some verbs are followed by the infinitive:
- ▸ *Oh no! I forgot to lock the door!*
- ▸ *I really want to learn to drive.*

Verbs followed by an infinitive

agree	hope	offer	seem
ask	learn	plan	wait
decide	mean	promise	want
expect	need	refuse	wish
forget			

I CAN'T WAIT TO FIND A CLEAN CAR!

Verb + gerund or infinitive

Some verbs combine with a gerund or infinitive with little change in the meaning:
- ▸ *She **started driving** when she was 17. / She **started to drive** when she was 17.*
- ▸ *He **continued talking** for hours. / He **continued to talk** for hours.*

Verbs followed by a gerund or an infinitive

begin	continue	like	prefer
	hate	love	start

Use the **infinitive** as the second verb if:
- ▸ the first verb is in the *-ing* form: *I am **continuing to** learn new things every day.*
- ▸ the second verb is a **state verb**: *He's **starting to love** his new course.*
- ▸ *I'm **beginning to understand** English grammar!* NOT ~~I'm beginning understanding English grammar!~~
- ▸ *We're **starting to feel** hungry.* NOT ~~We're starting to feeling hungry.~~

6A

1 Match 1–5 to a–e.

1 Jogging is
2 Smoking is not
3 I'm excited about
4 Karen's got a terrible cold. She keeps
5 Can I have your newspaper when you've finished

a starting college next year.
b reading it?
c coughing.
d permitted in this building.
e a good form of exercise.

2 Order the words in 1–5 to make sentences or questions.

1 a / sport / be / can / dangerous / diving / .
2 you / a / have / getting / new / considered / job / ?
3 watching / how / a / movie / about / ?
4 in / living / he / city / the / misses / really / .
5 doing / you / do / enjoy / what / relax / to / ?

6B

1 Complete 1–4 with the correct form of these verbs. There's one extra verb.

cook   cry   go   have   make   take

1 Marie suggested _____ to a restaurant, but Joel felt like _____ at home.
2 Can you imagine _____ a party on the moon? It would be a lot of fun!
3 My grandpa can't help _____ when he watches *Titanic*.
4 When you don't enjoy _____ a class, it's hard to do well.

2 Match photos a–f to 1–6. Then complete 1–6 with the correct form of the verbs.

1 She has just finished _____. (**eat**)
2 They have agreed _____ business. (**do**)
3 She is asking _____ home. (**go**)
4 She is practicing _____ first aid. (**give**)
5 He forgot _____ his coffee and left it on the car. (**pick up**)
6 They really enjoy _____ video games. (**play**)

3 Correct two mistakes in each of 1–5.

1 After drive all night, we had to stopping to sleep a little.
2 I really dislike to wash the dishes and never do if I can avoid to have to do it.
3 I recommend to go to Rome for your honeymoon. You can sightseeing in many romantic places.
4 Mike wants to learn cooking so he needs buy some books.
5 To be a teacher is a good job if you are interested in to help people.

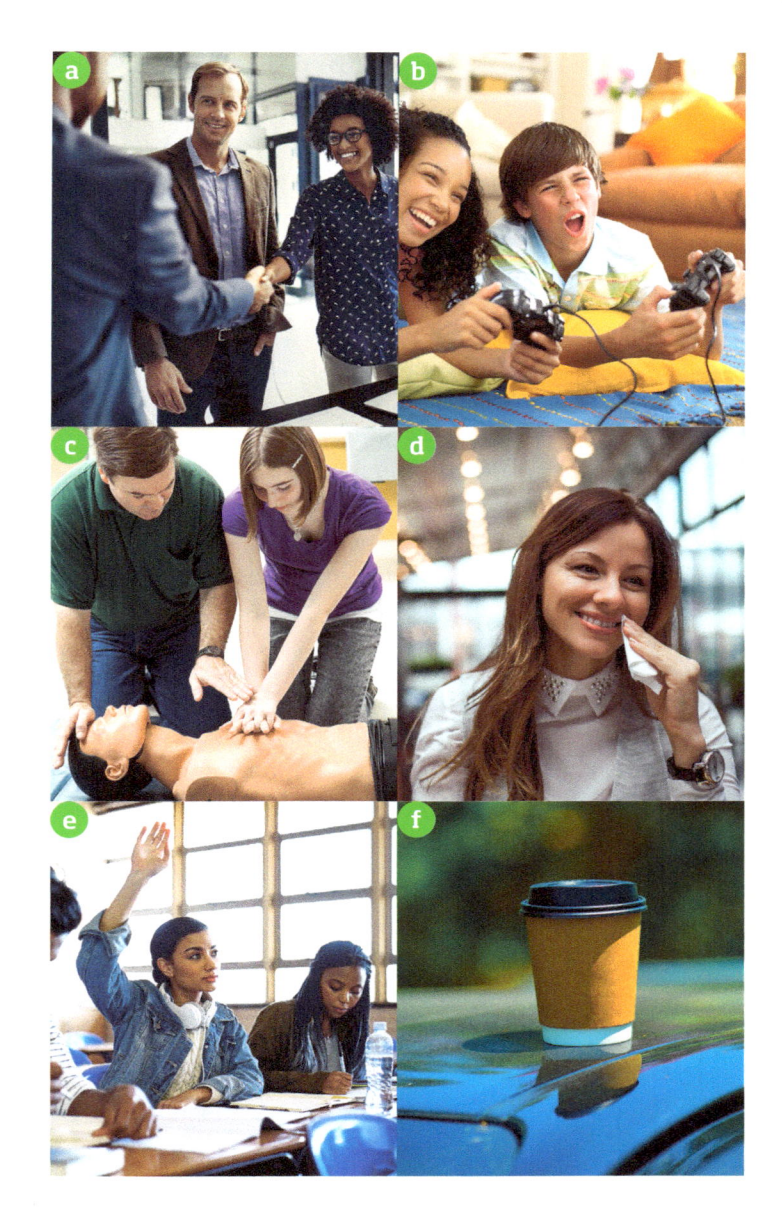

4 Circle the correct options in 1–5.

1 I asked him not **to play** / **playing** his music so loud.
2 If she wants **to continue** / **continuing** her piano lessons, she'll need to study!
3 Would you mind **to help** / **helping** me with this computer program?
4 I never thought I'd quit **to smoke** / **smoking**, but I've finally done it!
5 He decided **to leave** / **leaving** class early and go home to rest.

5 ◐ Make it personal Complete 1–4 about yourself.

1 My friends like me because I enjoy _____.
2 I'm learning to _____ at the moment, because _____.
3 I usually avoid _____, because _____.
4 I prefer _____ to _____, because _____.

Grammar Unit 7

7A Pronouns: *some-, any-, every-, no-*

See **nothing**.

Hear **nothing**.

If you hear **something**, don't tell **anyone**.

- I put my keys **somewhere**. Where are they?
- There's **something** in the way she moves.
- I know **someone** that looks like you.
- Ask Julia. She knows **everything** about baseball.
- There was **no one** in the room when I got here.
- They don't know **anything** about physics.
- Do you have **anything** valuable in your bag?
- Does **anyone** want a drink?
- Is there **anywhere** to sit?

⊕ Verbs

	Unidentified	All in a group	⊖ meaning	⊖ & ❓
For a **person**	someone	everyone	no one	anyone
	somebody	everybody	nobody	anybody
For a **thing**	something	everything	nothing	anything
For a **place**	somewhere	everywhere	nowhere	anywhere

- Almost everybody has a cell phone these days. NOT ~~Almost everybody have a cell phone these days.~~
- I didn't do anything fun on the weekend. NOT ~~I didn't do nothing fun on the weekend.~~

Use *-one* or *-body* to talk about people. The meaning is the same.

All the pronouns in this section use the singular form of the verb.

Note: *All* uses a plural verb:

- **All** the students in my class **are** Mexican. / **Everyone** in my class **is** Mexican.

7B *So* and *such*

- It's **so hot**! It's almost 40° C.
- I knew **so many** people at that party!
- There was **so much** traffic **that** I was late this morning.
- That's **such a** tragedy! I can't believe **that** happened.
- We had **such a** great time at your party **that** we didn't want to go.

Use:

- *so* to intensify adjectives and adverbs.
- *such* to intensify the characteristics of nouns.
- *so* / *such ... that* is often used to express a result.

"I've been so busy reading books on walking and running that I haven't had time to walk or run."

- We have such wonderful neighbors. NOT ~~We have so wonderful neighbors.~~

7C Passive voice: present and past

- These sweaters **are made** by hand.
- This fabulous dress **was designed** by Vera Wang.
- Thousands of shoes **are sold** every day in the U.S.

	S	V	O	Complement / agent of the passive
Active	J.K. Rowling	wrote	Harry Potter	in a café.
Passive	Harry Potter	was written		by J.K. Rowling in a café.
Active	Security guards	don't protect	this building	at night.
Passive	This building	isn't protected		by security guards at night.
Active	People	eat	a lot of pasta	in Italy.
Passive	A lot of pasta	is eaten		in Italy.

Form: *be* + past participle.

Use: when the object or event is more important than who did it.

When it's necessary to say who / what did the action, use *by*.

Four easy steps to transform an active voice into a passive:

- The **object** of the active voice becomes the subject of the passive.
- Use verb *be* in the same tense as the main verb of the active voice.
- Put the main verb in the past participle.
- If necessary, use *by* + the subject of the active voice to insert the **agent** of the passive.

7A

1 Complete 1–6 with *anyone, anything, someone, something, everyone, everything, no one,* or *nothing.*

1 Do you know _____ that lives in Chile?
2 _____ tastes better than chocolate. It's my favorite food.
3 I'll wait until _____ has stopped talking before I start.
4 Excuse me, can I ask you _____?
5 My new girlfriend and I want to go to a place where ____ knows us and we can be alone!
6 There was a power outage at work and _____ stopped working, even the lights. We couldn't see _____, until _____ found a flashlight.

2 Match 1–5 to a–e. Then add the correct verb to a–e.

1 I can't cook because there's
2 I don't have
3 It was a great party.
4 Someone phoned earlier,
5 Does anyone

a have a pencil I could _____?
b but they didn't _____ their name.
c nothing in the fridge. Let's _____ out to eat.
d anything to _____. I'm so bored.
e Everyone _____ they enjoyed it.

3 Correct one mistake in each of 1–5.

1 He didn't do nothing on Sunday. He just stayed at home.
2 Someone have taken my cell phone!
3 I left my window open in the storm! Now everything I have are totally wet.
4 I didn't tell someone your news. Your secret is safe.
5 At the airport, they ask, "Do you have something to declare?"

4 ○ **Make it personal** Write your ideas about 1–5 in complete sentences.

1 Name something you can't live without.
2 Name someone you love.
3 Name somewhere you go often.
4 Did you eat anything before class? What?
5 Did you go anywhere on your last vacation? Where?

7B

1 Complete 1–4 with *so* or *such.*

1 That movie is _____ fantastic! I've seen it twice.
2 My boss is _____ a difficult person; he's obsessed with punctuality and order. It can be _____ annoying.
3 I didn't know she could be _____ brave! She's _____ a hero.
4 Our tutor is _____ an exceptional speaker. That was the best lecture I've ever heard.

2 Add *so* or *such* to 1–5 and match to a–e.

1 Are you angry that
2 Vera did a good job that
3 Their singing was impressive that
4 Rosa and Jorge went to Canada. It was cold that
5 John was a good player that

a they couldn't feel their feet.
b they were asked to perform at the concert.
c his team gave him a special medal.
d you can't even talk to her about it?
e she got a promotion.

3 ○ **Make it personal** Complete 1–5 so they are true for you.

1 _____ is such a great movie!
2 _____ is such an inspiring person!
3 _____ makes such good food!
4 I'm so happy when _____.
5 I'm so sad when _____.

7C

1 Rewrite 1–5, passive to active or active to passive. Which three sound more natural in the passive?

1 The law prohibits smoking in this area.
2 People make a lot of things in China these days.
3 *Once Upon a Time in Hollywood* was written and directed by Quentin Tarantino.
4 Jennifer Lopez and Angelina Jolie wore these beautiful dresses.
5 People downloaded one million songs from iTunes in its first week.

2 Circle the correct options in 1–5.

1 Miguel de Cervantes is **knew / known** for his book *Don Quijote.* The book **is / was** published in 1612.
2 A lot of The Beatles' songs **was / were** recorded at Abbey Road studios in London. Most of them **was / were** written by Lennon and McCartney.
3 Hamburgers **is / are** usually **make / made** from meat, a bun, salad, and cheese.
4 Thousands of phones are **find / lost** every year, but only some of them are **return / returned** to their owners.
5 Millions of movies **was / were** downloaded last year, but most of them **wasn't / weren't** paid for.

3 ○ **Make it personal** How is a hamburger made? Write a delicious description!

First, the hamburger is put on the grill. Then the bun is cut in half ...

Grammar Unit 8

8A Phrasal verbs

- *The TV volume is really low. Can you **turn** it **up**?*
- *It's getting dark. Do you want me to **switch on** the light?*
- *When will you **give back** my bike?*
- *I'll **give** it **back** tomorrow.*
- *I just lost my glasses. Can you help me **look for** them?*

Man: *Turn up the volume!*   **Woman:** *No! Turn it down!*
Boy: *Give it back! It's mine!*

A phrasal verb is a combination of a **verb** + **particle** (preposition or adverb) that usually has a different meaning to the original verb. For example, *look* = focus your eyes in a particular direction; *look for* = try to find. Phrasal verbs are very common in **informal** fluent speech and writing.

Most phrasal verbs are separable (the object noun can go between the verb and the particle).

- *She turned the light on. / She turned on the light.*

A few are inseparable – the object can only go after the particle.

- *Juan cared for his mother when she was sick.*

To *find out* if a phrasal verb is inseparable, *look* it *up* in a dictionary.

8B Future forms 1: *will* and *going to* for predictions

- *We probably **won't** be able to live on Mars. (prediction)*
- *I think there **will** probably be a lot of people at the concert. (prediction)*
- *I don't think it**'s going to be** hot tomorrow. (prediction)*
- *My sister**'s going to have** her baby very soon. (prediction based on evidence)*

Will

	S	Modal	Adverb	I	O phrase
+	He	will / 'll	definitely / probably	find	a job.
	S	**Adverb**	**Modal**	**I**	**O phrase**
−	We	definitely / probably	will not / won't	get	a promotion.
	Modal	**S**	**Adverb**	**I**	**O phrase**
?	Will	I		definitely	go	to Europe?

Going to

	S	Be	Adverb	(Not) going to	I	O phrase
+ −	I	am / 'm	probably	going to / not going to	have	fun.
	We	are / 're				
	He	is / 's				
	Be	**S**	**Adverb**	**Going to**	**I**	**O phrase**
?	Are	you	definitely	going to	live	on the moon?
	Is	she				

Use *going to* or *will* for predictions.
Going to is more common in spoken English and is usually pronounced *gonna*.
Use *going to* for predictions that are based on evidence.
Adverbs modify predictions: *possibly* → *probably* → *definitely / certainly*.

- *It's 7:30. You're going to be late for school. (prediction based on evidence) And you're probably going to miss the first class too. (modification)*

8C Future forms 2

- *You need a volunteer? I**'ll do** it! (quick decision)*
- *The package **will** arrive by 2 p.m. (fact)*
- *You can tell us. We **won't** tell anyone else. (promise)*
- *They**'re going to visit** their uncle in Paris. (fixed plans)*
- *I**'m not going to** go to that party. (intention)*
- *Look at that cloud! It**'s going to** rain any minute! (prediction based on evidence)*
- *They**'re flying** tomorrow. (arrangement with the airline)*
- *She**'s working** this weekend. (arrangement with her company)*
- *The show **starts** at 7 p.m. (schedule)*

Use:

- *will / won't* for statements of facts, quick decisions, promises, or predictions.
- *going to* for decided plans, intentions, and predictions based on evidence.
- **present continuous** for fixed plans, or arrangements with other people.
- **simple present** for scheduled events.

To differentiate **present continuous** for future from actions that are happening now, use a future time expression:

- *I'm leaving. (now)*
- *I'm leaving in half an hour. (future)*

8A

1 Complete 1–6 with these prepositions.

down   in (x 2)   off   on   out

1 Please switch _____ the lights when you leave.
2 Where can I plug _____ my cell phone? I need to charge it.
3 Can you turn the air conditioning _____ a little? It's really cold in here.
4 When you check in online for a flight, the company emails you the boarding pass so you can print it _____ at home.
5 Get _____ the car and I'll take you to the bus station.
6 It's getting cold. I'm going to put _____ a sweater.

2 Order the words in 1–5 to make sentences and questions.

1 horror / you / movies / are / into / watching / alone / ?
2 she / her / looking / glasses / for / is / reading / .
3 many / of / have / college / dropped / year / how / out / people / this / ?
4 money / did / put / much / the / vending / in / machine / he / how / ?
5 off / before / shoes / take / in / your / you / come / .

8B

1 Rewrite 1–6 as future predictions using the words in parentheses.

1 The party is a lot of fun. (**probably**)
   The party is probably going to be a lot of fun.
2 There are a lot more economic problems. (**definitely**)
3 We can take a vacation on Mars. (**in 2020**)
4 We don't have any fish in the oceans. (**probably / 100 years from now**)
5 NASA makes contact with an alien civilization. (**before 2050**)
6 We can't eradicate poverty before the end of this century. (**certainly**)

2 ⬤ Make it personal   Correct one mistake in each of 1–5. Do you agree with the statements?

1 We will can speak fluent English one day.
2 There won't probably be any homework today, so we'll have a free evening!
3 We definitely not going to find a cure for cancer soon.
4 Our country has the best soccer team and is definitely winning the next World Cup!
5 If I'm going to pass my exams, I'll be a teacher.

8C

1 Complete 1–6 with *will / won't* or *be + going to / not going to.*

1 _____ you _____ be back before dinner?
2 Sorry I didn't wash the dishes. I _____ do them tomorrow, I promise.
3 It's a long way to the airport and the bus is terrible. We _____ take you in our car.
4 I _____ go to school tomorrow because I have to go to the doctor.
5 I'm so sorry I hurt you. I _____ do it again.
6 A: What's that man doing on the bridge? Oh no! He _____ jump!
   B: Don't worry. It's a bungee-jumping platform.

2 Look at the ticket and circle the correct options in the dialogue.

A: Hey, Billy Sonic **plays** / **is playing** at The Arena this weekend, do you want to go?
B: I'd love to, but I**'m working** / **will work** on Saturday.
A: Really? What time **do you finish** / **are you finishing**?
B: I**'m going to finish** / **finish** at 5 p.m. What time's the show?
A: Uh, the doors **open** / **will open** at 7 p.m.
B: OK, cool. Can you get me a ticket and **I'm going to** / **I'll** pay you back?
A: No problem. It's going to **be** / **being** great!

3 ⬤ Make it personal   Write your answers to questions 1–4.

1 What are you doing this weekend?
2 When does your English course finish?
3 What will you do after that?
4 What are you going to do when you've learned enough English?

When I've learned enough English, I'm going to look for a job in California.

Grammar Unit 9

9A -ed and -ing adjectives

- *Wow, that movie was **terrifying**!*
- *Janet has traveled a lot. She seems really **interesting**.*
- *We are going to be **totally exhausted** after our vacation!*
- *The analyst is **bored** with his patient's dreams.*

Use:

- -ed or -ing adjectives after verbs such as *be, become, feel, get, look, seem,* etc.
- -ed adjectives to describe a feeling or a condition.
- -ing adjectives to describe what causes the feeling or condition.

The spelling rules are the same as for simple past (-ed) and continuous verbs (-ing). See Grammar 2A and 2B p. 140.

Use **intensifying adverbs** before a participle adjective to show the degree of feeling.

very	really	extremely	absolutely / totally / completely

Intensifying adverbs go before the main verb, auxiliary, or adjective they emphasize:

- *Kim **absolutely** adores hip hop.*
- *Jo is **extremely** tired of working on Sundays.*
- *I don't **really** like bananas.*
- *Rob cooks **very** well.*

Tiring is used to describe the thing that makes you feel tired.

- *Your husband looks really tired. Is he OK?* NOT *Your husband looks really tiring. Is he OK?*
- *I've had such a tiring day at work that I'm going to bed.* NOT *I've had such a tired day at work that I'm going to bed.*

9B Second conditional

- *If I had wings, I would fly.* (but I don't have wings = not real)
- *If my father didn't have to work, he would play more golf.* (but he has to work = not real)
- *She would enjoy school more if she didn't have to study math.* (but she has to study math = not real)
- *If you won the lottery, what would you buy first?* (but I don't think you will win = improbable)
- *Would you be scared if an earthquake happened here now?* (but I don't think it will happen = improbable)

Conditional clause			Result clause		
If / When	**S**	**Past verb** ⊕⊖	**S**	**Would** ⊕⊖	**I**
If	I / you / he / she / we / they	**were** taller,	I / you / he / she / we / they	would	play volleyball.
		didn't need money,		**wouldn't**	work.

Form: if + **past verb** + would + **infinitive**.

- *If cell phones didn't exist, how would your life change?* NOT *If cell phones wouldn't exist, how would your life change?*

The **conditional** clause uses a past tense to talk about an imaginary, unreal, improbable, or impossible present or future event.

When the result clause comes first, don't use a comma.

Use *were* with all subjects in formal English. In informal English, people increasingly use *was* with the first and third persons singular: *If I was you, I'd tell him.*

We often use the phrase *If I were / was you, I'd ...* to give advice.

9C May / might / could / must / can't + be

- *You've been on a plane for 15 hours. You **must** be tired!* (certain that it is true)
- *She went downtown, so she **might** be at the mall or she **could** be at the library.* (uncertain)
- *You **can't** be hungry. You just ate a big dinner!* (certain that it isn't true)
- *My dog is acting strangely. Do you think she's OK?* (asking for speculation / deduction) *She **may** be. But take her to the vet to check.*

Use:

- modals (*can't / might / may / could / must*) to speculate or make deductions based on evidence, and to express degrees of certainty.
- ***Do you think ...?*** to ask for speculation or a deduction:
  Do you think Liverpool are going to win? They might!

9A

1 Correct one mistake in four of 1–6. Be careful! Two have no mistakes.

1   It's a totally depressing movie about a young family that loses everything.
2   I get exciting at Christmas – I love all the food and the decorations.
3   Jane was feeling very stress because she has a job interview tomorrow.
4   She's been to the spa and now she feels very relaxing.
5   They can't even think about cooking dinner – they're totally exhausted.
6   The baseball game was a little bored. Nothing happened for hours.

2 Complete 1–5 with the -ed or -ing form of the verbs.

1   I have a three-month-old cousin. I'm totally _____ how much she cries! (**amaze**)
2   That was the most _____ flight I have ever been on! (**terrify**)
3   When he finished the race, he was so _____ that he collapsed. (**tire**)
4   Do you turn red easily when you are _____ ? (**embarrass**)
5   She read my work and said it was _____ . Is that good or bad? (**surprise**)

9B

1 Circle the correct options in 1–6, then match to a–f to make second conditional sentences.

1   If you **seen** / **saw** a crime,
2   If Ellen **had** / **was having** long hair,
3   If I found out my partner **was** / **is** cheating,
4   If you **could** / **was able to** time travel,
5   What would you **do** / **did**
6   If she **doesn't** / **didn't** want to go out with you,

a   would you visit the past or the future?
b   would you call the police?
c   she would look just like Alex Morgan.
d   she wouldn't and she'd make an excuse.
e   I'd dump him immediately.
f   if your parents told you not to marry someone you loved?

2 Use the prompts to make second conditional questions.

1   flight / what / if / you / do / miss / you / ?
    What would you do if you missed the flight?
2   how / away / you / win / the / give away / if / lottery / much / you / ?
3   if / emails / your / be cheating / you / partner's / think / if / you / read / ?
4   if / any / be / who / can / you / professional / if / you / sportsperson / you / be / ?
5   you / if / here / where / not / live / like / you / ?

3 🔘 **Make it personal** Write your answers to questions 1–5 in **2**.

9C

1 Correct two mistakes in each of 1–6. Be careful! Not all the mistakes are modals.

1   Jack isn't answering his phone. He can be in a meeting, or maybe he's leaving it at home.
2   You got a promotion! That's great news! You must to be such pleased!
3   Have you notice he's in really good shape? He must doing a lot of exercise!
4   I think that man look familiar. He can to be a famous actor.
5   Celia must be exhausting. She traveled all night and she was sit on the bus for hours.
6   Someone has took your wallet? Oh no! You could be really angry.

2 🔘 **Make it personal** Make at least two deductions about photos a–e using *must*, *could / might / may*, or *can't be*.

They could be tourists in Egypt. Or they might be guides who are showing tourists the pyramids.

Grammar Unit 10

10A Relative pronouns: *that* and *who*

- ▸ *Tessa loves a guy **who** lives in a different city.*
- ▸ *These are the videos **that** you asked me to send you.*
- ▸ *Are those the people **that** used to work with you?*

Sentence 1	Sentence 2			Relative clause
	S	**V**	**O**	
He's the actor.	I	love	him.	That's the actor **who** / **that** I love.
I live in a house.	It	has	two pools.	I live in a house **that** has two pools.

A relative pronoun refers to a noun mentioned previously. **Use** relative pronouns to join two sentences or ideas.
The relative pronoun is optional when it refers to the object of a sentence.

- ▸ *The city I love the most is Rome. / The city that I love the most is Rome.*

One / ones

- ▸ *Which are your **keys**? Are they the **ones** with the Mickey Mouse key ring?*
- ▸ *Which **one** is better for me? A **Mac** or a **PC**?*
- ▸ *"Where's your **car**?" "It's the old black **one** over there."*
- ▸ *"I've heard that **joke** before." "Yeah, the old **ones** are the best."*
- ▸ *"Have you read **Harry Potter**?" "Which **one**?"*

Use: to avoid repeating singular and plural nouns.
Don't use *one / ones* after a **possessive** (*my, your, his, her, Julia's*):

- ▸ *You do **your job**, and I'll do **mine**. NOT ~~You do your job, and I'll do the my one.~~*

Don't use *one / ones* directly after a **number** or a **quantifier** (*some, many, a few*):

- ▸ *When we're getting ready to go out, I only need **10 minutes** but my boyfriend needs **20**.*
- ▸ *"Can I have **some cookies**, please?" "Oh! Can I have **a few** too?"*

10B Asking questions: review

- ▸ *How many times have I told you not to do that?*
- ▸ *How much time do we have for the test?*
- ▸ *How long did you stay in New York?*
- ▸ *How old is your father?*
- ▸ *How tall are you?*
- ▸ *How far (away) is your house?*
- ▸ *What do you call this in English?*
- ▸ *What are you going to do this weekend?*
- ▸ *What should we do to stop climate change?*
- ▸ *What's glass made of?*
- ▸ *Which shoes do you like? The black ones or the red ones?*

- ▸ *Who did you go on vacation with?*
- ▸ *Why don't we go for a coffee?*
- ▸ *Is she working this weekend?*
- ▸ *Do you often eat hot peppers?*
- ▸ *Don't you like this cake? Come on! It's delicious!*

Q	O	A	S	I	
How much	money	do	I	need?	
How many	friends	does	your brother	have	on Facebook?
How fast		can	you	run?	
How often		do	you	work out?	
Which	colors	does	your partner	like	best?
Where		will	you	go	after class?
What	music	would	you	choose	to hear?
Who		did	she	meet	last night?
Where		don't	they	want	to live?
What	food	doesn't	he	like?	
		Do	we	have	any money left?
		Doesn't	your city	have	a metro?

Use:

- ▸ ***how much*** for quantity + U nouns.
- ▸ ***how many*** for quantity + C nouns.
- ▸ ***how + adj. / adv.*** to ask about quantity or degree.
- ▸ ***which*** to ask about things when there is a limited choice.
- ▸ ***what*** for general questions.
- ▸ ***who*** to ask about people.
- ▸ only an auxiliary for *Yes / No* questions.
- ▸ negative **ASI** questions to confirm information you think you know or to show surprise.

"So, how far is the restroom?"

10A

1 Add *who* or *that* in the correct places in the dialogue. Which three pronouns are optional?

A: Hello, we'd like to check in. My name's Cristina and this is my husband, Clive.

B: Ah, hello! You're the people booked online. Welcome to Hotel Flamingo.

A: Thank you. Could you tell me a little about the area?

B: Sure! There are some great restaurants you'll love. There's one around the corner has live music every night. I think there's a musician plays traditional songs tonight. And here we are, this is your room.

A: Oh! Uh … this isn't the room we saw on the website.

B: No. I'm afraid the room you booked has a problem with the shower. But this room is even bigger and has the same view.

2 Combine the two sentences in 1–5 using *who* or *that*.

1 This is the gym. This gym was on the website.
2 She is a girl. I knew her in high school.
3 That is the taxi driver. I met him at the basketball game.
4 There are five books. You have to read the books this semester.
5 Do you know a club? A club has good music.

3 Rewrite five of these sentences to avoid repetition and use *one / ones* correctly. Be careful! One sentence has no mistakes.

1 "Mom, can I eat those apples?" "Which?"
2 My dad's looking for a new car, a car with seven seats.
3 Look! We've got two letters. This one is my one and that one is your one.
4 Those earrings are nice, but I like the big earrings better.
5 I have seven cousins. The young ones are still at school and the old ones are already working.
6 I like the Fast and Furious movies but some ones are better than others.

10B

1 Complete dialogues 1–5.

1 **A:** _____ was your computer?
 B: About $900. But it has a massive memory.
2 **A:** _____ people are coming to the reunion?
 B: About 30 I think. Nearly everyone.
3 **A:** _____ your best friend dating anyone?
 B: No, she _____. Do you want to ask her out?
4 **A:** _____ pie are you going to have?
 B: Not the chicken one. Can I have a vegetable one, please?
5 **A:** _____ have you been in the line?
 B: Over 20 minutes. It's taking a long time.

2 Correct the mistakes in 1–7. There are eight mistakes.

1 What are those ladies over there? They look like friends I knew in college.
2 How often you eat fast food?
3 How much time did you live in New Mexico before you moved to Boston?
4 Do he change his status on Facebook every hour? How often he tweets?
5 Has you met many interesting new people recently?
6 How much people do you stay in touch with every day?
7 What juice will you having? Orange or pineapple?

3 🔵 **Make it personal** Order the words in 1–6 to make questions. Write your answers to the questions.

1 often / newspaper / do / you / a / how / buy / ?
2 bus / the / take / school / how / does / long / ?
3 how / bags / are / your / heavy / ?
4 every day / do / coffee / how / you / much / drink / ?
5 center / is / city / it / to / far / how / the / ?
6 been / beach / year / times / you / many / have / to / the / how / this / ?

Verbs

Irregular verbs

Irregular verbs can be difficult to remember. Try remembering them in groups with similar sounds, conjugation patterns, or spellings.

Simple past and Past participle are the same

Base form	Simple past	Past participle
bring	brought /brɔt/	brought
buy	bought	bought
catch	caught /cɔt/	caught
fight	fought	fought
teach	taught	taught
think	thought	thought
feed	fed	fed
feel	felt	felt
keep	kept	kept
leave	left	left
mean	meant /mɛnt/	meant
meet	met	met
sleep	slept	slept
lay	laid	laid
pay	paid	paid
sell	sold	sold
tell	told	told
send	sent	sent
spend	spent	spent
stand	stood /stʊd/	stood
understand	understood	understood
lose	lost	lost
shoot	shot	shot
can	could	could
will	would	would
build	built /bɪlt/	built
find	found /faʊnd/	found
hang	hung	hung
have	had	had
hear	heard /hɜrd/	heard
hold	held	held
make	made	made
say	said /sɛd/	said
sit	sat	sat
swing	swung /swʌŋ/	swung
win	won /wʌn/	won

Base form and Past participle are the same

Base form	Simple past	Past participle
become	became	become
come	came	come
run	ran	run

No changes across the three forms

Base form	Simple past	Past participle
cost	cost	cost
cut	cut	cut
hit	hit	hit
let	let	let
put	put /pʊt/	put
quit	quit /kwɪt/	quit
set	set	set
split	split	split

Special cases

Base form	Simple past	Past participle
be	was / were	been
draw	drew /dru:/	drawn /drɔn/
fly	flew /flu:/	flown /floʊn/
lie	lay	lain
read	read /rɛd/	read /rɛd/

Simple past + -*en*

Base form	Simple past	Past participle
beat	beat	beaten
bite	bit	bitten
break	broke	broken
choose	chose	chosen
forget	forgot	forgotten
freeze	froze	frozen
get	got	got / gotten
speak	spoke	spoken
steal	stole	stolen
wake	woke	woken

Simple past + -*en*

Base form	Simple past	Past participle
beat	beat	beaten
bite	bit	bitten
break	broke	broken
choose	chose	chosen
forget	forgot	forgotten
freeze	froze	frozen
get	got	got / gotten
speak	spoke	spoken
steal	stole	stolen
wake	woke	woken

Base form + -*en*

Base form	Simple past	Past participle
drive	drove	driven /drɪvən/
eat	ate	eaten
fall	fell	fallen
give	gave	given
ride	rode	ridden /rɪdən/
see	saw /sɔ/	seen
shake	shook	shaken
take	took	taken
write	wrote	written /rɪtən/

Base form ending in *o* + -*ne*

Base form	Simple past	Past participle
do	did	done /dʌn/
go	went	gone /gɔn/

i - a - u

Base form	Simple past	Past participle
begin	began	begun
drink	drank	drunk
ring	rang	rung
sing	sang	sung
swim	swam	swum

ow - ew - own

Base form	Simple past	Past participle
blow	blew /blu:/	blown
grow	grew	grown
know	knew	known
throw	threw	thrown

ear - ore - orn

Base form	Simple past	Past participle
swear	swore	sworn
tear /tɛr/	tore	torn
wear	wore	worn

Sounds and usual spellings

▶ To listen to these words and sounds, and to practice them, go to the pronunciation section on the Richmond Learning Platform.

Vowels

/iː/	three, tree, eat, receive, believe, key, B, C, D, E, G, P, T, V, Z
/ɪ/	six, mix, it, fifty, fish, trip, lip, fix
/ʊ/	book, cook, put, could, cook, woman
/uː/	two, shoe, food, new, soup, true, suit, Q, U, W
/ɛ/	pen, ten, heavy, then, again, men, F, L, M, N, S, X
/ə/	bananas, pajamas, family, photography

/ɜr/	shirt, skirt, work, turn, learn, verb
/ɔr/	four, door, north, fourth
/ɔ/	walk, saw, water, talk, author, law
/æ/	man, fan, bad, apple
/ʌ/	sun, run, cut, umbrella, country, love
/ɑ/	hot, not, on, clock, fall, tall
/ɑr/	car, star, far, start, party, artist, R

Diphthongs

/eɪ/	plane, train, made, stay, they, A, H, J, K
/aɪ/	nine, wine, night, my, pie, buy, eyes, I, Y
/aʊ/	house, mouse, town, cloud

/ɔɪ/	toys, boys, oil, coin
/oʊ/	nose, rose, home, know, toe, road, O

Voiced
Unvoiced

Consonants

TO MAKE THESE SOUNDS WE USE				
our lips	p	b	m	w
our teeth + another articulator	f	v **S**	θ **S P**	ð **P**
the tip of the tongue	t	d **S**	n **P**	l **P**
the front of the tongue	s	z	ʃ	ʒ
the back of the mouth	k	g	ŋ **S P**	h
the tooth ridge	tʃ **S**	dʒ **S**	r **P**	j **S**

/p/ pig, pie, open, top, apple
/b/ bike, bird, describe, able, club, rabbit
/m/ medal, monster, name, summer
/w/ web, watch, where, square, one
/f/ fish, feet, off, phone, enough
/v/ vet, van, five, have, video
/θ/ teeth, thief, thank, nothing, mouth
/ð/ mother, father, the, other
/t/ truck, taxi, hot, stop, attractive
/d/ dog, dress, made, adore, sad, middle
/n/ net, nurse, tennis, one, sign, know
/l/ lion, lips, long, all, old

/s/ snake, skate, kiss, city, science
/z/ zoo, zebra, size, jazz, lose
/ʃ/ shark, shorts, action, special, session, chef
/ʒ/ television, treasure, usual
/k/ cat, cake, back, quick
/g/ goal, girl, leg, guess, exist
/ŋ/ king, ring, single, bank
/h/ hand, hat, unhappy, who
/tʃ/ chair, cheese, kitchen, future, question
/dʒ/ jeans, jump, generous, bridge
/r/ red, rock, ride, married, write
/j/ yellow, yacht, university

Audioscript

Unit 6

▶ 6.1 Notice /dʒ/, /g/, and /ng/.

Welcome to fabulous Florida, the Sunshine State! It's the perfect place for all kinds of exciting outdoor activities. You can go hiking, fishing, or camping, and you can go diving or climbing. We have thousands of square miles of beautiful parks and countryside for you to explore. Or, if you prefer indoor activities, why not go bowling, go clubbing, or work out at one of our many great gyms? If you like exercising and enjoy sunny weather at the same time, you can even work out on our lovely beaches. And at the end of a fantastic day ... just hang out with your friends or the friendly locals! That's Florida – the Sunshine State.

▶ 6.2 Notice pronunciation and spellings of /f/, /v/, and /b/.

R = Rosie   B = Ben

R   Oh hi Ben! We just got back. It was such a great vacation!
B   I bet! I'd love to go to Florida. Did you stay just in Miami?
R   No. Martin and I went camping in the Everglades National Park. That was amazing.
B   That's, uh ... interesting. How did it go?
R   Well ... we were having a great time for the first few days. We went fishing and hiking.
B   Did you catch anything? A cold maybe?
R   No! But it was relaxing. And we saw alligators!
B   Wow! Really?
R   Yes. Then we went diving and saw more animals. We saw dolphins and a manatee and turtles.
B   What's a manatee?
R   Like a really big, fat, slow dolphin. Beautiful.
B   Sounds like you had a great time!
R   Yeah, we did – at first!
B   What happened?
R   Well, it's the rainy season and, uh, three days before the end of our vacation, it rained really hard, and our tent flooded and everything got wet.
B   Oh no! That's why I never go camping!
R   Yeah! At first we didn't know what to do – it was awful! Like, we were cold and our clothes and all our things were wet. But then we decided to stay the last two nights at a hotel in Miami and it was just fantastic. Totally.
B   Right, so what did you do?
R   Oh, we went bowling and we went clubbing. It was cool!
B   Sounds like you had a really ... varied vacation.
R   We sure did! Overall, it was great, but our tent is ruined forever!

▶ 6.5 Notice /θ/ and /ð/.

W = woman   M = man

W   My boyfriend Charlie did a triathlon the other day.
M   Oh yeah?
W   Yeah, but it was kind of extreme. Even more challenging than a standard triathlon! First he ran five kilometers along a beach.
M   Uh-huh.
W   Then he climbed up a rope, over a wall, and down the other side ... before running through fire.
M   He what?
W   Yeah, really! Then he jumped into the river and swam around an island, under a bridge, and past the stadium.
M   Whoa!
W   Then, he got out of the river and cycled 15 kilometers towards the finish.
M   15 kilometers!
W   And after finally running across the finish line, he collapsed!
M   I'm not surprised!

▶ 6.6 Notice /aɪ/ and /iː/.

M = Martin   J = Jo

M   Hey, do you want to go surfing this weekend? We could go to the beach and stay at that nice hotel.
J   Hmm ... not really, I don't feel like getting hot and tired, and I don't really enjoy surfing.
M   But, but I thought you did! Well, we could go swimming instead? They have a lovely pool at the hotel.
J   I hate swimming – it's worse than surfing – it's so boring!
M   I really miss going to the beach. I don't remember the last time we went.
J   I have to say that I don't miss the beach, sorry, Martin. I like to stay cool – I'd rather stay inside. Do you want to go bowling this weekend? I adore bowling. You can stay inside and you don't get hot when you're bowling.
M   You keep asking me that! You know I can't stand bowling. You know, I just don't get it. When I met you, you started swimming and surfing with me and you loved it!
R   I suppose I did, but I guess I've changed. Right now I can't imagine getting onto a surfboard. Umm ... what about the movies? Let's go to the movies. We both enjoy doing that.
M   OK – I guess so, but let's go surfing soon.
R   Uh ... maybe.

▶ 6.9 Notice the schwa /ə/.

A = adult   C = child

C   So, you need a ball?
A   Yeah, and two big goals.
C   Right.
A   And, um, you pass the ball from one player to another.
C   Ooh, is it soccer?
A   No, sorry. You pass the ball with your hands.
C   OK.
A   Yeah, and you have to put the ball down over the line to score.
C   Oh! Is it American football?
A   No, no, you, don't wear a helmet. But it's similar. Um, you can kick the ball too.
C   I see ... I think.

A   It's popular in Australia, New Zealand, Argentina, South Africa, Europe, and, uh, ...
C   Got it! I know, it's ...

Review 3

▶ R3.2 Notice /æ/.

PS = pool supervisor   C = child

1 PS   Hey! You can't run in here.
2 PS   Hey! You can't dive in the pool. No diving!
3 PS   Sorry. You can't have food and drink in here.
4 PS   The showers are over there. You have to take a shower before you swim.
5 PS   How old are you?
  C   I'm six.
  PS   I'm sorry, children have to swim with adults. Where's your mom?

▶ R3.3 Notice pronunciation and spelling of /s/ and /z/.

Hi, my name's Clara Bush and I'm 22 years old. I'm from Phoenix, Arizona, but, uh, I'm living and studying in Mexico City for the summer. I really need to learn Spanish fast as I'm majoring in Spanish and have my final exams as soon as I get back, uh, at the end of August.

▶ R3.4 Notice to /tə/, at /ət/, and of = /əv/.

I absolutely adore, uh, traveling, I always have, and so when I turned 21 I decided, uh, to go and live in Mexico, um, to study Spanish. At first my parents didn't want me to leave the States, but in the end they agreed, uh, to pay for my studies here in Mexico City. Anyway, so now I'm here and it's great 'cos I can practice, uh, speaking every day, and I think my Spanish is really improving, and I hope, uh, to pass my final exam in two months. I kind of miss, uh, going to the mall with my friends back home, and of course my family, but I know I'll see them again soon. When I have finished, uh, studying here, I think I'm going to travel down south and maybe see some temples before I go home.

▶ R3.6 Notice /w/.

M = man   W = woman

W   Would you like to get into a crocodile tank with just a two-inch thick plastic cage around you?
M   What? Of course not, I'm not crazy! Why?
W   I think it sounds amazing! It's totally safe.
M   What are you talking about?
W   In Australia, you can get in a plastic tank and then you're lowered into the water.
M   And what's in the water?
W   Saltwater crocodiles!
M   That's ridiculous!
W   It's not. I think it sounds cool.
M   When did you start wanting to do ridiculous things?
W   It's not ridiculous – it would be fun. It's only for about 15 minutes.
M   That 15 minutes would seem like a lifetime!

W And you get really close to the animals. They swim really close to you and you have a 360° view of them as they swim around you.

M And try to eat you, I suppose!

W But they can't get through the plastic! And the organizers photograph you and film you as you do it.

Unit 7

◯ 7.1 Notice pronunciation of the -d endings, /d/ or /ɪd/, and their spelling.

Tune in to the Classic Movie Channel – we have something for everyone this week – here's the best of the week. For horror fans we have *Hereditary* – be prepared to be scared! If a drama is more to your taste we have *Boyhood*, or if you're in the mood for a comedy there's *Bridesmaids*. For all the family we have the adventure movie *The Hunger Games*, and for fantasy fans there are the *Fantastic Beasts* movies. If you like animated movies, don't miss *Inside Out*, or if you feel like watching a documentary, we have *Senna* – don't miss it!

◯ 7.2 Notice /s/ and /z/ endings.

J = Jack K = Kelly

J OK, Kelly, you go stand in line for the tickets, I'll buy the popcorn.

K I already bought the tickets online – we don't need to stand in line.

J Cool, but we need to for popcorn.

K Uh huh. ... Oh, no, the movie's about to start!

J OK, well you buy the sodas – there's no one waiting – and I'll stand in line and get the popcorn.

K OK, I'll go into the theater after I've bought the sodas, and you join me when you've got the popcorn.

J OK – make sure you get us good seats.

K I already chose the seats online, Jack, after I bought them! When was the last time you went to the movies?

J Oh, yeah, I forgot you could do that. What movie are we seeing again?

K I've told you five times, it's a classic horror movie called *Hereditary*.

J But I don't like horror movies!

K It's too late, Jack! I'll see you inside – in the dark .... Wooooooo

◯ 7.6 Notice the schwa /ə/.

M = Male presenter W = Female presenter

M ... Welcome back to "You must be joking!," the radio show about the unusual things we all do. This week, we're looking at unusual collections ... Next up on our top 10 list ... Number 5 ... Barbara Hartsfield from Georgia in the U.S. Barbara collects miniature chairs.

W What? You mean little chairs?

M Yes, little chairs. Barbara is such a huge miniature chair fan that she has her own museum with thousands of little chairs.

W Wow! That's funny.

M Yep. There are little chairs at the museum inside bottles, chairs made from toothpicks, chair earrings, everything is in the shape of a chair!

W Wow! Such a lot of little chairs! I'd like to see that.

M Well, that's nothing compared to number 4 on our top 10 ... Percival R. Lugue from the Philippines.

W ... and ... what does he collect?

M Fast food restaurant toys.

W What, those little toys that come with meals for kids?

M That's right. Well, Percival is so careful with his toys that he has over 15,000 of them.

W That's so sweet!

M Yep. Apparently, he is trying to collect all the fast food toys that exist in the world!

W That's a lot of fast food!

M So wait till you hear about the next collection in our top 10. Number 3 ... This one is a man called David Morgan from the UK. The man's such a passionate traffic cone fan that he has a collection of over 500.

W You mean traffic cones that you see on the street?

M Yes, that's right.

W So, does he steal them?

M Nope – he says he would never consider stealing one as they are so important for safety.

W Wow! People really collect unusual things, don't they!

M You betcha! After our commercial break, we're gonna ...

◯ 7.7 Notice /b/, /v/ and /w/.

M Welcome back ... You're listening to "You must be joking!" This week, we're looking at the unusual things that people collect. So, back to our top 10 countdown ... Number 2 ... Rainer Weichert from Germany enjoys bringing home a souvenir from all of his trips.

W So? Everyone likes to do that.

M Yes, but he doesn't bring a T-shirt or a key chain back he brings a "do not disturb" sign.

W You mean, those signs you put on your hotel door?

M Uh-huh.

W Wow! Hard to believe there are such strange collections out there! Do not disturb signs? There are so many better souvenirs!

M Yeah, I know! Really interesting, huh? Ready for number 1?

W Yeah. Can't wait.

M Our number 1 unusual collector is Nancy Hoffman from Maine in the U.S. She collects umbrella sleeves.

W You mean the cover for an umbrella? Not the umbrellas?

M No, just the sleeves. She likes them so much that she has collected them from 50 countries in the world.

W And how many does she have?

M Over 750.

W Oh, my goodness! That's such a strange thing to collect. I suppose some of them are pretty, but ...

◯ 7.9

1 three hundred billion / one hundred and six point nine billion / seventy-three point nine billion / fifty-three point two billion
2 seventy-one thousand six hundred
3 twenty-four percent
4 eight hundred and fifty
5 thirty-five percent
6 eighty-seven percent

◯ 7.12 Notice the short pauses and longer pauses.

B = Bruce J = Judy

B ... so why did I audition? I don't know. I was, uh, out of work, so I had all the time in the world to spend hours and hours camped outside the auditorium. Anyway, the big day arrived and I got there around 5, 5:30 a.m. – and Wow! it was such a huge place! Really huge! There were, what, 10,000 people standing in line. It was raining torrentially and they only let us in at 9! Can you believe those guys? Where was I? Oh, yeah, well, in the end, they only selected 200 people to audition in front of the show's producers. If your voice was good enough, you'd then advance to the next round and finally sing in front of the celebrity judges ... You know, the bad, cruel guys. I made it to the top 200, but during my audition there was something wrong with the audio and I didn't get to sing in front of the TV judges ... Actually, few people get that far – only 40, usually. Yeah, just 40. This was such a disappointment! I'd always wanted to meet the judges, you know. Guess I'll try again next year. Oh, by the way, my name's Bruce and I'm from New Jersey.

J ... So my name's Judy Jackson, and I'm from Dallas. So, uh, I've always been interested in real estate and I have a blog about buying and selling houses – it's quite popular, with about 750 visits a day. Anyway, one day, someone from ABC – or was it NBC? – found my blog on the Internet and sent me an email asking me if I wanted to be considered for the show. You can imagine my surprise ... I was chosen to be on TV! Yes, me! She said they were looking for interesting families. "Why me?," I thought. "I have such a conventional family!" Well, my immediate reaction was to say no, of course. Why on earth would I want to have someone watch me and my family fighting over buying a new house? But then I read somewhere that families were paid $20,000 to appear on the show – and, you know, at the time, Mark was unemployed, so I thought it over for a week or so and – surprise, surprise – in the end, I said yes. So I gave the woman a call and left a message ... and again ... and again ... I called her at least 15 times. Guess what, all my calls were ignored! All of them! Anyway, two months later – ironically – my family had to move house because of work, but we were never on the show.

Unit 8

▶ 8.3 Notice the **connections**.

D1 = smart alarm and coffee maker
W1 = woman

D1 It's time to wake up. Would you like me to let you sleep a little longer?
W1 Yes!
D1 Are you sure? You do have a very busy day.
W1 I'll get_up in five minutes.
D1 I'm going to turn on the coffee maker.
W1 OK, ... no, wait! Don't turn_on the coffee maker! It's broken! Oh no! ... What_a mess!

2

M1 = man   D2 = Jack, housework robot

M1 Jack! Wash the dishes.
D2 I'm sorry, I can't. You forgot to charge me this morning. I'm running on economy mode so I can save enough battery power to make the beds.
M1 No problem. Let me plug_you in.
D2 Thank you. Oh, that feels nice ...

3

D3 = smart temperature control device
W2 = woman]

D3 It's way too cold in here. This is not good for your body. I'm going to turn up the thermostat.
W2 No way! I like it when_it's cool.
D3 Turning up the thermostat in 3, 2, 1 second.
W2 Hey, what_are you doing? Please, turn the thermostat down! Turn it down!

4

C = car computer   M = Michael

C Please, look at the face detection device ... I'm sorry. I can't recognize you.
M What do_you mean?
C I can't recognize your face. Please, look straight into the face sensor ... I'm sorry. I still can't recognize you.
M Oh no! Not again. You know what, I'm going_to switch_you off.
C Michael, you know you can't switch me off. You need to answer a few security questions.

▶ 8.4 Notice the **intonation in questions** ↗ ↘.

C = computer   M = Michael

C May I ask you a few security questions? ↗
M Yes, I suppose so!
C What's your full name? ↘
M Michael Jay Huff.
C How do you spell "Huff"? ↘
M H-U-F-F.
C Correct. Are you American? ↗
M No, I'm from Canada.
C When were you born? ↘
M October 5.
C Correct.
M This is unbelievable.
C How long have you had this vehicle? ↘

M What? ↘
C How long have you had this vehicle? ↘
M Since June.
C Information mismatch.
M June, July, who cares? ↘ Just start the car. Please.
C Did you say July? ↗
M Yes.
C Correct. Did you use this car on Tuesday? ↗
M Yeah.
C What were you wearing? ↘
M I can't remember what I was wearing. A white T-shirt, I think.
C Try again.
M Come on! Why are you doing this to me? ↘

▶ 8.9

1 Notice the /t/ and silent **t**.

S = Sue   B = Bob

S Guess what! I just bought a new car.
B Really? That's cool. I, uh, I'm going to try to sell mine in October or November. It's got over 80 thousand miles on it, I think – time to get a new one.
S Wow, that's a lot. Anyway, it's a brand new Prius and I was looking at ...
B A Prius? No way! My Dad drives a Prius, too, you know ...
S Really? That's a coincidence. I ...
B Yeah, must be his third or fourth ... You know what? I'll call him right now and tell him. He'll like that you're getting the same car as him. I have to ...

2 Notice /t/ and /h/.

R = Regis   A = Ann

R Hey, wanna have lunch on Friday?
A I can't. I'm seeing the doctor on Friday.
R Oh yeah? Anything serious?
A No, just my annual check-up.
R That's good. You know it's important to always go to the doctor, don't you? I have a friend, she works long hours, gets no exercise and has such a bad diet, and I tell her "living like this, you're going to make yourself ill". So as I've told you before, you have to look after your health and get regular health checks.
A Regis! You know I have a health check every year!!
R Yeah, um ... I'm going to get a check-up too. Maybe I've been working too hard and not looking after myself. You know, I really don't think you do enough exercise, you should ...

3 Notice /g/ and /j/.

S = Sally   Y = Yuko

S Hi, Yuko! Just saw your tweet. Calling to wish you a safe trip.
Y Thanks. The plane leaves at two and I haven't started packing yet.
S Oh, don't worry. You still have about five or six hours ...
Y I'm really excited. I'd like to know if all the stuff we see in movies ...
S ... is true? Oh, you bet it is ... By the way, there's this great little restaurant on the corner

of Broadway and 47th or 48th that you simply must try. Seriously, you've got to go there. I think it's called La Pasta ... La Pasta something ... Google it.
Y What about the Guggenheim? Teri says ...
S Oh, there are some great museums. The last time I was there I went to the Museum of Modern Art and it was fabulous ...

▶ 8.12

J = Joe   C = coach

1 Notice the **sentence stress** and unstressed **auxiliary verbs**.

C1 Of course. **Joe**, what **can I help** you **with**?
J It's about **my career** ... You see, I've worked at the **same company** for five, no, **six years now** and it feels like ... well, it feels like I'm getting **nowhere**, you know what I mean? So, I guess **my question to you is** ... Will I ever **get a promotion**?
C1 Don't worry, this is a very **common problem**. We'll need to talk more about why you feel like this. If you've been **there six years**, you **might get a promotion soon**, but I think you also need to **consider your future** with the company.
J Yes, I've thought about that too. I've been **there so long**.
C1 There's a good chance that **you'll decide** it's **time to move on**.
J I think that's a good idea!
C1 Well, I can help you **make that transition** too ...

2 Notice the spelling of /e/ and /iː/.

J I just feel so tired all the time.
C2 Hmmm ... tell me more about this. How's your sleep?
J Uh, not that great – sometimes I find it difficult to go to sleep, and I'm always tired when I wake up in the morning.
C2 That's not so good. Are you looking at a screen before bed?
J Well, yes, I always check my messages in bed.
C2 Well, if you put your phone away at least two hours before bedtime, you'll find that you sleep better.
J You think so?
C2 Absolutely.
J Thanks, I'll try that ... and what about my headaches ...?
C2 Well, possibly your headaches will stop as well if you stop looking at your phone before bed, but there may be other reasons ...Tell me more about your headaches ...

3 Notice pronunciation and spelling of /l/ and the -ls ending /lz/.

C5 So, how can I can help you, Joe?
J Um, well, you see, I've been seeing Emma for over a year now and I really like her ... no, I love her, but I'm not sure she feels the same. Sometimes I can't sleep because I'm frightened she's going to leave me.

C5 I see. And why are you frightened about that, Joe? Has she given you any reason to feel like this?

J Not really, no, but my last two girlfriends left me and I don't understand why.

C5 All right. The first thing you have to do is talk to Emma and tell her how you feel. Communication is essential in a relationship.

J Do you really think that will help?

C5 For sure. If you don't talk to Emma, you won't find out how she feels.

J But I'm not good at talking to people ... and what if she says something I don't want to hear? How about I tell her I love her on Facebook? Is that a good idea?

C5 Probably not, Joe. You have to be brave and learn to say how you feel.

Review 4

▶ R4.1 Notice /d/ and /t/ endings.

... mostly cloudy during the day. So, if you've just tuned in, here are the answers to today's music quiz. Are you ready?
Number 1: "Imagine" was written by John Lennon in 1971, but it was only released four years later, in 1975. Pretty easy, wasn't it? Number 2 may surprise you, but nearly 1.5 billion smartphones are sold around the globe every year – that's a lot of phones. Yep, you heard it right: 1.5 billion. How 'bout that? Third question ... Beyonce's first solo album was called *Dangerously in Love*. It was released in 2003 and went to number 1 in several different countries.
Question 4 ... Amy Winehouse was only 27 when she was found dead in her apartment in London. Interestingly, singers Janis Joplin, Jim Morrison, and Kurt Cobain also died at age 27. And finally, here's our last question ... American singer Ariana Grande is considered to be one of the world's best vocalists. Her albums have sold millions around the world.

▶ R4.2 Notice the sentence stress.

1
A ... **hurry up**. We're going to **be late**. The movie starts **at nine. Oh no**! Your **battery's** almost **dead**.
B Is it? Uh oh – 2%. I'll **plug it in** – don't worry.
A **Where?**
B **In the car. Let's go.**
2
C I'm going **to bed**.
D But it's **only 8:30**!
C I know, but I'm going to **get up at 5 a.m.**
D **Why?**
C I have to **finish a project** and my **laptop is at the repair shop**, so I'm **going to school early**.
D **Seriously? 5 a.m?**
3
E ... Anyway, then **she told me** that I should ...
F What?
E **She told me** that I should **look for another job** and ...

F Look **for what?**
E Bill, why **do you always** have to have your music **so loud when I'm talking?**
F Oh, alright, I'll turn it down.
E Thank you. That's **much better**.
4
G ... that's really **exciting!** I've never been there. Oh, you'll have a **wonderful time**.
H Yeah, we're **really excited**. The plane **leaves at ten**. I'm counting the minutes.
G What if I **need to speak to you?** You know, about the project ... You're going to leave **your cell phone on**, right?
H Well, **actually, no**. I'm going to **turn it off** and only turn it **back on when I'm back home**.
G Really? But can I **call the hotel at least?**

▶ R4.3 Notice /ð/ and /θ/.

1 ... and for the fourth consecutive month, unemployment has increased by 13.7%, twice as much as the same period last year. A spokesman for the ...

2 ... the governor's chances of reelection. Now, on to local news. A three hour power outage left the state of Michigan in the dark last night. 248 cities were affected and there are ...

3 ... won last night's Emmy for best actor. Pineapple is in trouble with their latest tablet – the pTab. Over the past two weeks, there have been numerous reports of pTabs exploding and catching fire. Apparently, two thirds of all pTabs produced in May were considered defective. A spokesman for Pineapple has ...

4 ... the largest in history. A small town in Brazil has also made history this week, as new evidence emerges that some of its inhabitants were contacted by extraterrestrials on April 12. The town, with a population of only 40,540, was visited by UFOs in the past and according to a local TV station ...

Unit 9

▶ 9.2 Notice /iː/ and /ɪ/.

WP = wedding planner   M = Michaela

WP OK, Michaela. Here's how it's going to work.
M Um, I don't want anything very fancy, just ...
WP How long was your engagement?
M Er, three years.
WP Then you need something fancy. We'll have invitations like this – black with gold letters.
M Hmm – we actually just wanted plain white.
WP Then we'll have the wedding ceremony at your home and – we'll keep it small, just 200 guests.
M 200?! But that's not very small. We want the ceremony at the beach.
WP 200 is small, sweetie. Then we'll have the reception in a fantastic big restaurant that I know, for say 500 people.
M But we can't afford that! You know, we're thinking, like about 50 guests in a small restaurant for the reception.

WP OK, just 400 guests at the reception then. And then your dress – I see it something like this: white and very feminine.
M Uh, I was thinking of something more simple, just a nice dress – blue or green.
WP ... and let's see ... about ten bridesmaids all carrying mountains of flowers.
M Ten! No, I just want my sister and my niece.
WP ... and the groom in white also – a white suit – and you'll both have huge gold rings – it's going to be fabulous!
M Um ... Andy hates wearing a suit and we want to have silver rings.
WP Details, details! We'll worry about that later ... And then the honeymoon on a remote island ... a big ecological tour.
M Well ... erm... that's not really what we had in mind ... we probably won't have time for a honeymoon until next year – and then we just want to go to a nice resort.

▶ 9.7 Notice the connections.

M = man   W = woman

M Hey, Sarah.
W Hi, Max. What's_new?
M Not much – you?
W I'm waiting for Tony. Have you seen him?
M Umm ... no.
W He's_always late these days and he never answers my calls.
M He's probably really busy_at work.
W Yeah, that must be it. I saw him with_a woman from work earlier. They were probably talking about work.
M Uh ... there's_something I want to ask you, Sarah.
W What is it? What's_up?

▶ 9.8 Notice the silent letters.

M = man   W = woman

M Uh ... Sarah, what would you do if Tony cheated on you?
W Well, it depends. If I saw him with another person, I'd confront him. We've been dating for a year, so I think I know him.
M Uh huh. What if a friend told you, what would you do?
W Mmm. ... If I didn't know for sure, I'd ask Tony first.
M Would you follow him, if you thought he liked someone else?
W No, I wouldn't. I'd trust him to tell me the truth, if he wanted to date someone else.
M I see ...
W Why? Is there something you want to tell me? You're his best friend.
M No ... I was just wondering.

M = man   W = woman

M Would you like to be famous?
W I'm not sure. Uh, yes, I guess I'd like to be some kind of performer.
M And if you could be any kind of performer, what would you be?
W Hmm ... I don't know, maybe an actor or a singer? Or a musician?
M Really? But you don't play any instruments and you can't sing!
W Don't be so sure – I might have hidden talents!
M Hmm. They must be well hidden! I see you as an athlete or a dancer. You're so sporty.
W Uh, you think so? Really? I might be a good gymnast or a skater, something like that.
M Yeah, I can see that. Well, uh, um, I'd like to be a comedian or a magician.
W No way! What about a clown?
M Ha ha ha ha! What! What are you saying?
W Just that you're always falling over and you really make me laugh!

▶9.15 Notice the **sentence stress** and schwa /ə/.

J = Jane   M = Michael

J What's the **matter**, Michael?
M Uh ... nothing.
J Come on – **I know you** pretty well, **what's wrong**?
M Well, it's **dumb really**. You know **my brother**, David?
J Of course. He's your **only brother** and he's **a doctor, right**?
M Yeah, that's right. And **I'm a teacher**.
J So **what about** David?
M Well, he's just **got a promotion** and he's **bought a new car**.
J That's **great**!
M Yeah, it is, except that I **can't help feeling jealous. I** want **a** new car and I **can't afford one**, because my **job doesn't pay** as well as his!
J I see ... Is he **older or younger** than you?
M He's **younger – I should be** the one who **makes more money** and who buys **a** new car first!
J It's perfectly **natural for you to feel jealous** of your brother, especially because you're older than him, but really, is it **that important**?
M I suppose it's **just a car**.
J Yes, and think about all the **stress he has** in his job and the **long hours he works**.
M You're right – I **never wanted to be a doctor**.
J You see! You **like your job**, right? And you **have a really nice life**.
M That's **true**.
J Come on – let's **go for a walk**!
M **If I had a new car**, I'd **take you out** somewhere really nice.
J You **don't need a** new **car**.

▶9.16 Notice **sentence stress** and **weak forms**.

S = son   Mo = Mom   W = woman   M = man
D = daughter   F = father

1
S I**'ve lost my phone**.
Mo Why don't you **go upstairs** and **look in your room**?
S That's a **good idea. I was using it there** earlier.

2
W1 I'm so fed up with **my boyfriend**. He always **works on weekends**.
M1 If I were you, I'd **talk to him and explain** that it's **not fair**.
W1 Thanks for the suggestion, but, uh, you don't **know my boyfriend. I'm not sure that's the best** thing to do.

3
M2 I have a really **bad headache**.
W2 You should **go home and lie down**. You **shouldn't be at a party**.
M2 You're right. I**'m going home**.

4
M3 I**'m trying really hard**, but, man, my **job is** so **boring**.
W3 What about **looking for a new job**? My **brother has a restaurant** and he **might have a job**.
M3 Hey! **Thanks** for the tip – I**'d** like to **work in a restaurant**.

5
D I**'m failing math** class.
F You**'d** better **start working harder** or you **won't get into college**.
D Yeah, I **guess so**.

Unit 10

▶10.1 Notice /v/, /b/ and *have to* = /hæftə/.

Int = Interviewer

Int Hello! I'm conducting a survey for the Institute for Meditation and Relaxation. Do you have time to answer a question for me? What's the biggest stressor for you in your daily life?

1
W1 Hmm ... Well, in general, I would say that I always have so much work – my boss always gives me deadlines – I have to start and finish things with very little time. In fact, I have to do a report by the end of today, so, sorry, I have to go.

2
M1 My kids – I have two children – I love them, don't get me wrong, but it's just so hard caring for them all the time. I never get a break! Melissa! Stop that!

3
W2 It would have to be school – there's so much pressure to succeed – we have exams all the time and I need to do well to get into grad school.

4
M2 Uh ... well, I never seem to have enough money. I have a job, but I'm overworked and underpaid, and I'm in school too, and by the end of the month I have no money and I have to pay for things with my credit card – it's just a vicious circle.

5
W3 Food and eating is the biggest problem for me – I don't have time to eat well and so I eat fast, easy food and this is a really poor diet – I don't eat well when I'm stressed, then I get sick.

6
M3 Definitely lack of sleep – when I don't sleep well, I get worried about not sleeping and that stops me from sleeping and then I get more stressed. Then, when I do sleep, I oversleep! I'm late for class ... I have to go!

7
W4 I really need to exercise every day to get energy, but I'm always so tired when I get home at night that I just fall in front of the TV because I have no energy, so lack of exercise is my biggest problem.

8
M4 OK, great, thanks, talk to you later, bye ... So, I try to do so many things at the same time, I'm answering the phone and writing emails and reading reports all at the same time. Multitasking is really stressful! Excuse me ... This is John Maley.

▶10.5 Notice /m/, /n/ and /ng/.

P = Patrick   M = Molly

P Look! This is the hotel that was on the website.
M Wow! It's right on the beach. Cool. Is that where you stayed?
P No, when we got there they said it wasn't ready yet. So we stayed in this hotel, which was 30 minutes from the beach!
M Oh! Was the hotel nice at least?
P Yeah, it was great. You can see the swimming pool that was right outside our room.
M It looks awesome!
P And this is the lifeguard who told us to get out of the water because there was a storm coming.
M Wow! That was exciting.
P Yeah, there was thunder and lightning for about half an hour and lots of rain. This is the bar that was next to the pool. We watched the storm from there.
M That sounds like fun.
P Yeah. Look – these are some of the birds that were flying around outside.
M You sure do take a lot of photos!
P I know! Do you want to see some more?
M Um ... Oh, wow, look at the time! I've gotta go! Maybe you can show me later.

◉10.9 Notice spelling and pronunciation of /g/, /dʒ/ and /z/.

Part of the lifestyle involves salvaging discarded food, clothing, and furniture from stores or other people's garbage! I happen to participate in one part of freeganism quite often: the part where you salvage furniture from the trash. Now I live in New York City, where I think it's pretty common to pick up trashed furniture or electronics, because people here just leave that stuff on the sidewalk for you to grab. And when you're on your way home and you walk by a perfectly good piece of furniture that you can use, why not just scoop it up and schlep it back to your abode? A huge percentage of the furniture in my house is actually from other people's trash. Recently I told that to some people who don't live in New York and they were like, "ewww", disgusted by it. While they understand the saving money, recycling side of it, they couldn't get past the other side of it. The "Someone-else-who-could-have-bedbugs-or-disgusting-hygiene-owned-that" side of it.

◉10.10 Notice /s/ and /z/.

There are some things I won't pick up — bedding, anything with a fabric covering, or just furniture that looks too dirty, but generally, if it looks like it works and it just needs a little cleaning — that crap is mine and I'm psyched! So how about you? What would you take out of the garbage and bring to your home, if anything? Is there a freegan in you? This week let's talk about that.

◉10.11 Notice /r/ and the intonation.

Hi, it's Nicki Mitchell and I was in the class of 2004. I was looking at my old school photos and I realized that we haven't had a reunion for ages. There are some people I haven't seen for years and we used to have a lot of fun together — remember? Do you know what happened to Kyle Rodriguez? I'd like to find him and I know you two were friends. Anyway, the reunion's going to be at Pete's Pizza on Friday night. I'll put this info on Facebook too, so please reply there if you can come. Can't wait to see you, bye!

◉10.12 Notice intonation in exclamations and questions.

K = Kyle   N = Nicki

K   Hi, Nicki! Great to see you. When did we last see each other? ↘

N   Around 10 years ago — when we finished high school. It was so cool to find you on Facebook and awesome that you could meet me. How are you? ↘

K   Good — how about you? ↘ Are you married yet? ↗

N   Yeah, married with two kids. Jason is five and Scott is three. Um … I married Rick Respini.

K   No way! ↘ That's uh … wonderful.

N   Do you have any kids? ↗

K   Yes, my wife Jessie and I had twins last year.

N   That's awesome! ↘

K   Yeah … so how many people do you still see from high school? ↘

N   Oh, around 50 maybe. We're having the next reunion in a pizza restaurant downtown.

K   Oh yeah? ↘ Which restaurant is it at? ↘

N   Pete's Pizza — they do great food. Do you want to come? ↗

K   Yeah, I love their pizza! How often are the reunions? ↘

N   Around every six months or so. The last one was a lot of fun. Your ex, Mindy, was there.

K   Really? ↘

N   Yeah, did you know she divorced her husband? ↗

K   No! That's sad. Did they have kids? ↗

N   No, no kids, but I don't know much about it. But you can find out all about it at the reunion.

◉10.13 Notice the **sentence stress**.

1   Hey! I'm **so happy** to **see you**! What's **new**?
2   How **much time** do you **spend studying or working**?
3   How **often** do you **check Facebook**?
4   How **long** have you **lived in your current house**?
5   How **long ago** did you **start learning English**?
6   How **many people** have you **met online**?

Review 5

◉R5.2 Notice /æ/ and /ɔr/.

P = presenter   C = Carla   B = Dr. Brayman

P   Now for our next caller. Carla, you're through to Dr. Brayman.

C   Hello, Dr. Brayman.

B   Hi, Carla. What's your question?

C   It's kind of hard to talk about …

B   Don't worry, that's why you called. And that's why I'm here. Relax, really, it's fine.

C   Thanks, Doctor. Well, OK, my question is about jealousy. My partner, Jack, calls me all the time to find out where I am and what I'm doing.

◉R5.3 Notice /oʊ/ and /ɔr/.

B = Dr. Brayman   C = Carla   P = presenter

B   Well, Carla — this is a difficult problem. If a jealous partner calls all the time, the natural thing to do is not answer the phone calls. You know, just ignore them.

C   Yes, yes, that's exactly what I'm doing.

B   And then you start to grow apart and have secrets from each other. Have you found that happening?

C   Yes, totally! I mean, sometimes, he calls me every hour, even when I'm at work! I don't answer the phone, or I sometimes tell him that I left my phone at home — anything so that I don't have to answer his calls.

B   And I understand that, but this makes Jack more jealous and he calls you even more … and so you have to find other ways not to take his calls and the problem becomes worse, not better.

C   That's right, so what would you do Dr. Brayman?

B   The best way to deal with a jealous partner is to talk about where the jealousy is coming from. Your partner may feel jealous because he's afraid of losing you. Try talking to him about his fears and worries. Tell him how you feel about him. Tell him that his jealousy is having a negative effect on your relationship.

C   I see, so you think I should talk to him instead of ignoring his phone calls?

B   Yes, but remember that he's not going to change from one day to the next. A problem like this could take months or even years to resolve, so you also need to decide if you want to take this time. If your partner agreed, I would recommend that you both go and talk to an expert.

C   Yeah, maybe he would go to a counselor. I'll try it. Thanks, Dr. Brayman.

B   Good luck, Carla.

P   And our next caller is on line two …

PAUL SELIGSON
TOM ABRAHAM
CRIS GONTOW

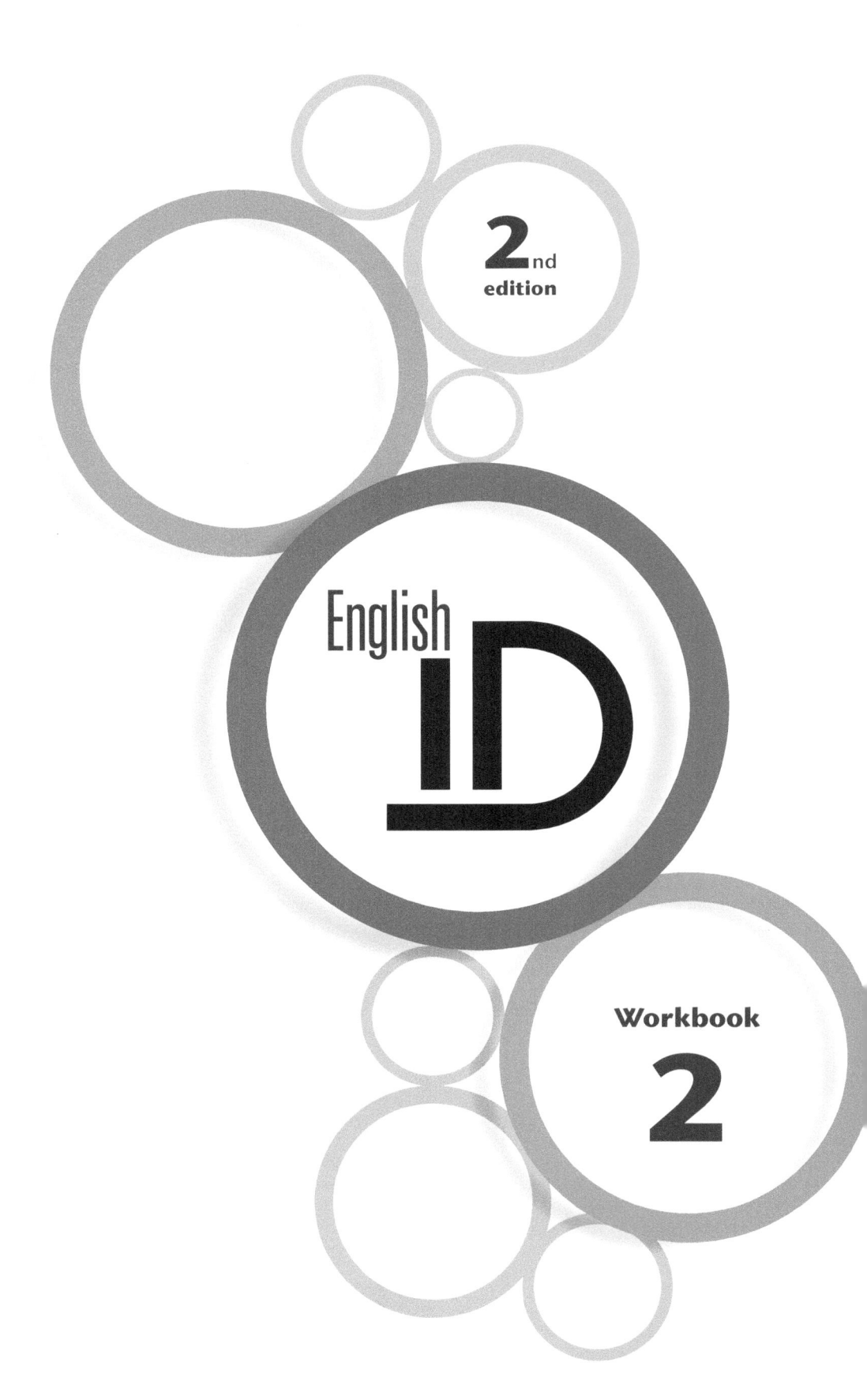

2nd edition

English **ID**

Workbook 2

Richmond

6.1 Have you ever been to Florida?

1 ▶6.1 **Practice the picture words and a–e. Then listen to check your pronunciation.**

a I'm going shopping tomorrow morning.
b We go clubbing every Friday evening.
c I went swimming and diving last weekend.
d We're going fishing next spring.
e Let's go bowling in Washington!

/ɪ/

2 **Complete the posts with these verbs in the correct form. Add *go* or *went* if necessary.**

bowl   camp   climb   club   dive   fish   hang out   ~~hike~~   work out

Visit Florida!

a My husband and I love to _go hiking_ so this spring we decided to walk part of the Florida Trail. We carried a tent with us and _____ under the stars. Absolutely fantastic, and we saw some alligators! ⚲ Posted by Sue

b Man, I love Florida! I _____ with my friends on the beach all day, enjoying the sun, the sea and the beautiful, beautiful people. And every night we _____. They have some of the best DJs in the world here. ⚲ Posted by EZ

c I've read a lot of the comments on your site, and Florida sounds great. I'm really excited because I'm visiting in a couple of months. I want to have scuba lessons and _____ in the ocean. I hope I see a lot of cool fish! ⚲ Posted by Anya

d Awesome vacation guys! Thanks a lot. Oh, and I stayed in a great hotel so I was able to go to the gym and _____ every day before I hit the beach. I'm looking really fit right now! Check out my pics! Awesome! ⚲ Posted by Brad

e "Great!" I thought. "A cheap holiday in Florida." Well, it was cheap for a reason. And the reason is called Gabrielle, Hurricane Gabrielle. I wanted to come down here, go out on a little boat and _____, maybe catch a big tuna. But no, I have to stay inside. I can _____ if I want, but I don't really enjoy throwing a ball at ten pieces of plastic. I'm _____ up the walls in frustration! ⚲ Posted by Angryman13

3 **Reread and answer a–e.**
  a Which two people mention the weather?
  b Which person is writing about a future vacation?
  c Which two went on vacation with friends or relatives?
  d Which person is happy with their body?
  e Is Angryman13 really climbing up the walls?

4 🔴 **Make it personal** **Write your answers to the questions.**
  1 Which experience, a–e in **2**, would you most like to try? Why?
  2 Are there any you definitely wouldn't like to try? Why not?
  3 Have you ever had any similar experiences? What happened?

📶 **Connect**

Record your answers on your phone. Send them to a classmate or your teacher.

6.2 Would you like to try hang gliding?

1 Read the blog posts and label the photos with the names.

_____ _____ _____

Travel blog spot   🔍 Baños

I had a cool experience in Baños. There are a few tour companies that organize "canyoning" trips. Basically you just climb _____ waterfalls, but it is so exhilarating as the water rushes past you.
On the trip I went on, we climbed three waterfalls. The first was only about five meters, but the final one was giant—35 meters down! One piece of advice, wear gloves 'cause the rope can hurt your hands.
Posted 29 November by Frederico

Amazing day in Baños! We went white-water rafting _____ the Pastaza river. OMG! I have never been so terrified. At one point I thought the raft was going to turn over and leave us all in the river. Apparently, the rapids are usually a class two, but the water level was unusually high so some parts were class five rapids—there are only six classes! Anyway, although it was scary it was also really fun. I would recommend it to anyone.
Posted 29 July by Heitor

After a week of hiking in the mountains, Baños was a welcome relief for my aching muscles. This Ecuadorean town is full of hot spas, that are heated by the local volcano! The spas range from around 18°C to 55°C and are full of natural minerals. After a couple of days submerged _____ the hot water and then jumping _____ the refreshing cold water pools, my legs feel ready for the next challenge. Bring on the mountains!
Posted 10 February by Jillian

2 ▶6.2 Complete the posts with the words in the box. Listen to check.

> down   in   into   on

3 Reread and complete a–c.

a   If you go canyoning, wear _____ to protect your _____.

b   The rapids were class five because the _____ was _____.

c   Jillian was _____ in the _____ before she arrived in Baños.

4 Use clues a–h to make compound nouns and complete the puzzle.

a   coffee / World – *c u p*
b   pass / air / computer – ___ ___ ___
c   class / living / bed – ___ ___ ___
d   news / toilet / sand – ___ ___ ___ ___
e   skate / surf – ___ ___ ___ ___
f   ___ ___ ___ – glasses / bathing
g   ___ ___ ___ ___ – bag / ball / shake
h   ___ ___ ___ ___ ___ – son / father / mother

a	C	u	p
b	O		
c	M		
d	P		
e	O		
f	U		
g	N		
h	D		

5 Label these pictures with words from the puzzle.

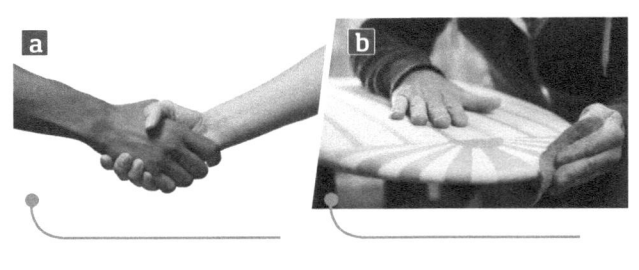

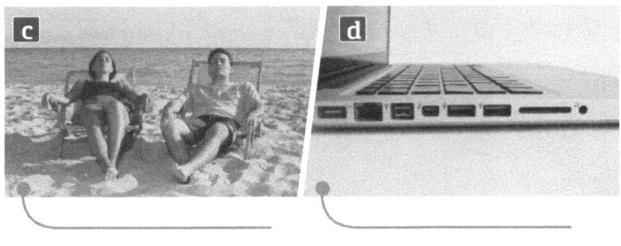

6 Complete the verbs of movement with the missing letters.

a   d _ v _
b   r _ n
c   sn _ wb _ _ rd
d   j _ mp
e   f _ ll
f   sw _ m
g   cl _ mb

7 🔴 **Make it personal** Write your answers to the questions.

1   Would you like to visit Baños? Why (not)?
2   Which of the experiences in **1** would you most like to try? Why?

6.3 Do you feel like going out tonight?

1 Look at the pictures and complete extracts *a* and *b* with the correct prepositions.

a over   under   ~~along~~   towards   into   out of

It's very easy, really. At first you run *along* the course, _____ the big wall. Then you climb _____ the wall and jump _____ the big pool of mud on the other side. Once you get _____ the mud pool, it's just straight _____ the electric fence and then the bridge.

b up   down   past   across

Last night I went to the movies. While I was waiting for the movie to start, I looked _____ the theater and saw an old school friend walking _____ the steps. She didn't see me and walked straight _____ me then sat _____ in her seat. I wanted to call out to her, but then it went quiet and the movie started.

2 ▶ 6.3 **Match a–g to 1–7. Listen to check.**

a During school vacations, I really miss …
b I have exams this year, so I have to start …
c I haven't finished …
d I want to practice …
e I'm a great student, but my teacher keeps …
f I really can't stand …
g I don't feel like …

1 giving me bad grades. I don't know why.
2 waiting for the bus. I'm too impatient!
3 studying seriously if I want to pass.
4 seeing my school buddies every day.
5 cooking tonight. Let's order some pizza.
6 listening, so I rented a movie in English.
7 reading that book yet. Don't tell me the end!

3 Make pairs with similar meanings. Check the strongest in each pair.

a adore   ☐ can't stand
b beautiful   ☐ enjoy
c large   ☐ hilarious
d dislike   ☐ pretty
e funny   ☐ huge

4 🔲 **Make it personal** Use the verbs in **3** and the prompts to make true sentences.

a I _____*enjoy cooking*_____ (cook).
b My mom _____ (clean the house).
c I _____ (go clubbing).
d My best friend _____ (shop).
e I _____ (travel long distances).
f I _____ (work out).

5 ▶ 6.4 **Say sentences a–c and listen to check your pronunciation. Notice the voiced /ð/ and unvoiced /θ/. Then match the bold words to pictures 1 and 2 and answer question b.**

a I'll always be **there**, **with** or **without** you.
b Who is my **father**'s **brother**'s **mother**'s grandchild?
c She **threw the toothbrush through** the window.

/ð/   /θ/

6.4 What do you enjoy doing on your birthday?

1 Complete definitions a–e with prepositions and match them to the sports.

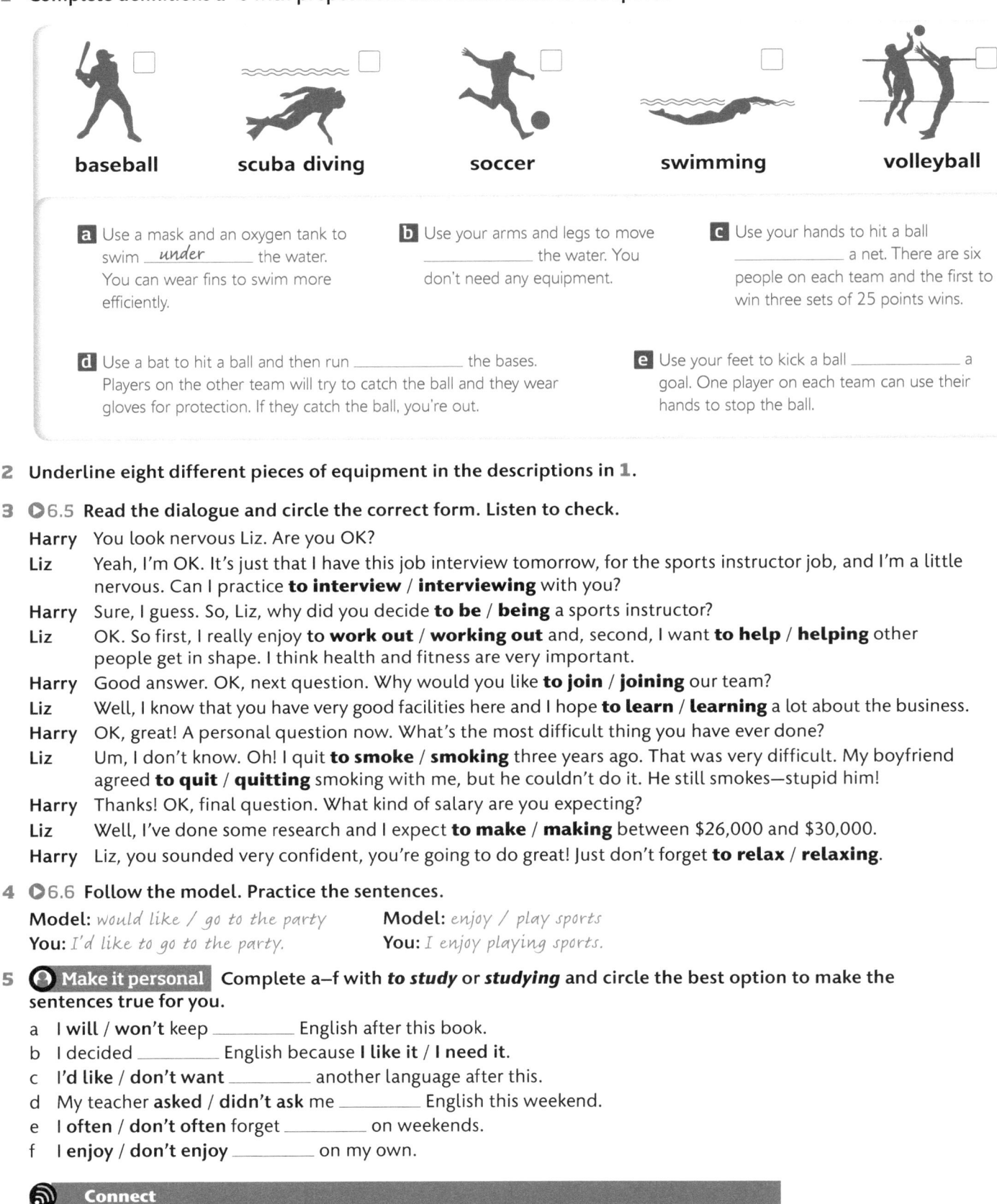

baseball scuba diving soccer swimming volleyball

a Use a mask and an oxygen tank to swim ___under___ the water. You can wear fins to swim more efficiently.

b Use your arms and legs to move _____ the water. You don't need any equipment.

c Use your hands to hit a ball _____ a net. There are six people on each team and the first to win three sets of 25 points wins.

d Use a bat to hit a ball and then run _____ the bases. Players on the other team will try to catch the ball and they wear gloves for protection. If they catch the ball, you're out.

e Use your feet to kick a ball _____ a goal. One player on each team can use their hands to stop the ball.

2 Underline eight different pieces of equipment in the descriptions in **1**.

3 ▶6.5 **Read the dialogue and circle the correct form. Listen to check.**

Harry You look nervous Liz. Are you OK?

Liz Yeah, I'm OK. It's just that I have this job interview tomorrow, for the sports instructor job, and I'm a little nervous. Can I practice **to interview / interviewing** with you?

Harry Sure, I guess. So, Liz, why did you decide **to be / being** a sports instructor?

Liz OK. So first, I really enjoy **to work out / working out** and, second, I want **to help / helping** other people get in shape. I think health and fitness are very important.

Harry Good answer. OK, next question. Why would you like **to join / joining** our team?

Liz Well, I know that you have very good facilities here and I hope **to learn / learning** a lot about the business.

Harry OK, great! A personal question now. What's the most difficult thing you have ever done?

Liz Um, I don't know. Oh! I quit **to smoke / smoking** three years ago. That was very difficult. My boyfriend agreed **to quit / quitting** smoking with me, but he couldn't do it. He still smokes—stupid him!

Harry Thanks! OK, final question. What kind of salary are you expecting?

Liz Well, I've done some research and I expect **to make / making** between $26,000 and $30,000.

Harry Liz, you sounded very confident, you're going to do great! Just don't forget **to relax / relaxing**.

4 ▶6.6 **Follow the model. Practice the sentences.**

Model: *would like / go to the party*
You: *I'd like to go to the party.*

Model: *enjoy / play sports*
You: *I enjoy playing sports.*

5 🎤 Make it personal **Complete a–f with *to study* or *studying* and circle the best option to make the sentences true for you.**

a I **will / won't** keep _____ English after this book.
b I decided _____ English because **I like it / I need it**.
c **I'd like / don't want** _____ another language after this.
d My teacher **asked / didn't ask** me _____ English this weekend.
e I **often / don't often** forget _____ on weekends.
f I **enjoy / don't enjoy** _____ on my own.

🔊 **Connect**

Interview your partner about what they like doing on their birthday and record it on your phone.

6.5 Would you rather stay in or go out?

1 Read and match the highlighted words to items a–c in the photo.

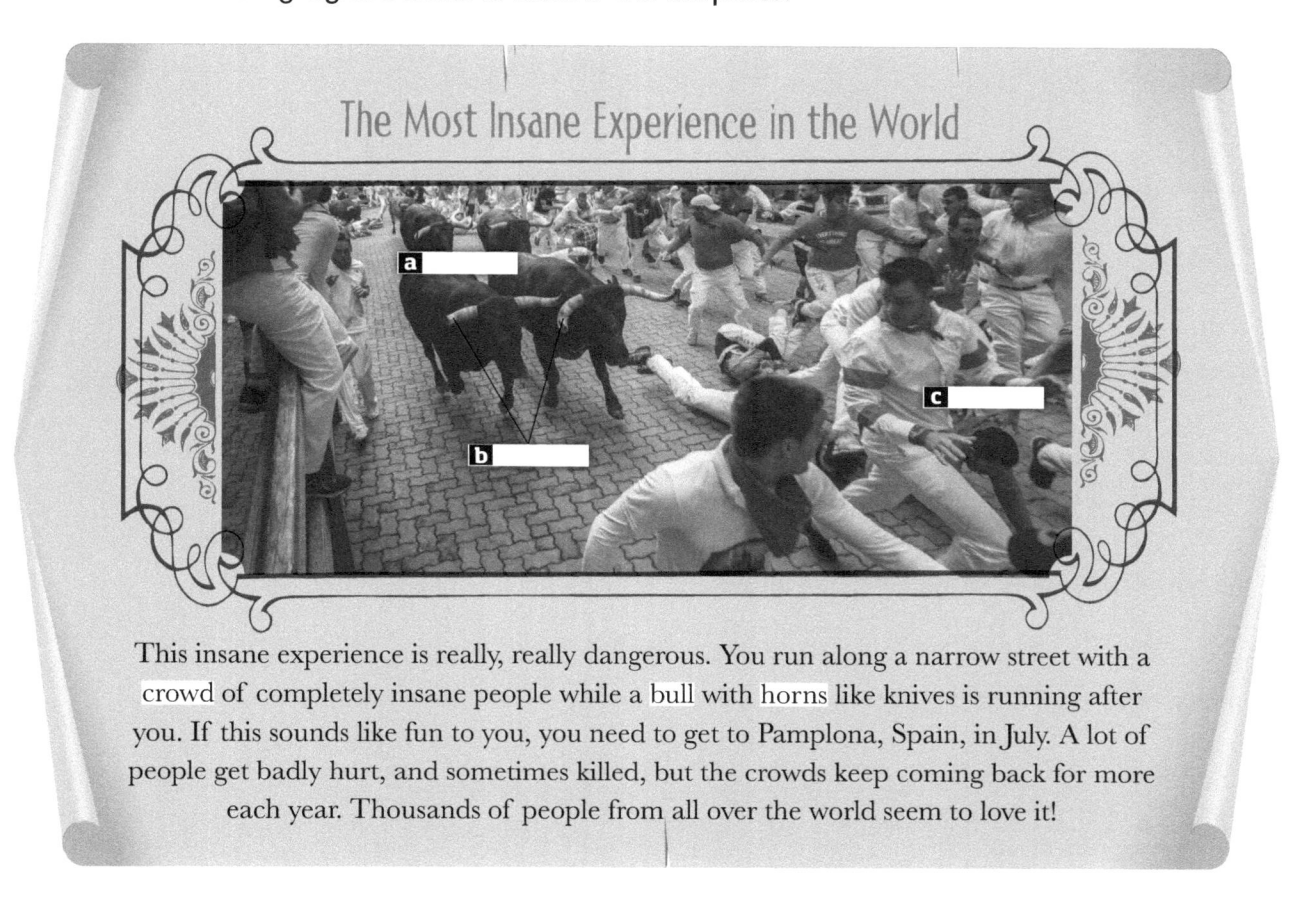

The Most Insane Experience in the World

This insane experience is really, really dangerous. You run along a narrow street with a crowd of completely insane people while a bull with horns like knives is running after you. If this sounds like fun to you, you need to get to Pamplona, Spain, in July. A lot of people get badly hurt, and sometimes killed, but the crowds keep coming back for more each year. Thousands of people from all over the world seem to love it!

2 ▶6.7 Listen to interviews 1–4. Who has run with the bulls?

3 ▶6.7 Who said these things? Listen again and match.
1	Shane	☐ I guess …
2	Petra	☐ … you know?
3	Jake	☐ Not in a million years!
4	Lucia	☐ It looks really crazy.

4 ▶6.8 Order dialogues *a* and *b*. Listen to check.

a **At home**
- ☐ **M** I don't feel like watching a movie. Let's go and see the band.
- ☐ **W** It's OK, but I've seen it before. I'll turn it off.
- ☐ **M** So, what do you want to do this evening?
- ☐ **W** Hmm, I don't know. Do you want to go to the movies? Or, there's a band playing.
- ☐ **M** I'm bored with this program, aren't you?

b **At the bar**
- ☐ **W** No thanks. I'm on an alcohol-free diet.
- ☐ **M** OK, one orange juice coming up.
- ☐ **W** Would you like a drink?
- ☐ **W** Uh, I'd rather have an orange juice, please.
- ☐ **M** Oh. So, how about a Coke?
- ☐ **M** It's OK, I'll get it. Would you like a beer?

5 ▶6.9 Listen to the end of the dialogue and fill in each blank with two words.

The man didn't like the band. He _____ to _____.

The woman liked the band. She _____ to _____ again.

> **Can you remember …**
> - ➤ 9 leisure time activities? SB➔p.72
> - ➤ 5 extreme sports? SB➔p.74
> - ➤ 5 verb / adverbial preposition combinations? SB➔p.75
> - ➤ 5 common compound nouns? SB➔p.75
> - ➤ 12 prepositions of movement? SB➔p.76
> - ➤ 8 verbs that are followed by *-ing*? SB➔p.76
> - ➤ 11 pieces of sports equipment? SB➔p.78
> - ➤ 5 sports verbs? SB➔p.78
> - ➤ 7 verbs that are followed by *to* + infinitive? SB➔p.79

1 Read the funny definitions and complete them with the words in the box.

| box office | stunt | plot | review | sequel | soundtrack | subtitles |

Diabolical Definitions!

a _____ noun [C] when you have to pay twice to see one story.

b _____ noun [C] something a brave (or just stupid) person does.

c _____ noun [C] a place where you pay a lot of money and get a small piece of paper.

d _____ noun [C] something you read if you want to talk about the movie but don't want to watch it.

e _____ noun [C] things that allow you to talk to friends and understand the movie at the same time.

f _____ noun [C] a series of increasingly incredible events that you have to believe.

g _____ noun [C] if you can't remember the story, maybe you'll remember the music.

2 Complete the ten movie genres with the missing letters.

a m _ _ _ _ _ y   c _ n _ m _ _ _ d   e _ _ _ _ l _ _ r   g _ _ r _ _ r   i c _ _ _ d _

b _ _ a _ a   d a _ _ _ _ n   f d _ _ _ m _ _ _ _ _ _   h _ _ v _ _ t _ _ _   j _ _ _ t _ s _

3 Read three movie reviews and match them to the genre and the stars. There is one extra genre.

Movie Reviews

| ☐ Comedy | ☐ Gangster |
| ☐ Sci-Fi | ☐ Suspense |

a ★
b ★★★
c ★★★★★

1 At 158 minutes, this movie is about 150 minutes too long. It starts well and there are some genuine laughs in the opening sequence, but after that it gets worse. This was not as funny as the first movie, let's hope that the next in the series isn't a disappointment too.

2 I don't usually enjoy this actor, so when I bought my ticket at the box office I wasn't expecting a lot, but I have to say this movie really impressed me. The plot slowly increases the tension through the entire movie and I couldn't guess the ending at all. It is a very intelligent story with some superb acting.

3 This is the story of Danny's fight to the top against his rivals in crime. The violence is sometimes very strong—don't watch this movie if you are sensitive to blood. The plot is a little predictable but there are also some emotional scenes, for example, when Danny discovers that his brother is a traitor working for the police. Danny's reaction is inevitable and is also the cause of his ruin.

4 Reread and answer a–e. Which movie ...

a is good at the start?

b had an unpredictable story?

c was surprisingly good?

d is probably not good for young children?

e is a sequel?

5 Correct two mistakes in each of a–c.

a The *Terminator 2* is one old movie starring Arnold Schwarzenegger.

b The most actors want to win the Oscar.

c I watched a great movie on the TV the last night.

6 🔊 **Make it personal** Complete the review about a movie you have seen. You can expand this short review if you have more to say.

The last movie I saw was _____ (name). It's a _____ (genre) movie starring _____ (actor). I **liked / didn't like** it because it is _____ (adjective). I **would / wouldn't** recommend it to you.

7.2 Are you crazy about music?

1 Choose the best word / phrase to complete the sentences.

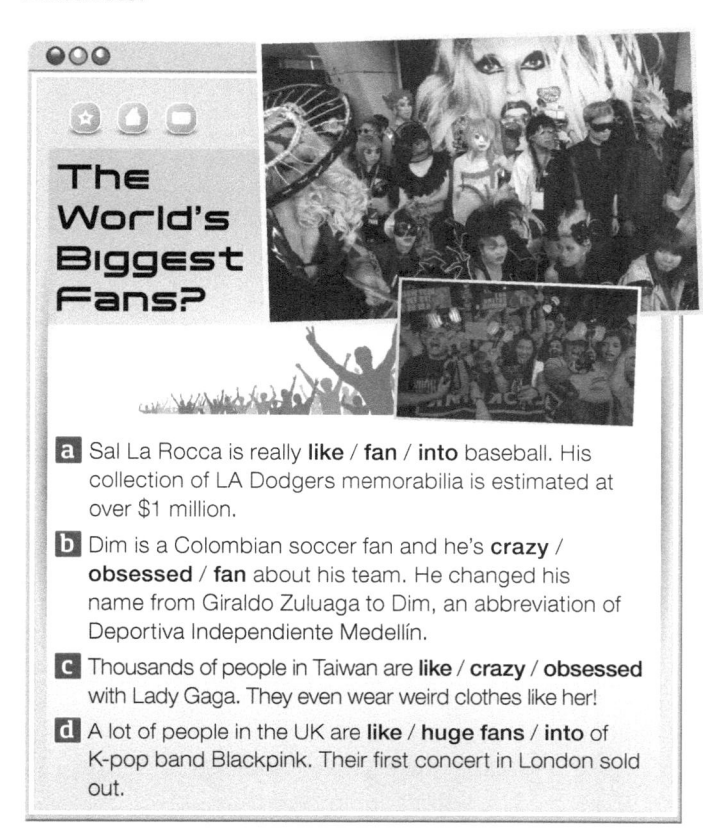

The World's Biggest Fans?

a Sal La Rocca is really **like / fan / into** baseball. His collection of LA Dodgers memorabilia is estimated at over $1 million.

b Dim is a Colombian soccer fan and he's **crazy / obsessed / fan** about his team. He changed his name from Giraldo Zuluaga to Dim, an abbreviation of Deportiva Independiente Medellín.

c Thousands of people in Taiwan are **like / crazy / obsessed** with Lady Gaga. They even wear weird clothes like her!

d A lot of people in the UK are **like / huge fans / into** of K-pop band Blackpink. Their first concert in London sold out.

2 Cross out the word that doesn't fit the group.

a video / DVD / ~~photo~~
b earrings / sunglasses / haircut
c general public / paparazzi / journalist
d huge / really / very
e love / adore / obsessed

3 Complete the sentences with **some**, **any**, **every** or **no**.

a There's _____ thing we can do about this, it's impossible to fix.
b I've never met _____ one like you before.
c Can I have _____ thing to eat, please? I'm hungry.
d We asked _____ body, but _____ body knows anything, I'm afraid.
e We need to find _____ one for the job.
f You can sit _____ where you want.

4 ▶7.1 Read the story and circle the correct word. Listen to check.

My Birthday

I got up in the morning and checked the mail. There were some letters for my parents, but there was **nothing / something** for me.

I got to work and said "Hi" to my colleagues, but **no one / anyone** said **nothing / anything** to me.

At lunch, I went to the cafeteria. It was very busy and there wasn't **nowhere / anywhere** to sit. I had to wait for **someone / anyone** to finish his food before I could sit down.

I was a little angry because I never forget **anyone's / everyone's** birthday and **anyone / everyone** was ignoring mine, so after work I went to the park to try and relax.

It was a beautiful sunny afternoon, and I tried to find **anywhere / somewhere** to sit, but it was very crowded and there were people **everywhere / somewhere**.

After dark, I drove home, but my street was full of cars and there was **anywhere / nowhere** for me to park my car. What a terrible day! **Everything / Anything** was going wrong.

I parked my car two streets from my house and walked home. There was **anything / something** very strange happening, but I didn't know what it was.

I arrived home and when I opened the door, I couldn't believe it. **Someone / Everyone** was there. It was a surprise birthday party, and they were all waiting for me!

🔊 Connect

Record yourself describing your last birthday on your phone, then send it to a classmate or your teacher.

5 ▶7.2 Circle the word where the bold letter has a different sound. Listen to check.

a s**o**mewhere   n**o**   n**o**thing
b **a**nything   **e**verything   f**a**n
c n**o**where   **o**ne   **o**nly

6 👤 **Make it personal** What did you do for your last birthday? Write a short story like the one in **4**.

7.3 What do you have a lot of at home?

1 Read and match a–d to their endings to complete the four world records. Then match them to photos 1–4.

Crazy World Records!

(a) Freddie is the world's tallest dog measuring 40.75 in. and weighing 196 lbs. He is so…

(b) The Insano in Fortaleza, Brazil, is the world's tallest waterslide: 41 meters. It has such…

(c) Kazuhiro Watanabe is in the world record books with the world's tallest Mohican. It took him 15 years to grow such…

(d) The Giant Weta is a kind of insect from New Zealand. In fact, it is the world's largest insect and, although its legs are designed for jumping, it is so…

- ☐☐ … heavy that it can't jump!
- ☐☐ … an impressive hairstyle.
- ☐☐ … big that small children think he is a horse.
- ☐☐ … a sudden fall that people can go up to 105 km/h before arriving in the pool.

2 Read and complete the diary with *so* or *such*. Add *a* or *an* if necessary.

Monday
My boss is _____¹ idiot. She made a lot of mistakes today and then she made me stay late to help her make everything right again!

Tuesday
There was _____² much traffic this morning that I arrived 30 minutes late. My boss looked a little angry but she didn't say anything because I helped her yesterday. HaHaHa!

Wednesday
Vicki and I wanted to go to the movies after work, but when we got to the mall the line for tickets was _____³ long that we decided to go shopping instead!

Thursday
Mario came to deliver some things to the office today. He is _____⁴ good-looking and he is _____⁵ friendly guy too. I have to find out if he has a girlfriend!

Friday
It was _____⁶ beautiful day that I went to the park at lunchtime. It was _____⁷ hot and I was _____⁸ tired that I fell asleep! Luckily I was back in the office before my boss.

3 ▶ 7.3 Make sentences with *so* or *such*. Follow the model.
Model: *He's lazy.*   **Model:** *He's a good cook.*
You: *He's so lazy.*   **You:** *He's such a good cook.*

4 🔊 Make it personal   Write questions a–d. Each / means one word. Then choose the best answer for you and complete them if necessary.

a / / collect anything?
- ☐ Yeah, I have a collection of _____.
- ☐ No, I don't collect anything.

b / / into sports?
- ☐ Yeah, I love _____.
- ☐ No, I don't do any sports.

c / / have / favorite artist?
- ☐ I'm really into _____. I also like _____.
- ☐ No, I don't have a favorite.

d Which soccer team / / support?
- ☐ I'm a _____ fan.
- ☐ I don't like soccer.

🔊 Connect

Interview your partner with the questions and record it on your phone.

5 ▶ 7.4 Listen to four dialogues. Complete follow-up questions a–d and match them to the answers.

a _____ do you have?
b _____ do you play?
c _____ seen her perform?
d Have you ever _____?

- ☐ Yeah, I went last year.
- ☐ Unfortunately, no, I haven't.
- ☐ About 50.
- ☐ About once a week.

7.4 Who was Instagram created by?

1 **Read the introduction to the article. Is it about:**

a an animated movie? b a group of animated movies?

A Success STORY

Animated movies are becoming more and more sophisticated and often adults enjoy them as much as children do. In this article, we will look at one of the most popular and successful animated series of all time.

2 **Read the rest of the article and cross out the incorrect verb form.**

The **TOY STORY** series **is loved / loves** by children and adults all over the world and each of the three movies has received fantastic reviews globally too. The first movie **is released / was released** in 1995 and became the first movie to **create / be created** entirely with CGI (computer-generated imagery). In the movie, Andy **gets / is gotten** a new toy, Buzz Lightyear. The old toy, Woody, worries that Andy doesn't like him anymore.

TOY STORY 2 didn't intend / wasn't intended for the movie theaters. The original plan was for a short video sequel. However, the voice actors were so enthusiastic about the movie that they **persuaded / were persuaded** the executives to make a full movie. In this movie Woody **captures / is captured** by a toy collector and the other toys go on a mission to save him.

TOY STORY 3 was released in 2010, eleven years after **TOY STORY 2**. This movie **made / is made** more than $1 billion in the box office, the first animated movie to do so. In this movie Andy is leaving to go to college and his toys **accidently throw / are accidently thrown** in the garbage. The toys' adventures take them to a kindergarten, and a garbage truck before they **find / are found** Andy again.

In 2019, **TOY STORY 4** came out. In this fourth movie, the characters **joined / are joined** by Forky, a spork that Bonnie makes into a toy, and go on a road trip adventure. It has made even more money than **TOY STORY 3**, and is another wonderful movie full of humor and emotion!

MOVIE MAGAZINE | P. 101

3 ▶ 7.5 **Listen and complete the statistics.**

a In total, the first three movies made $_____ worldwide.
b The review website Rotten Tomatoes ranks the movies as the most acclaimed series ever. On average, the movies have a _____% positive review rates.
c *Toy Story 2* is the shortest in the series. It is a little over _____ hours.
d The _____ movie had _____ new characters.
e *Toy Story 3* won _____ of the Oscars it was nominated for.
f *Toy Story 4* was released in theaters in the United States on June _____, 2019.

4 ▶ 7.6 **Write complete sentences in the past passive. Then listen to check. Mark the participles regular (R) or irregular (I).**

a *Game of Thrones* / write / George R. R. Martin
b "Live it up", the official song of the 2018 World Cup, / sing / Nicky Jam featuring Will Smith & Era Istrefi
c The World Wide Web / invent / Tim Berners-Lee
d Microsoft / found / Bill Gates and Paul Allen

5 ▶ 7.7 **Listen to the sound of -*ed* + *a* in sentences a-f. Do you hear (1) /də/ or (2) /dɪdə/?**

a He download<u>ed a</u> movie. 2
b They design<u>ed a</u> car.
c They play<u>ed a</u> game.
d She found<u>ed a</u> company.
e They stu<u>died a</u> book.
f The scientists captur<u>ed a</u> monster.

6 🔴 **Make it personal** **What are your three favorite movies? Why do you like them? Record your answers.**

7.5 Are you a good singer?

1 ▶7.8 **Listen and match these words to the pictures according to the sound of the <u>underlined</u> letters.**

audi<u>ti</u>on · ca<u>tch</u> · <u>ch</u>ur<u>ch</u> · conclu<u>si</u>on
deci<u>si</u>on · expre<u>ssi</u>on · illu<u>si</u>on · ki<u>tch</u>en
participa<u>ti</u>on · pronuncia<u>ti</u>on
ques<u>ti</u>on · <u>sh</u>ow

/ʃ/
shorts
shark
audition

/tʃ/
cheese
chair

/ʒ/
treasure
television

2 ▶7.8 **Listen again and mark the stress in 1. Can you notice a stress pattern in -*ion* words?**

3 ▶7.9 **Order the words in a–c to make questions. Then listen and answer.**
a is / on / watching / what / TV / Jess / ?
b show / the / Helen / like / does / ?
c nervous / does / Helen / why / feel / ?

4 ▶7.9 **Listen again and count how many times you hear these expressions.**
☐ As I was saying   ☐ Anyway   ☐ You know

5 ▶7.10 **Make a–c more tactful. Listen to check.**

a I expected the movie to be good. In fact, it was terrible! I'm really disappointed!

_____ wasn't as _____ as _____.

b Everyone says the soundtrack is great! I thought it was absolutely awful!

_____ didn't _____ all that great.

c I didn't think the movie was terrible, but it certainly wasn't fantastic.

Well, _____ OK, but not really five stars.

6 🔵 Make it personal **Complete sentences a–c. Use these ideas to help you.**

a book · a movie · a place
a restaurant · a sporting event

a I **thought / didn't think** _____ was **great / interesting / fun**.
b I thought _____ was OK, but nothing special.
c _____ **was / wasn't** as **good / interesting / useful / fun** as I expected.

7 ▶7.11 🔵 Make it personal **Listen and match questions a–e to the answers. Then write or record your own answers. Add more details too.**
a Do you ever download movies?
b What's the last movie you saw?
c Did you like the last movie you saw?
d Do you have any posters in your room?
e What do you collect?

☐ I collect money from different countries.
☐ Yeah, I have an old Spider-Man poster from when I was younger.
☐*a* Sometimes, but my Internet connection is kind of slow.
☐ I watched a horror movie on TV last night.
☐ It was OK, but it was a little predictable.

8 **Rewrite the sentences using** *such*.
a The place was so noisy.
It _____.
b My car is so slow.
I have _____.
c The movie was so disappointing.
It _____.
d The documentary was very interesting.
It _____.
e The radio station is very popular.
It _____.
f Her collection of chairs is so strange.
She has _____.

Can you remember ...
➤ 10 movie genres? SB→p.86
➤ 6 movie words? SB→p.87
➤ 6 ways to talk about your passion? SB→p.88
➤ 3 compounds with -*thing*? SB→p.89
➤ present and past ⊕ ⊖ *be* + past participle? SB→p.93
➤ 3 ways to improve your speaking fluency? SB→p.94
➤ 3 ways to give your opinion politely? SB→p.95

8.1 Are you into science fiction?

8

1 Complete the sentences with *at*, *in* or *on*.

a Neil Armstrong was the first man on the moon _____ 02:56 GMT _____ July 21, 1969.

b The first email was sent _____ October 1971.

c The first Twitter message was "just setting up my twttr" and was posted _____ 09:50 PST _____ March 21, 2006.

d Facebook started _____ 2004.

2 Read the article and use the <u>underlined</u> phrases to write descriptions of the inventions.

<u>A door that can lock itself</u> = *A self-locking door*

New Inventions

a _____
Nobody likes waking up to the sound of an alarm clock beeping angrily at them in the morning. That's why this <u>alarm clock that can produce smells</u> provides a much nicer experience. You can wake up to the smell of freshly-baked bread, for example, or peppermint.

b _____
This amazing development allows you to heat your lunch without a kitchen. It connects to an app on your phone, and when you tell it to, the <u>lunch box can heat itself</u>, and your lunch. You can take it to work or when you go camping, and enjoy delicious hot food wherever you are.

c _____
A 17-year-old developer from London has released his fourth smartphone application (app). He started writing apps when he was 12 and now has his own company, but he still goes to school and he has exams to worry about. The new <u>app summarizes news</u> stories so that users can read news more easily on their smartphones.

3 Reread the article. True (T), False (F) or Not mentioned (N)?

a The alarm clock makes an angry beeping noise.

b People can choose the smell they want to wake up to.

c The food in the lunch box doesn't need to be cooked in an oven.

d The teenage software developer was born in London.

e The young inventor has dropped out of school.

🔊 Connect
Look up new inventions online and choose your favorite one.

4 Match words / phrases a–g to definitions 1–7.

a smart vending machine
b GPS
c surveillance camera
d a button
e facial recognition device
f speaker
g active contact lenses

1 Something that records video in order to help with security.

2 You can buy something from this device, which has a touch screen.

3 Something which produces sound.

4 Something you press on a machine.

5 Things which help you see and are connected to a computer.

6 A system that helps you use software maps in real time.

7 A special camera which recognizes your face.

5 Complete the sentences with one missing word.

a Welcome to the Happy Days Hotel. If you're hungry in the night we have a range of smart _____ machines which sell food.

b I think we're lost. Switch on your _____ so we can find the way.

c Sit near the _____ and you'll hear the music better.

d These active contact _____ make it much easier to see.

e My new cell phone uses a _____ recognition device to unlock it.

6 😀 **Make it personal** Number the items below, 1–4, and do the same with all the pictures on this page.

1 I use it every day.

2 I use it more than once a week.

3 I use it more than once a month.

4 I have never used it.

☐ contact lenses
☐ a button on a remote control
☐ a surveillance camera
☐ a vending machine
☐ speaker
☐ a facial recognition device

8.2 Do you ever switch off from technology?

1 Study these sentences from ID **2**. Match phrasal verbs a–g with their definitions.

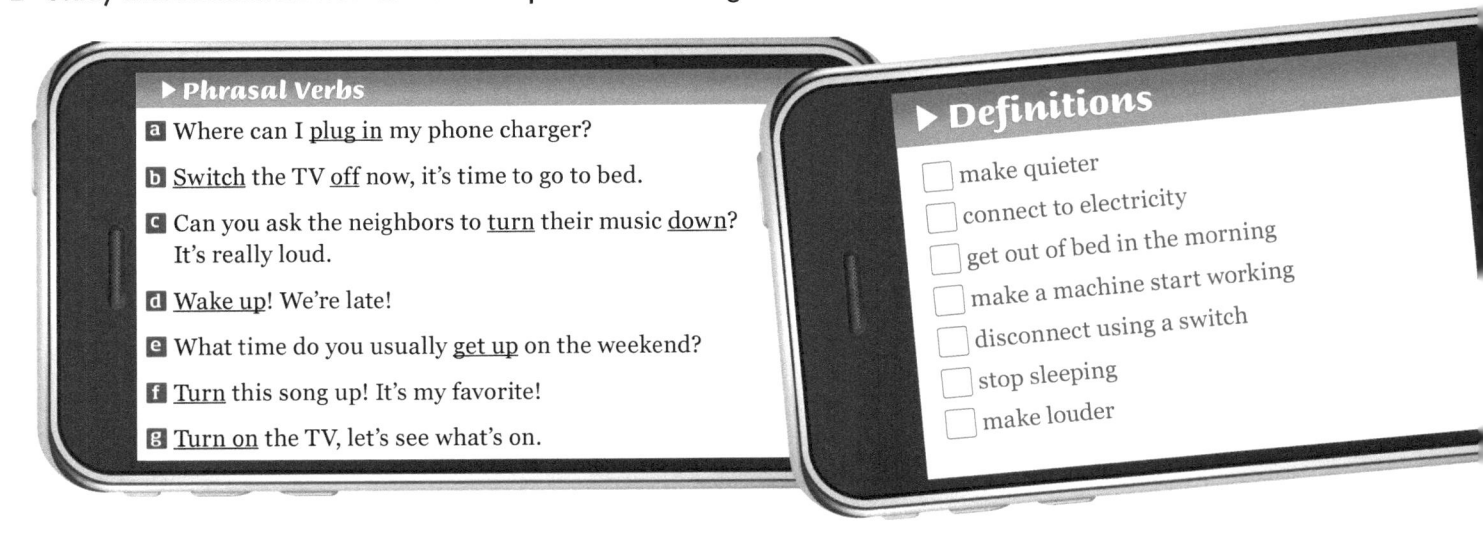

▶ **Phrasal Verbs**

a Where can I <u>plug in</u> my phone charger?

b <u>Switch</u> the TV <u>off</u> now, it's time to go to bed.

c Can you ask the neighbors to <u>turn</u> their music <u>down</u>? It's really loud.

d <u>Wake up</u>! We're late!

e What time do you usually <u>get up</u> on the weekend?

f <u>Turn</u> this song up! It's my favorite!

g <u>Turn on</u> the TV, let's see what's on.

▶ **Definitions**

☐ make quieter
☐ connect to electricity
☐ get out of bed in the morning
☐ make a machine start working
☐ disconnect using a switch
☐ stop sleeping
☐ make louder

2 Match a–d to their continuations 1–4.

a Shall we go out tonight?
b Can you pick up my bag please? Sorry, I can't reach.
c Put on your hat, it's sunny outside.
d Everyone stand up, please.

1 OK. Let me just take my hairband off first.
2 No, I'm tired. Let's just stay in and watch a movie.
3 Now find your partner and sit down next to them.
4 Sure. Where shall I put it down?

3 ▶8.1 Listen to phrases a–d in **2** then read the correct phrase, 1–4, after the beep.

4 Read the instruction manual and label the diagram with the bold words. Then complete the instructions with **down**, **on**, **off** or **up**.

To start using your new phone simply press the **on / off button** to turn it _____. When you want to turn it _____ just press the same button for three seconds.
To adjust the volume, touch the **volume icon** in the top right corner of the screen. The standard volume is four. To turn it _____ choose a higher number, and to turn it _____ choose a lower number. To mute the phone, select 0.
When the battery is low you can use the **USB cable** to attach your phone to a computer. You need three hours to fully charge _____ the battery.

5 ▶8.2 Order the words in a–f to make questions about the cell phone. Predict the intonation and add ↗ or ↘. Listen to check and write the answers.

a your / cell phone / is / new / that / ?

d it / with / I / can / play / ?

b buy / you / where / it / did / ?

e have / apps / you / do / how many / ?

c the / last / battery / how long / does / ?

f do / does / this / what / app / ?

6 🔵 **Make it personal** Write instructions on how to use an app on your cell phone.

📶 **Connect**

*Send your instructions in **6** to a friend. Can she / he understand them?*

8.3 Will space vacations be popular soon?

1 ▶8.3 Listen and match these words to the pictures according to the sound of the <u>underlined</u> letters.

syn<u>th</u>etic	telepa<u>th</u>y	<s><u>th</u>at</s>	<u>th</u>e	<u>th</u>emselves	<s><u>th</u>eory</s>	<u>th</u>ere
<u>th</u>ey	<u>th</u>ink	<u>th</u>irty	<u>th</u>is	<u>th</u>oughts	<u>th</u>ree	<u>th</u>rough

/θ/
theory

/ð/
that

Remember, when you say "father" or "teeth" you need to touch your teeth with your tongue.

"Th" can be voiced /ð/ or unvoiced /θ/.

Touch your throat when you say "fa<u>th</u>er" and "tee<u>th</u>." Can you feel the vibration in "father"?

2 Read these predictions and add the adverbs in parentheses in the right place.

> ▶ **What will cell phones be like in the future?**
>
> **a** Cell phone software will *definitely* get better, but the design *probably* won't change a lot. (<s>**definitely** / **probably**</s>)
>
> **b** We will be able to download personalities for our cell phones and will have celebrity voices to read our texts. (**probably / possibly**)
>
> **c** There have been big developments in screen technology and this will continue. (**certainly**)
>
> **d** I think governments and organizations will use cell phone technology to collect information about individuals. (**possibly**)
>
> **e** We won't use cell phones in the future. Using microchip technology, we will be able to communicate through telepathy. (**probably / possibly**)

3 Use the prompts to write more predictions about cell phones.
a   Cell phones / have / bigger screens ⊕ probably *Cell phones will probably have bigger screens.*
b   Cell phones / can / clean themselves ⊕ possibly _____
c   Cell phones / be / "phones" ⊖ definitely _____
d   We / need to touch / the screens ⊖ probably _____
e   Cell phones / can / recognize our voices ⊕ certainly _____

4 ▶8.4 **Correct the mistakes in a–f. Listen to check.**
a   3D TV will be common in five years?
b   Will have a World War 3?
c   Did we had homework from the last class?
d   Are we go to have a test this week?
e   Is going to be sunny this weekend?
f   Will we be able to talk with aliens one day?

5 ▶8.5 **Listen and circle the answers to the questions in 4. What else do the speakers say?**

a	I think so.	I hope not.	(I don't think so.)	*Maybe in 10 years.*
b	I hope so.	I don't think so.	I hope not.	
c	I think so.	I don't think so.	I hope so.	
d	I hope so.	I hope not.	I think so.	
e	I hope not.	I think so.	I don't think so.	
f	I hope so.	I hope.	I hope not.	

6 ▶8.5 **Listen again. After the beep, say the answer and listen to check your pronunciation.**

7 🔵 **Make it personal**   What are your plans for next week? Write at least five plans.

8.4 Is technology making us more, or less, social?

1 Replace the <u>underlined</u> mistakes in a–g with these words.

> answer   arguments   intends   ~~now~~
> sensitive   take   take place

a   I used to work in a restaurant but <u>actually</u> *now* I work in an office.
b   When I was young my parents used to fight and have really angry <u>discussions</u>. It was terrible.
c   Your cell phone is ringing, please <u>attend</u> it outside.
d   The Coldplay concert will <u>realize</u> next weekend.
e   People who do extreme sports <u>assume</u> a lot of risks.
f   My smartphone screen is <u>sensible</u> to touch.
g   My brother <u>pretends</u> to be a lawyer when he is older.

2 Now use the correct form of the <u>underlined</u> words from **1** to complete these sentences.

a   I saw a great documentary the other day. Two scientists were having an interesting *discussion* about the future of technology.
b   I don't know if she is at home but I _____ she is because the lights of her house are on.
c   He has a good job but he isn't very _____ with his money. He always spends it on stupid things.
d   Julia _____ that she couldn't move her leg so she didn't have to go to school.
e   I was walking to the bus stop when I suddenly _____ that I forgot to lock my front door.
f   Is Benicio Del Toro Mexican? I think he's Puerto Rican, _____.
g   If you don't _____ all of your classes you will probably get a bad grade.

3 Read Valerie's vacation plans, then complete her email with the verb in the *simple present*, *present continuous* or *going to*.

4 ▶8.6 Look at the photos and choose the best form. Listen to check and repeat after the beep.

a   Can U take me 2 the airport l8r? Pleeeeease!
    Of course **I will** / **I'm going to**. C U after work. Sue
b   **I'll** / **I'm going to** have the risotto, please.
c   **He'll** / **He's going to** score! Yes! A beautiful goal!
d   It definitely **won't** / **isn't going to** rain today.
e   Don't worry. **I'll** / **I'm going to** pay for you.

5 🔵 **Make it personal**   Use the *simple present*, *present continuous*, *going to* or *will* to make four questions. Email them to a friend and share answers.

a   What time / your next lesson / start / ?
    _____
b   What / you do / this weekend / ?
    _____
c   Do you think we / stop driving cars in the future / ?
    _____
d   You / do any homework tomorrow / ?
    _____

Friday 29
As usual, work until five p.m. but then... vacation! Yeah!
Hotel address: Hotel Orion, 263 W. 16th Street, Manhattan.

Saturday 30
Meet Joe, Times Square, noon.

AmericanAirlines · **Boarding Pass**
PASSENGER NAME
BUSHELL / VALERIE
FROM: SEATTLE   TO: NEW YORK   FLIGHT: AA187   DATE: 29NOV   TIME: 2010

New York — Friday 29° · Saturday 30° · Sunday 31°

Hi Joe,
Only one more day at work! I'm so excited! My last day at work is Friday, I _____ (finish) at five p.m.—the usual time. My plane _____ (leave) at 20:10 so I'm _____ (have to) hurry to the airport. I _____ (ask) my colleague, Sue, if she can take me to the airport in her car, I hope she can! Anyway, I've booked a hotel, I _____ (stay) at the Hotel Orion, on 16th Street. Do you know it? I've checked the weather in New York, it _____ (be) sunny on Sunday so maybe we can go to the park, what do you think?
See you in Times Square!!!
XX
Valerie

8.5 Who do you talk to when you need help?

1 ▶ 8.7 **Listen to these words and cross out the ones where the bold letter has a different sound.**

a ma**j**or intelli**g**ent **g**ive langua**g**e
b **h**ouse **h**our **h**eart **h**otel
c bu**s** su**n** bu**s**y **s**omething

2 Reduce the Internet ads a–c to ten words each.

a	~~I have a~~ bike for sale. It is five years old. It is in very good condition. It costs $80.	
b	A waiter is needed. We are a busy downtown restaurant. Experience is required. You will receive good pay.	
c	A babysitting service is being offered. I can work on weekdays only. You have to pay $10 per hour. Please call me at 733-383-6876.	

3 Read the horoscopes, then circle predictions *a*, *b* or *c* in 1–4.

Leo (Jul. 23 – Aug. 23)
You are sometimes a little aggressive and this can cause problems for you. If you argue too much, your colleagues won't want to talk with you. Try to pause before you speak and you will be OK.

Virgo (Aug. 24 – Sep. 22)
You have had a very busy life recently so now you need to relax. You will feel a lot better if you go on a short vacation. You'll probably spend more than usual but you will enjoy it. Worry about your bank account next month!

Libra (Sep. 23 – Oct. 23)
You'll feel very romantic this month. If you're in a relationship, your partner will be very surprised. If you're single, there's a good chance you'll meet someone new, so get out and have fun!

Scorpio (Oct. 24 – Nov. 21)
You will get some great career opportunities, but because of this you won't have much free time. Don't forget the important people in your life. If you give some time to them they will probably be able to help you.

1 Hi, I'm a Libra. Could you tell me if I'll meet a new boyfriend this month? Thanks.
   a) Definitely. **b)** There's a good chance. **c)** I doubt it.

2 Hi. I'm a Virgo, and I want to know if I will be rich this month.
   a) For sure. **b)** Probably. **c)** I doubt it.

3 Help! I had a lot of problems at work last month. Will this month be the same? By the way, I'm a Leo.
   a) Absolutely. **b)** Perhaps. **c)** Definitely not.

4 Hello. I'm a Scorpio, and I need to know if I'll be very busy this month.
   a) Definitely. **b)** Maybe. **c)** I doubt it.

4 ▶ 8.8 *Fortune-Teller!* Now listen to people 1–4 from **3**, respond after the beep and check your pronunciation.

5 ▶ 8.9 🎧 **Make it personal** Match questions a–e to the answers. Listen to check and share your own answers with a friend.

a Do you have a dishwasher?
b Do you have a new phone?
c Do you think 3D TV will be common?
d Do you have any appointments this week?
e Do you ever read your horoscope?

☐ I don't think so. I don't think people would like it.
☐ No I don't, but I wish I did. I hate doing the dishes.
☐ Only sometimes, for a laugh.
☐ Yes, I'm going to the dentist on Thursday.
☐ No, I've had this one for about a year now.

Connect
Look up your horoscope for today or this week online.

Can you remember …

➤ 6 appliances and devices? SB→p. 99
➤ how to use *-ing* to describe machines? SB→p. 99
➤ 7 technology phrasal verbs? SB→p. 100
➤ 5 adverbs to modify *will*? SB→p. 102
➤ the opposite of *I hope so*? SB→p. 103
➤ 5 false friends? SB→p. 104
➤ 4 verb forms to talk about the future? SB→p. 105
➤ 4 words for *fifty-fifty*? SB→p. 107

9

9.1 What do you think of marriage?

1 Complete the puzzle with wedding words. Each symbol represents a letter.

E ◆ N ⇲ G ∿ ✋ ∿ ◆ 🄿 ◆ ⊢ ✝

H ✎ ⊢ ◆ Y ☺ 🄿 ✎ ✎ ⊢

C 🄱 ◆ R ✿ ◆ M 🄿 ✎ ✎ ☺

∿ U ◆ S ☀ T 🄿 L I ☀ ⊛ ✝

∿ ☀ F 🄿 | ✿ ◆ ◆ ∿ ☀ ⊛ ✝ ✿ ☺

☀ ⊢ V ☀ 🄿 A ✋ ✝ ☀ O ✎ ⊢

✿ ◆ 🄱 ◆ P ✝ ☀ ✎ ⊢

B ♌ ✿ ☀ D ⊛ ◆

∿ ✿ ✎ ✎ 🄿

♌ ✿ ☀ ⊛ ◆ ⊛ 🄿 ✋ ☀ ❄ ⊛

2 ▶9.1 **Match a–e to 1–5 to make funny quotes about marriage. Listen to check.**

a Marriage is like a phone call in the night.
b Marriage is a wonderful invention,
c The secret of a happy marriage
d Men marry women and hope they won't change.
e My wife and I were happy for 20 years.

1 remains a secret.
2 First the ring, and then you wake up.
3 Women marry men and hope that they will.
4 Then we met.
5 but then again, so is the bicycle repair kit.

3 Complete a–e with **get** + one of these adjectives.

better   dark   dressed   lost   wet

a What time does it _____ in the evening in winter?

b I use the GPS on my smartphone so I don't _____.

c Take two of these a day and you will _____ quickly.

d You can stand under my umbrella so you don't _____.

e In the mornings, I take a shower and then I _____.

4 Read the article. Are a–g True (T), False (F) or Not mentioned (N)?

Wedding Traditions Around the World

China
In China today, it's common for the bride to wear several dresses on her wedding day. At the beginning of the wedding banquet the bride wears a traditional Chinese dress. This dress is red because that's a lucky color in China. In the middle of the banquet, she leaves and changes into a white Western-style wedding dress. After the banquet the bride will change into the final dress, a cocktail dress in her favorite color.

Peru
Peruvian weddings have a nice tradition involving the cake. Small gifts are put inside the wedding cake and attached to ribbons. Each unmarried female guest pulls a ribbon and one lucky woman will find a wedding ring. She will be the next bride.

South Africa
Zulu weddings are often very vibrant events. There are dance competitions between the bride and groom's families that symbolize the traditional antagonism between them. In very traditional weddings, the groom has to pay the bride's father before they can get married.

UK
An old tradition in the UK is that brides wear "something old" to symbolize continuity with the bride's family, "something new" to symbolize optimism for the future, "something borrowed" to symbolize good fortune, and "something blue" because that color was traditionally connected with love.

a Chinese brides often wear four dresses in a day.
b The dresses are usually different colors and styles.
c In Peru, all of the single females receive a ring.
d The guests have to eat the cake to find the gifts.
e In South Africa, the best dancer gets a cake.
f Zulu brides usually have to pay the groom's family.
g In the UK, blue is traditionally a romantic color.

5 *Celebrity Marriage!* Order the words in a–c to make sentences. Complete them with a preposition + one of the names from the photos.

a got / 2012 / Jessica Biel / to / married / _____ / _____ / .
b Mark Zuckerberg / their garden / _____ / married / _____ / .
c got / Michael Bublé / _____ / Luisana Lopilato / to / married / _____ / and Buenos Aires / .

Justin Timberlake

Vancouver

Priscilla Chan

6 🟠 **Make it personal** Which of the wedding traditions in **4** do you like best? Why?

9.2 Do you think romantic movies are entertaining?

1 Read Jen's diary and circle the correct adjective.

● *Sep. 13*

*What a day! I was sitting in Mr. Stanton's science class, feeling **bored / boring** as usual. I was also **tired / tiring** because I'd been up late studying for an exam the night before. Then a new boy, Connor, came into the classroom and sat down next to me. He looks **amazed / amazing**, really good-looking. Anyway we talked and he's really **fun / funny** too, he made me laugh a lot. After class we sat together in the canteen and talked all the way through lunch time. I really like him!*

● *Sep. 14*

*The worst day ever! I had to do my presentation today, in front of about 400 people. I didn't know what to say and my stomach felt bad and my head felt dizzy. It was so **terrified / terrifying**! But then Viv did her presentation and I was really **surprised / surprising** 'coz it was really good. Usually she feels **scared / scary** in front of crowds of people but she said it was **excited / exciting**. Well done Viv!*

● *Sep. 15*

*Miss Innes said she was really **interested / interesting** in my presentation. I thought it was terrible but she said she was really **satisfied / satisfying** with it. Miss Innes said Viv's presentation was "entertained" / "entertaining". I don't know if that's good or bad!*

2 Reread the article and circle the best option in a–d.

a Jen's writing about her **classes / school** in general.
b Mr. Stanton is a **teacher / the director**.
c Jen **likes / doesn't like** Mr. Stanton.
d Miss Innes **liked / didn't like** Jen's presentation.

3 ▶9.2 Listen to the sound effects. After the beep, say the full phrase with the best adjective.

a soccer match   boring / exciting / terrified
b she   bored / tiring / tired
c the result   surprised / surprising / excited
d he   scared / interesting / irritated
e the movie   terrifying / interested / bored

4 Complete the chart with adverbs. Which three mean the same?

Adjective	Adverb
absolute	absolutely
complete	
extreme	
real	
very	
total	

5 🔵 Make it personal Complete a–c with noun or gerund phrases and d–f with adjectives.

a For me, the most stressful day of the week is _____ because _____.
b The most exciting movie I've seen recently is _____.
c I'm really interested in _____.
d In my opinion, watching TV is _____.
e I usually feel _____ when I arrive at school.
f I feel _____ if I miss a bus or train.

6 ▶9.3 Listen and categorize the past tense forms of these verbs by number of syllables. Which two are irregular?

attract   break   cheat   date
dump   fall   flirt

1 syllable	2 syllables	3 syllables
lived	needed	remembered

7 ▶9.4 Listen and number the words from 6 in the order you hear them. Be careful! The verbs are not all in the same tense.

8 ▶9.4 Listen again. What do these numbers relate to? There's one extra number.

6   16   60   2003   2005

9.3 If you had three wishes, what would they be?

1 ○9.5 **Listen to a teacher at a job interview and complete the interviewer's questions.**

a   What would you do if _____?
b   If your students _____, how would you control them?
c   _____ if there was a power outage?
d   _____, would you give yourself this job?

2 ○9.6 **Order the words in Mike's replies and match them to a–d in 1. Listen to check.**

a   I / anything / wouldn't / do / .
b   I / of / yes / would / , / course / .
c   the / definitely / run / out / would / classroom / of / I / .
d   would / home / I / send / the / probably / students / .

3 🔘 Make it personal **Write complete second conditional questions using the prompts in a–e.**

a   you (be) the interviewer you (give) Mike the job?   *If you were...*
b   you (be) the teacher what you (do) next class?
c   you (can) travel anywhere where you (go)?
d   how you (feel) you (lose) your cell phone?
e   you (have) a million dollars what you (spend) it on?

4 ○9.7 **Match a–g to the cartoon pictures to make a joke. Listen to check.**

a   The first man closed his eyes and said, "If I were in New York, I'd be the happiest man in the world."
b   They were very surprised when a genie appeared and gave them three wishes, one each.
c   "What's the matter?" asked the genie. "I'm so lonely," said the last man. "If my friends were here, I'd feel better."
d   "Poof!" The man disappeared. "Wow! That's amazing!" said the woman. She closed her eyes and said, "My wish is that... I were in Paris!"
e   There were three people stuck on a desert island in the middle of the Pacific Ocean. One day, they found a lamp on the beach, so they picked it up and rubbed it.
f   The genie immediately gave the man his wish and brought his friends back to the island.
g   "Poof!" The woman disappeared, and the last man immediately started crying.

5 ○9.8 **Match the bold letters in a–e to the sound pictures. Listen to check and repeat the sentences.**

a   An interesting **g**eography **j**ournal.
b   He is a **j**ealous e**d**itor.
c   The i**d**ea of marria**g**e terrifies him.
d   The e**dg**e of my **d**iary is beautiful.
e   It's **g**enuinely **d**ifferent.

1 /d/   **2** /dʒ/

9.4 Have you ever performed for an audience?

1 ○ 9.9 **Mark the** syllables and **stress in these words, as in the example. Listen to check.**

a actor ●●

c comedian

e gymnast

g runner

b athlete

d guitarist

f celebrity

h magician

2 ○ 9.10 **Listen to a couple talking. What has the woman lost? Why does she say "I must be getting old"?**

3 ○ 9.10 **Listen again and complete the chart.**

Location that the man suggests	Reason	The woman agrees ✓ or disagrees ✗	Reason
living room			
	She often leaves her glasses there.		
			She doesn't need them for typing.
	They must be somewhere.	✓	

4 **Match a–f to 1–6 in the second column to make deductions. Then match three of them to photos 1–3.**

a You haven't eaten anything all day.
b Are you crazy? It's 35° C.
c Where's Angela today?
d I know Karen and Liz,
e You've been at school all day.
f That's absolutely ridiculous.

1 so you must be Ellie. Nice to finally meet you.
2 You must have learned something.
3 You must be really hungry.
4 You can't possibly be cold.
5 You can't be serious.
6 She might be sick. She didn't look very well yesterday.

5 ○ 9.11 **Cover the second column. Listen and, after the beep, make a deduction.**

6 🔵 **Make it personal** Who is a successful person you admire? Why are they successful? Write a paragraph about the person.

🔊 **Connect**

Record your paragraph on your phone and send it to a classmate or your teacher.

9.5 How do you get on with your siblings?

1 Read the article. True (T), False (F) or Not mentioned (N)?

a The twins have won over 50 singles titles each.

b The boys are exactly the same height.

c Their parents were worried about the way they communicated as children.

d They shared winning when they were younger.

e They watched a lot of tennis stars on TV when they were children.

f The twins' charity builds schools in the U.S.

Tennis Twins

Americans Bob and Mike Bryan are the most successful tennis doubles team in history. The guys have won multiple Olympic medals, including Gold in 2012 and have won more games, matches, tournaments and grand slams than any other team. They have been the number one team eight times and have won at least five titles per year for ten years. A very impressive record! _____ are also identical twin brothers, although Bob is about three centimeters taller. So, has being a twin helped _____ be so successful?

Well, their communication on the tennis court is amazing and this goes back to _____ shared childhood. _____ finish each other's sentences and know what the other is thinking. When they were around six their parents took _____ to therapy because they were speaking an "alien twin language"! They are so close that they don't need to speak to communicate. It just comes naturally, and this makes _____

very dangerous to their opponents. _____ parents thought it was important that their children had fun playing tennis and they didn't want the boys to compete with each other. If _____ played each other in singles competitions, they would share victories. In one competition Bob would win, and Mike would win in the next. Of course, being able to practice with an expert player every day has helped _____ become so good at tennis.

But tennis isn't the only thing _____ are good at. They have played music since they were young and they recorded _____ first album in 2004. One thing they didn't have when they were young was TV. _____ dad took it out of the house so they had lots of time to practice music and tennis. And this could be the reason why they are so successful today! The guys do a lot of charity work too. Their organization, Bryan Bros. Foundation, helps children around the world to have a better quality of life.

2 ▶9.12 Reread the article and complete with *they*, *them* or *their*. Listen to check.

3 Insert the missing word in suggestions a–e.

a Why you go to bed?

b If I you, I'd call her.

c should study more often.

d What putting an ad on the Internet?

e You better eat something.

4 ▶9.13 Listen to five problems and, after the beep, give some advice from **3**. Listen to check.

Can you remember ...

➤ 10 wedding words? SB→p.112

➤ 5 relationship words? SB→p.114

➤ the difference between *bored* and *boring*? SB→p.115

➤ 6 adverbs to make adjectives sound stronger? SB→p.115

➤ 3 performers ending -*or*, -*er* and -*ian*? SB→p.118

➤ 4 modal verbs for making guesses? SB→p.118

➤ 5 ways to make suggestions? SB→p.121

10.1 Do you often feel stressed?

1 ▶10.1 **Listen to a woman talking about stress and circle the correct word / phrase.**

a The woman is **stressed** / **an expert on stress** / **having stress therapy**.
b She talks about **two** / **three** / **four** types of stress.
c Acute stress is caused by **positive** / **negative** / **both positive and negative** experiences.
d Chronic stress is **sometimes** / **often** / **always** bad for you.
e She talks about the **financial** / **physical** / **emotional** effects of stress.

2 ▶10.1 **Listen again and complete the brochure with one word in each gap.**

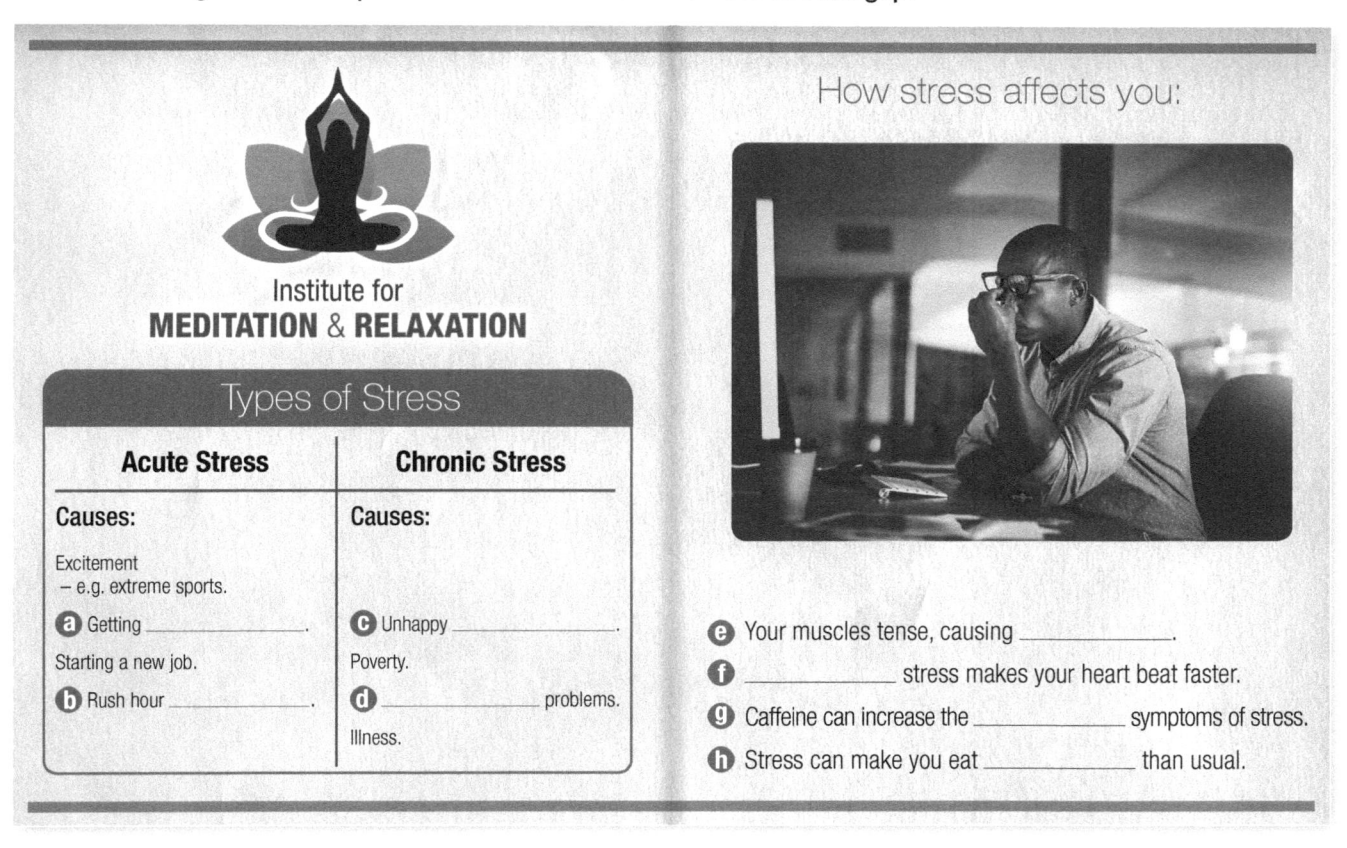

Institute for
MEDITATION & RELAXATION

Types of Stress

Acute Stress	**Chronic Stress**
Causes:	Causes:
Excitement – e.g. extreme sports.	
a Getting _____ .	**c** Unhappy _____ .
Starting a new job.	Poverty.
b Rush hour _____ .	**d** _____ problems.
	Illness.

How stress affects you:

e Your muscles tense, causing _____ .
f _____ stress makes your heart beat faster.
g Caffeine can increase the _____ symptoms of stress.
h Stress can make you eat _____ than usual.

🔊 **Connect**

Look up ways to reduce stress online.

3 👤 **Make it personal** **Using the brochure, decide what kind of stress these stressors cause, acute (A) or chronic (C). Have you ever experienced any of these?**

a Financial problems.
b Caring for a child every day.
c A deadline at work or school.
d Multitasking in the morning.
e Lack of sleep for two months.

4 **Use *over* or *under* + the verb in parentheses to complete these sentences.**

a These potatoes are _____ (**cook**). They are still hard.
b Most soccer players have too much money. They are incredibly _____ (**pay**).
c I always _____ (**eat**) at Christmas. There's so much delicious food!
d I can't use my credit card anymore, I have _____ (**spend**) this month.
e The coach _____ (**estimate**) the opposition team and didn't use his best players, so his team lost 4–1.

5 ▶10.2 **Words beginning *s* + consonant can be difficult to pronounce. Listen and repeat these two groups. Don't put a vowel sound before the *s*.**

a stressed   start   sleep   snack
b smoke   spend   spoiled   school   /s/

10.2 Would you like to change anything in your life

1 Study the chart and correct two mistakes in each of a–e.

✋ (completely stop)	➖ (change)	➕ (change)
I want to <u>quit</u> *my job.* (noun)	I want to *work* <u>less</u>. (verb)	I want to *exercise* <u>more</u>. (verb)
I need to <u>quit</u> *smoking.* (verb + *-ing*)	I want to *eat* <u>less</u> *salt.* (verb + noun)	I want to *get* <u>more</u> *sleep.* (verb + noun)

a   That's a cough bad. Why don't you quit to smoke?
b   Ugh! Your cooking is so salty. You should to use salt less.
c   I'm not going lend you any money so you'd better spending less.
d   You don't play any sports and you drive everywhere. Why you don't exercising more?
e   You won't pass your school test if you don't study more and to watch TV less.

2 ⏵10.3 **Listen and respond to each statement after the beep using the advice in 1. Follow the model.**

Model: *Ugh! Your cooking is so salty!*   **You:** *You should use less salt.*

3 Complete the clues with **who** or **that**. Match six of them to photos a–f and do the crossword.

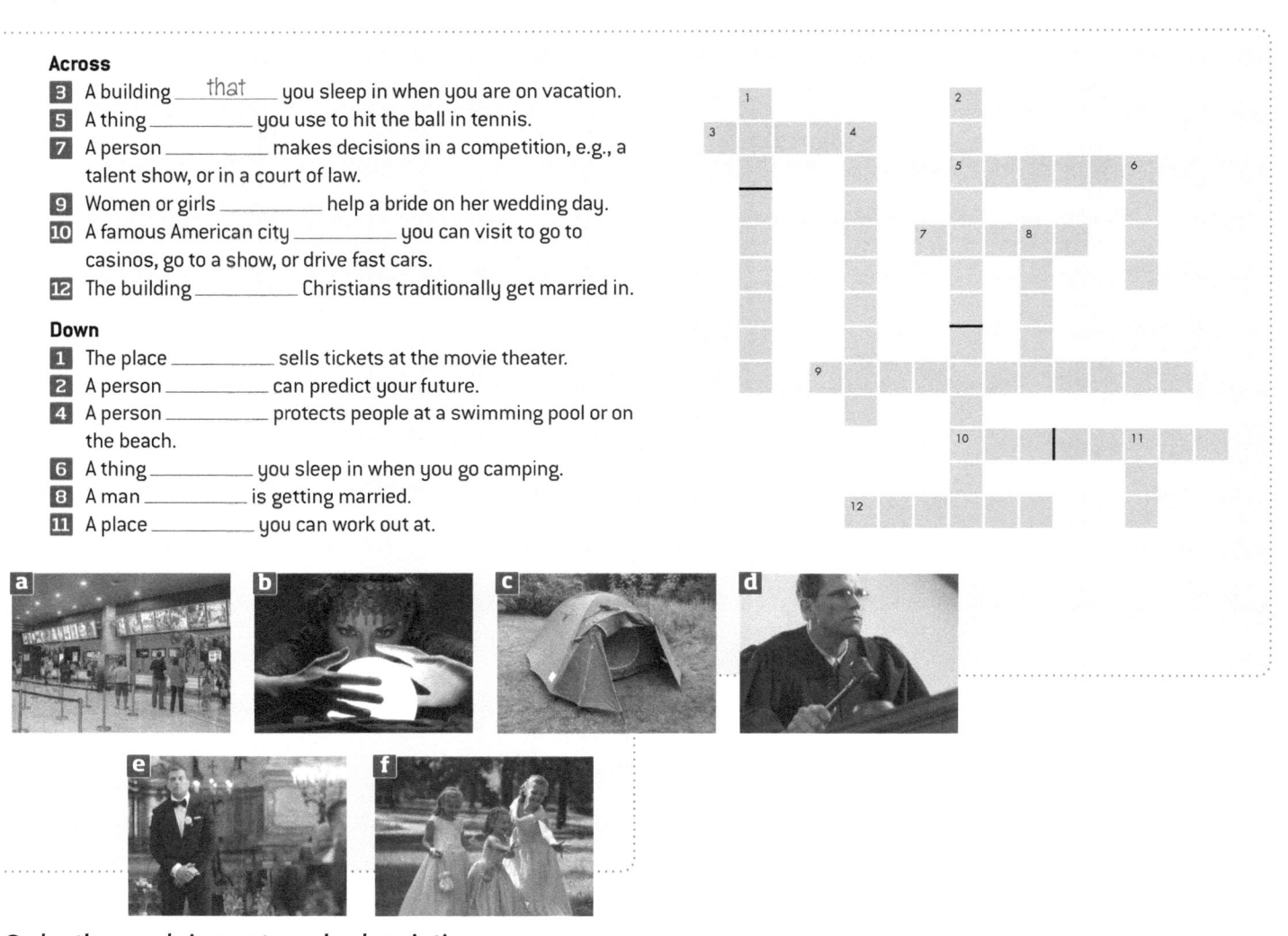

Across

3 A building ___that___ you sleep in when you are on vacation.
5 A thing _____ you use to hit the ball in tennis.
7 A person _____ makes decisions in a competition, e.g., a talent show, or in a court of law.
9 Women or girls _____ help a bride on her wedding day.
10 A famous American city _____ you can visit to go to casinos, go to a show, or drive fast cars.
12 The building _____ Christians traditionally get married in.

Down

1 The place _____ sells tickets at the movie theater.
2 A person _____ can predict your future.
4 A person _____ protects people at a swimming pool or on the beach.
6 A thing _____ you sleep in when you go camping.
8 A man _____ is getting married.
11 A place _____ you can work out at.

4 Order the words in a–c to make descriptions.

a   place / books / that / lends / a / .
b   clean / that / a / use / house / you / your / to / thing / .
c   new / who / constructs / person / a / houses / .

5 ⏵10.4 **Listen to check and write down the name of the person, place, or object.**

6 🎤 **Make it personal** Think of three things you'd like to change in your life. Why do you want to change them? How would you change them? Record your answers.

10.3 What's your attitude to money?

1 Read the article and put the paragraphs a–c in the correct order. Then complete paragraph *a* with the correct form of these verbs. There's one extra word.

> afford   cost   earn   pay for   spend   win

From the Streets to Success

a Topitop is successful because it constantly produces new styles at prices customers can _____. For example, a surf shirt from Topitop _____ approximately US$10, half the price of an imported equivalent. Middle-class Peruvians, families that _____ on average US$550 a month, can _____ their money at Topitop and still have enough money to _____ a movie ticket.

b Aquilino Flores was born in poverty, high up in the Andes mountains. He was 12 when he left home and traveled to Lima, the capital of Peru, to work, and his first job there was washing cars. He earned just enough money to live and nothing more, but Aquilino was a good worker and a friendly guy, and one day one of his customers suggested that he sell T-shirts. The man gave Aquilino 20 T-shirts and he sold them in one day. That is how Aquilino Flores started in the fashion industry.

c Now his company, Topitop, is the largest clothes producer in Peru and makes over US$275 million a year. The company has stores all over Peru, as well as Venezuela, and also exports clothes to Brazil, Europe and the U.S., where the clothes are sold as Hugo Boss, North Face and other famous and expensive brand names.

2 Read the website and match the titles to a–e.

> Bargain   Earn Money   Lend Your Money
> Save Your Money   Win Money

Top Ways to Get Rich

a _____
The traditional way to make money is to get a job and spend all day working. This has its disadvantages. It can be… `click to read more`

b _____
The lottery is a good way to make a lot of money very quickly. All you have to do is buy a ticket and hope. Of course, you will… `click to read more`

c _____
Don't pay more for things than you have to. Before you go shopping, find out how much different items cost in different places and on the Internet. NEVER spend more than you can afford and don't be scared to ask for a discount. Although this can be… `click to read more`

d _____
When you get some money, don't spend it—it's that simple. Some bank accounts will even pay you a percentage to leave your money in the bank. Of course, it will be… `click to read more`

e _____
If the banks can do it, why can't you? Let people borrow money from you and then make them pay a large percentage on what they borrow. This can be… `click to read more`

3 ▶10.5 **🅐 Make it personal** Listen to check and find one disadvantage to each suggestion. Which suggestion is the best for you?

4 Read the extracts from the freeganism video on p. 129 of the Student's Book. Then replace the underlined slang words with their synonyms.

> carry   abandoned   excited   house
> pick it up   take   those things

"I live in New York City, where I think it's pretty common to pick up <u>trashed</u> furniture or electronics, because people here just leave <u>that stuff</u> on the sidewalk for you to <u>grab</u>. And when you're on your way home and you walk by a perfectly good piece of furniture that you can use, why not just <u>scoop it up</u> and <u>schlep</u> it back to your <u>abode</u>?"

"I'm <u>psyched</u>!"

10.4 How often do you post on social media?

1 Read the text about Bruno Mars and order the words in a–f to make questions.

24k **Magic!**

Bruno Mars has been a performer for _____ years. He has had _____ number-one singles and he's won nearly _____ awards, including eleven Grammys and four Guinness World Records. Amazingly, over _____ people watched Bruno perform at Morumbi Stadium in São Paulo in _____ . That concert alone made over $ _____ !

a   long / singer / been / has / a / how / Bruno / ?
b   singles / how / had / he / number-one / has / many / ?
c   he / awards / many / has / won / how / ?
d   São Paulo / many / how / people / him / watched / in / ?
e   in / when / he / São Paulo / perform / did / ?
f   how / money / make / did / concert / the / much?

2 ▶10.6 Listen to an interview to check the questions and complete Bruno's biography.

 **Connect**
Go online and find information about a musician or band you like.

3 Use the prompts to write questions about units 6–9. Do the quiz and look back to check.

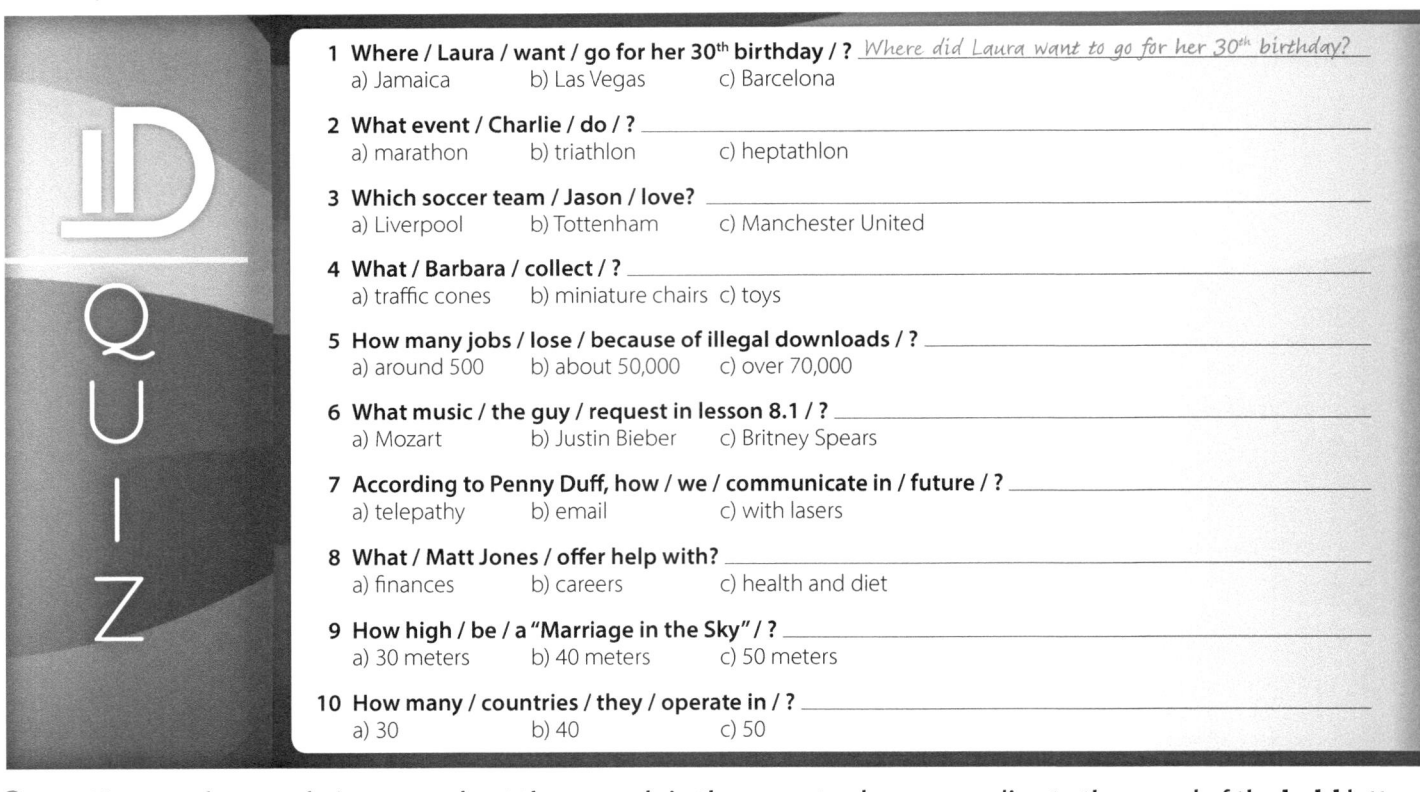

1 Where / Laura / want / go for her 30ᵗʰ birthday / ? *Where did Laura want to go for her 30ᵗʰ birthday?*
   a) Jamaica   b) Las Vegas   c) Barcelona

2 What event / Charlie / do / ? _____
   a) marathon   b) triathlon   c) heptathlon

3 Which soccer team / Jason / love? _____
   a) Liverpool   b) Tottenham   c) Manchester United

4 What / Barbara / collect / ? _____
   a) traffic cones   b) miniature chairs c) toys

5 How many jobs / lose / because of illegal downloads / ? _____
   a) around 500   b) about 50,000   c) over 70,000

6 What music / the guy / request in lesson 8.1 / ? _____
   a) Mozart   b) Justin Bieber   c) Britney Spears

7 According to Penny Duff, how / we / communicate in / future / ? _____
   a) telepathy   b) email   c) with lasers

8 What / Matt Jones / offer help with? _____
   a) finances   b) careers   c) health and diet

9 How high / be / a "Marriage in the Sky" / ? _____
   a) 30 meters   b) 40 meters   c) 50 meters

10 How many / countries / they / operate in / ? _____
   a) 30   b) 40   c) 50

4 ▶10.7 Listen to the sound pictures and put these words in the correct column according to the sound of the **bold** letters.

consump**ti**on   conven**ti**onal   deci**si**on   lei**su**re   occa**si**on   participa**ti**on

1 /ʃ/
2 /ʒ/

5 ▶10.8 Listen to check and repeat the words.

10.5 Do you enjoy reading in English?

1 Read the story and, as you read, answer 1–5.

Class of '99

The taxi drove downtown and Nick looked at the low gray building. Has it really been twenty years since he was last here? Through the double doors, everything was exactly as he remembered it, although a little smaller now, and strangely quieter. The Principal's office was on the right, next to the nurse's room. He turned left and followed the signs: "Class of '99 Reunion."

1 What is the low gray building?

He found the gym and waited in the doorway watching the middle-aged people standing in uncomfortable groups of 4, 5 or 6. Who did he remember? That tall man holding two glasses of orange cocktail in his big hands, and drinking from both, must be Jed, the football star. The girls loved him, almost as much as he loved himself.

2 Why should Nick remember the middle-aged people?

Nick picked up a glass of orange cocktail from the table and walked slowly around the room, trying hard to remember faces. The cocktail had a sour, toxic taste. "Nick, is that you?" said a quiet voice. Turning, he saw a small man in an expensive suit, his blue eyes behind thick glasses. Marcus! Nick smiled, happy to see a face that he knew and happy also that the quiet, shy, hardworking kid was now apparently a successful adult.

3 Why does Nick think that Marcus is successful?

"Isn't that cocktail awful? Try this," said Marcus as he replaced Nick's glass. Nick took the beer and the two started talking. Nick was divorced and working in a hotel, Marcus was unmarried and working for a pharmaceutical company.
Suddenly a loud voice: "Well, little mouse Marcus… squeak, squeak!" and a massive hand hit Marcus in the back. For a second, Marcus's face showed terror, then anger, before returning to calm.

4 Who do you think hit Marcus?

"Jed?" said Marcus. Suddenly Nick remembered the horrible names, the broken glasses, the physical and mental torture that was Marcus's life and Jed's amusement for four years of adolescent prison. "Of course it is. I'll be back to talk with you later, Mouse." said Jed, pressing Marcus's glasses with his finger. As Jed walked away laughing, Marcus watched him, his eyes burning with anger.

5 How does Marcus feel about Jed?

"Nick, I have to go now," said Marcus. "You were always so kind to me, but I don't think we'll meet again." He paused and then added "And Nick, don't drink any more of that cocktail."

6 What do you think Marcus did to Jed's cocktail?

2 This story is approximately 400 words long. Try to reread it in two minutes.

3 These workbook texts are approximately 200 words long each. Time yourself and see how fast you can read them. Then try again another day and see if you are faster.

Text and lesson	Target time	1st reading	2nd reading	3rd reading	4th reading
A Success Story (7.4)	60 seconds				
Horoscopes (8.5)	75 seconds				
Wedding Traditions (9.1)	75 seconds				

4 ▶10.9 Add *one* or *ones* in three places in each dialogue. Listen to check.

a **Customer** I'd like to buy some shoes.
Salesperson Of course. Which would you like to try?
Customer I like the black in the window.
Salesperson Certainly. What size are you?
Customer I'm a 13.
Salesperson Ah. I'm afraid we don't have size 13, but our other store might have them. The next to the movie theater.

b **Customer** I'm making a fruit salad. Do you have any grapes?
Salesperson Yes, we have purple and green. Which would you like?

c **Customer** Do you have any guidebooks for the city?
Salesperson Yes. This has a good map and this has lots of historical information.
Customer I'll take the with the map, please.

Can you remember …

➤ 9 common causes of stress? SB→p.124
➤ 12 suggestions for relieving stress? SB→p.125
➤ 2 relative pronouns? SB→p.127
➤ 8 money verbs? SB→p.128
➤ 3 adverbs that can go after *how* in a question? SB→p.130

Audioscript

Unit 6

▶ 6.7

I = interviewer

I Today we are asking tourists on the streets of Madrid what they think about Spain's famous bull-running.

1 S Hi, Shane here. I love running with the bulls, it's a real adrenaline rush, you know? I go every year if I can. Last year I actually touched a bull on the head. It was so cool!

2 P Hi there. I'm Petra, from New Orleans. I've seen the bull running on TV and there's no way I would ever do that. Not in a million years! I think it's really stupid and the bulls are obviously tormented by all the people around them. Poor animals!

3 J Hi, I'm Jake, from St. Louis, in the U.S. Yeah, I'd love to run with the bulls. It looks really crazy. I used to play college football, so I think I would be good at it.

4 L I'm Lucia. Hmmm, I guess I'd like to try it. Maybe just once though. And I would want to practice running in a crowded place first, maybe in a metro station or somewhere like that.

▶ 6.8

M = man   W = woman

a M1 I'm bored with this program, aren't you?

W1 It's OK, but I've seen it before. I'll turn it off.

M1 So, what do you want to do this evening?

W1 Hmm, I don't know. Do you want to go to the movies? Or, there's a band playing.

M1 I don't feel like watching a movie. Let's go and see the band.

b W2 Would you like a drink?

M2 It's OK, I'll get it. Would you like a beer?

W2 No, thanks. I'm on an alcohol-free diet.

M2 Oh. So, how about a Coke?

W2 Uh, I'd rather have an orange juice, please.

M2 OK. One orange juice coming up.

▶ 6.9

M = man   W = woman

W1 So, what did you think of the band?

M1 Uh... well... they were OK, I guess.

W1 You mean you didn't like them?

M1 Well, uh... they were kind of loud and I prefer listening to quieter bands.

W1 Oh. Well, I thought they were great. I'd love to see them again!

Unit 7

▶ 7.4

M = man   W = woman

a M Do you collect anything?

W Yeah, I have a collection of coffee cups.

M How many do you have?

W About 50.

b W Are you into sports?

M Yeah, I love tennis.

W How often do you play?

M About once a week.

c M Do you have a favorite artist?

W I'm really into Beyoncé.

M Have you ever seen her perform?

W Unfortunately, no, I haven't.

d W Which soccer team do you like?

M I'm a United fan.

W Have you ever been to a game?

M Yeah, I went last year.

▶ 7.9

J = Jess   H = Helen

J Hi Helen, how's it going?

H Hi Jess, yes, I'm good thanks. Hey, I was hoping you could do me a favor next week. I've got this interview and... uh Jess, are you OK? What's going on there?

J Oh, I'm just watching Big Brother. I don't know where they find these people, they are just so stupid, you know?

H What? Big Brother! That's a terrible show, they're just idiots. Anyway, uh, Jess. Could you...

J I mean, this man on here now is crying because he tried to cook something and it burned and the other people are screaming because there is smoke in the kitchen. They are all idiots! Anyway Helen, how can I help?

H So, as I was saying, I have this interview next week and I'm kind of, you know, kind of nervous. So I was hoping I could practice interviewing with you, you know, just so I feel more confident.

J Yeah, sure, no problem. Come whenever you want.

H Thanks Jess.

Unit 8

▶ 8.4

a Will 3D TV be common in five years?

b Will there be a World War 3?

c Did we have homework from the last class?

d Are we going to have a test this week?

e Is it going to be sunny this weekend?

f Will we be able to communicate with aliens one day?

Unit 9

▶ 9.2

M = man   W = woman

a M1 GOAL!!!

M2 The soccer match is exciting.

b W1 I'm going to bed, good night.

M2 She is tired.

c M3 That was the weather report and now the sports. The result of today's friendly match between France and Switzerland is... France 1 – Switzerland 5.

M2 The result is surprising.

d M4 Come on!

M2 He is irritated.

e W2 No, please no...

M2 The movie is terrifying.

▶ 9.4

Actor and model Ashton Kutcher met actress Demi Moore at a dinner party in New York in 2003, they were extremely attracted to each other and they talked all night. Many people were surprised because Demi is 16 years older than Ashton.

They fell in love and got married in 2005. Rumors started in the media that Ashton cheated on Demi almost immediately after the wedding.

Ashton's friends say that he was very loyal to Demi and never flirted with other women when he was with her.

However, after six years Demi decided to break up with Ashton. Why did she dump him? Were the rumors true? Or was the age difference too much? Who knows, but the new rumors are that he is dating another Hollywood actress.

▶ 9.5

P = principal   M = Michael

P Well Michael, you have a very interesting résumé and a lot of experience. Now we would like to ask some questions about classroom management, OK? Now the first question is: What would you do if the school caught fire?

M If the school caught fire? Oh, I would definitely run out of the classroom as quickly as possible. I don't want to get hurt!

P Oh, I see. OK, if your students were making too much noise, how would you control them?

M Oh, I wouldn't do anything. I would just wait for them to stop. If they were shouting for a long time, maybe I would read a book or something. I think it's important that students express themselves naturally in the classroom.

P Hmmm. OK, Michael. What would you do if there was a power outage?

M Ummm... I would probably send the students home. I can't teach if I don't have a computer.

P Hmm, OK. Now, the final question. If you were me, would you give yourself this job?

M Yes, of course I would. I'm a fantastic teacher.

▶ 9.10

M = man   W = woman

W Have you seen my glasses?

M Have you lost them again? Well, they could be in the living room. We were watching TV last night.

W No, they can't be in there. I'm sure I've had them today.

M Ummm, they might be in your bag. You often leave them in there.

W No, I've already checked.

M Well... they might be next to the computer. You were using the Internet earlier.

W No, I don't think they are there. I don't need my glasses for typing.

M Well, they must be somewhere. Have you looked in the car?

W Ah! You're right! They must be in there. I had them when I went to the store. I must be getting old!

▶ 9.13

M = man   W = woman

1 M1 I'm trying to sell my car.
   W1 What about putting an ad on the Internet?

2 M2 I had a big argument with my girlfriend and now we are not speaking.
   W2 If I were you, I'd call her.

3 W3 I'm so tired.
   M3 Why don't you go to bed?

4 W4 I'm really hungry, I haven't eaten since breakfast.
   M4 You'd better eat something.

5 M5 I'm a bit worried because I keep failing my exams.
   W5 You should study more often.

Unit 10

▶ 10.1

Let's start by finding out what stress is. So, stress is your body's way of reacting to situations around you. There are two main kinds of stress: acute, or sudden stress, and chronic stress. Acute stress is very common and it usually isn't dangerous to our health. It can be caused by short, positive experiences, such as excitement, getting married, starting a new job, or negative experiences, like rush hour traffic.

Umm, chronic stress is very different and it is always very unhealthy. It is caused by long experiences like, uh, unhappy relationships or poverty, uh, career problems or sickness.

Now, stress can have emotional or physical symptoms and, ummm, I'd like to talk about the physical side of stress.

So, first, when you get stressed your muscles tense, causing headaches and other muscle problems, and, aahh, this can make you feel very tired.

One interesting effect of acute stress is that your heart beats faster. This is why extreme sports are so exciting. However, if it happens too often, you may develop heart problems.

A lot of people feel tired when they get stressed, so they drink a lot of coffee to stay awake. Unfortunately, many scientists believe that caffeine increases the physical symptoms of stress, like your heart beating faster.

Another thing is diet. Stress can change the way you eat and can make you eat more than usual.

OK, and next, I'd like to talk about the emotional side of stress...

▶ 10.6

G = Gary   P = Pete

G I'm talking today to a big music fan, Pete.

P Hi Gary, well I'm a huge fan of Bruno Mars. He's an amazing singer and has been a superstar for years.

G That's right. Exactly how long has Bruno Mars been a singer?

P Fifteen years, and in that time he has had so many fantastic songs.

G How many number ones has he had?

P He's had seven! I mean, that is an incredible number. And he's won lots of awards.

G How many awards has he won?

P Nearly forty! And that includes eleven Grammy awards and four Guinness World records.

G Wow, that's amazing! Has he ever performed in South America?

P Yes he has. The largest concert was at Morumbi Stadium in São Paulo.

G How many people watched him there?

P Over 80,000 people went to see him play.

G Amazing. When did he perform in São Paulo?

P In 2017. That concert made a lot of money.

G I can imagine. How much money did the concert make, exactly?

P That concert alone made over six million dollars.

G Wow!

Answer Key

Unit 6

6.1

2 a went camping b hang out, go clubbing c go diving d work out e go fishing, go bowling, climbing

3 a EZ and Angryman13. b Anya. c Sue and EZ. d Brad. e No, "climbing up the walls" means he is frustrated.

4 Personal answers.

6.2

1 Jillian, Frederico, Heitor

2 down / on / in / into

3 a gloves / hands b water level / unusually high c hiking / mountains

4 b port c room d paper e board f sun g hand h grand

5 a handshake b sandpaper c sunbathing d computer port

6 a dive b run c snowboard d jump e fall f swim g climb

7 Personal answers.

6.3

1 a towards / over / into / out of / under b across / up / past / down

2 a 4 b 3 c 7 d 6 e 1 f 2 g 5

3 Verbs: *adore* and *enjoy* = similar, positive meaning. *Adore* is stronger.
dislike and *can't stand* = similar, negative meaning. *Can't stand* is stronger.
Adjectives: *beautiful* is stronger than *pretty*; *huge* is stronger than *large*; *hilarious* is stronger than *funny*.
d, a, e, b, c

4 Possible answers:
b My mom dislikes cleaning the house.
c I adore going clubbing.
d My best friend can't stand shopping.
e I dislike traveling long distances.
f I enjoy working out.

5 1 /ð/ with, there, without, father, mother, brother, the
2 /θ/ threw, toothbrush, through
b It could be me, one of my siblings, or one of my cousins.

6.4

1 a scuba diving b through – swimming c over – volleyball d around – baseball e into – soccer

2 a mask, oxygen tank, fins b – c ball, net d bat, gloves e goal

3 interviewing / to be / working out / to help / to join / to learn / smoking / to quit / to make / to relax

5 a studying b to study c to study d to study e to study f studying

6.5

1 a bull b horns c crowd

2 Shane has run with the bulls.

3 4, 1, 2, 3

4 a 5, 2, 3, 4, 1 b 3, 6, 1, 5, 4, 2

5 a prefers listening / quieter bands b would love / see them

Unit 7

7.1

1 a sequel b stunt c box office d review e subtitles f plot g soundtrack

2 a mystery b drama c animated d action e thriller f documentary g horror h adventure i comedy j fantasy

3 1 Comedy – a 2 Suspense – c 3 Gangster – b

4 a 1 b 2 c 2 d 3 e 1

5 a *Terminator 2* is **an** old movie...
b **Most** actors want to win **an** Oscar.
c I watched a great movie on **TV last night**.

6 Personal answers.

7.2

1 a into b crazy c obsessed d huge fans

2 a photo (the photo doesn't move) b haircut (you can't take it off) c general public (paparazzi and journalist are media jobs) d huge (an adjective – it means very / really big) e obsessed (an adjective, needs a preposition "with")

3 a nothing b anyone c something d everybody / nobody e someone f anywhere

4 nothing / no one / anything / anywhere / someone / anyone's / everyone / somewhere / everywhere / nowhere / Everything / something / Everyone

5 a no b fan c one

6 Personal answers.

7.3

1 d 1 c 2 a 3 b 4

2 1 such an 2 so 3 so 4 so 5 such a 6 such a 7 so 8 so

4 a Do you b Are you c Do you / a d do you

5 a How many – About 50.
b How often – About once a week.
c Have you ever – Unfortunately, no, I haven't.
d been to a game – Yeah, I went last year.

7.4

1 b

2 These verb forms must be **crossed out**: is released / create / is gotten / didn't intend / were persuaded / captures / is made / accidently throw / are found / joined

3 a 1.9 billion b 99.7 c one and a half d third / 14 e two fifths f 21st / twenty-first

4 a *Game of Thrones* was written by George R.R. Martin. (I)
b "Live it up", the official song of the 2018 World Cup, was sung by Nicky Jam featuring Will Smith and Era Istrefi. (I)
c The World Wide Web was invented by Tim Berners-Lee. (R)
d Microsoft was founded by Bill Gates and Paul Allen. (R)

5 b 1 c 1 d 2 e 2 f 1

6 Personal answers.

7.5

1

/ʃ/ shorts	/tʃ/ cheese	/ʒ/ treasure
ex**pre**ssion, partici**pa**tion, po**si**tion, pronunci**a**tion, **sh**ow	**c**atch, **ch**urch, **k**itchen, **ques**tion	con**clu**sion, de**ci**sion, il**lu**sion,

2 Check answers in 1. The syllable before -*ion* is stressed.

3 a What is Jess watching on TV? (Big Brother.)
b Does Helen like the show? (No.)
c Why does Helen feel nervous? (Because she has an interview.)

4 1, 2, 3

5 a It / good / I expected b I / think it was c It was

6 Personal answers.

7 e, d, a, b, c

8 a It was such a noisy place.
b I have such a slow car.
c It was such a disappointing movie/ disappointment.
d It was such an interesting documentary.
e It is such a popular radio station.
f She has such a strange collection of chairs.

Unit 8

8.1

1 a at / on b in c at / on d in

2 a a smell-producing alarm clock b a self-heating lunch box c a news-summarizing app

3 a F b N c T d N e F

4 a 2 b 6 c 1 d 4 e 7 f 3 g 5

5 a vending b GPS c speaker d lenses e facial

6 Personal answers.

8.2

1 a connect to electricity
b disconnect using a switch
c make quieter
d stop sleeping
e get out of bed in the morning
f make louder
g make a machine start working

2 a 2 b 4 c 1 d 3

4 1 on / off button 2 USB cable 3 volume icon on / off / up / down / up

5 a Is that your new cell phone? ↗
b Where did you buy it? ↘
c How long does the battery last? ↘
d Can I play with it? ↗
e How many apps do you have? ↘
f What does this app do? ↗

6 Personal answers.

8.3

1

/θ/	/ð/
synthetic, telepathy, think, thirty, thoughts, three, through	the, themselves, there, they, this

2 b We will **probably** be able to... / ... and will **possibly** have celebrity... c There have **certainly** been big... / ... this will **certainly** continue. d ... organizations will **possibly** use... e We **probably** won't use cell... / ... we will **possibly** be able to...

3 b Cell phones will possibly be able to clean themselves. c Cell phones definitely won't be "phones." d We probably won't need to touch the screens. e Cell phones will certainly be able to recognize our voices.

4 a **Will** 3D TV be common in five years? b Will **there be** a World War 3? c Did we **have** homework from the last class? d Are we **going** to have a test this week? e Is **it** going to be sunny this weekend? f Will we be able to **communicate** with aliens one day?

5 b I hope not. It would be terrible! c I think so. But I can't remember. d I hope not. I think it's next week. e I think so. They said it will be. f I hope so. They are usually cool in the movies!

7 Personal answers.

8.4

1 b arguments c answer d take place e take f sensitive g intends

2 b assume c sensible d pretended / was pretending e realized f actually g attend

3 finish, leaves, going to have to, 'll ask / 'm going to ask, 'm staying, 's going to be / will be

4 a I will b I'll c He's going to d isn't going to e I'll

5 a What time does your next lesson start? b What are you doing this weekend? / What are you going to do this weekend? c Do you think we will stop driving cars in the future? d Are you going to do any homework tomorrow?

8.5

1 a give b hour c busy

2 Suggested answers.
a Bike for sale. Five years old. Very good condition. $80.
b Waiter needed. Busy city center restaurant. Experience required. Good pay.
c Babysitting service offered. Weekdays only. $10 per hour. Call 733-383-6876.

3 1 b 2 c 3 b 4 a

5 c, a, e, d, b

Unit 9

9.1

1 engagement, honeymoon, ceremony, guest list, gift registry, invitation, reception, bride, groom, bridesmaids

2 a 2 (Evelyn Hendrickson) b 5 (Billy Connolly) c 1 (Henry Youngman) d 3 (Albert Einstein) e 4 (Rodney Dangerfield)

3 a get dark b get lost c get better d get wet e get dressed

4 a F b T c F d F e N f F g T

5 a Jessica Biel got married to Justin Timberlake in 2012.
b Mark Zuckerberg married Priscilla Chan in their garden.

c Michael Bublé got married to Luisana Lopilato in Vancouver and Buenos Aires.

6 Personal answers.

9.2

1 Sep. 13 – bored / tired / amazing / funny
Sep. 14 – terrifying / surprised / scared / exciting
Sep. 15 – interested / satisfied / "entertaining"

2 a classes b teacher c doesn't like d liked

3 a exciting b tired c surprising d irritated e terrifying

4 completely, extremely, really, very, totally; "absolutely", "completely", "totally" have the same meaning.

5 Personal answers.

6

1 syllable	2 syllables	3 syllables
broke, dumped, fell	cheated, dated, flirted	attracted

"Break" and "fall" are irregular.

7 1 attracted 2 fell 3 cheated 4 flirted 5 break up 6 dump 7 dating

8 1 After 6 years, Demi decided to break up with Ashton. 2 Demi is 16 years older than Ashton. 3 They met in 2003. 4 They got married in 2005.
The extra number is 60.

9.3

1 a the school caught fire b were making too much noise c What would you do d If you were me

2 a I wouldn't do anything. – b b Yes, of course I would. – d c I would definitely run out of the classroom. – a d I would probably send the students home. – c

3 a If you were the interviewer, would you give Mike the job?
b If you were the teacher, what would you do next class?
c If you could travel anywhere, where would you go?
d How would you feel if you lost your cell phone?
e If you had a million dollars, what would you spend it on?

4 e, b, a, d, g, c, f

5 a geography 2   journal 2
b **j**ealous 2   ed**i**tor 1
c **id**ea 1   marria**g**e 2
d e**dg**e 2   **d**iary 1
e **g**enuinely 2   **d**ifferent 1

9.4

1 b ath-lete   f ce-leb-ri-ty
c co-me-di-an   g run-ner
d gui-tar-ist   h ma-gi-cian
e gym-nast

2 She has lost her glasses. She says "I must be getting old" because she keeps forgetting things.

3

Location that the man suggests	Reason	✓ or ✗	Reason
living room	Watching TV last night.	✗	Sure she has had them today.
in her bag	She often leaves her glasses there.	✗	She has already checked.
next to the computer	She was using the Internet earlier.	✗	She doesn't need them for typing.
in the car	They must be somewhere.	✓	She had them when she went to the shop.

4 b 4 c 6 d 1 e 2 f 5
Pictures 1 d, 2 e, 3 b.

5 Personal answers.

6 Personal answers.

9.5

1 a N b F c T d T e F f N

2 They / them / their / They / them / them / Their / they / them / they / their / Their

3 a Why **don't** you go to bed?
b If I **were** you, I'd call her.
c **You** should study more often.
d What **about** putting an ad on the Internet?
e You**'d** better eat something.

4 1 d 2 b 3 a 4 e 5 c

Unit 10

10.1

1 a an expert on stress
b two
c both positive and negative
d always
e physical

2 a married b traffic c relationships d career e headaches f Acute g physical h more

3 a C b C c A d A e C

4 a undercooked b overpaid c overeat d overspent e underestimated

10.2

1 a That's a **bad** cough. Why don't you quit **smoking**?
b Ugh! Your cooking is so salty. You should **use less** salt.
c I'm not going **to** lend you any money so you'd better **spend** less.
d You don't play any sports and you drive everywhere. Why **don't** you **exercise** more?
e You won't pass your school test if you don't study more and **watch less** TV.

3 Across
3 hotel   5 that – racket   7 who – judge (d)
9 who – bridesmaids (f)   10 that – Las Vegas
12 that – church
Down
1 that – box office (a)   2 who – fortune-teller (b)
4 who – lifeguard   6 that – tent (c)
8 who – groom (e)   11 that – gym

4 a A place that lends books.
b A thing that you use to clean your house.
c A person who constructs new houses.

Answer Key

5 a Library   b Vacuum cleaner   c Builder

6 Personal answers.

10.3

1 Correct order: b, c, a.
afford / costs / earn / spend / pay for

2 a Earn Money   b Win Money   c Bargain
d Save Your Money   e Lend Your Money

3 a It can be boring.
b You will almost certainly lose.
c This can be a little embarrassing.
d It will be a very long time before you are rich.
e This can be a risky way to get rich.

4 abandoned / those things / take / pick it up /
carry / house / excited

10.4

1 a How long has Bruno been a singer?
b How many number-one singles has he had?
c How many awards has he won?
d How many people watched him in São Paulo?
e When did he perform in São Paulo?
f How much money did the concert make?

2 a 15   b seven   c 40   d 80,000
e 2017   f 6 million

3 1 b
2 What event did Charlie do? b
3 Which soccer team does Jason love? c
4 What does Barbara collect? b
5 How many jobs are lost because of illegal
downloads? c
6 What music did the guy request in lesson 8.1? a
7 According to Penny Duff, how will we
communicate in the future? a
8 What does Matt Jones offer help with? b
9 How high is a "Marriage in the Sky"? c
10 How many countries do they operate in? b

4 1 /ʃ/ **sh**ark, **sh**orts, consump**ti**on, conven**ti**onal,
participa**ti**on
2 /ʒ/ televi**si**on, trea**su**re, deci**si**on, lei**su**re, occa**si**on

10.5

1 1 It's a school.
2 Because he went to school with them.
3 Because he was wearing an expensive suit.
4 Jed – big hands.
5 Marcus feels angry.
6 He put something in it.

4 a Which **ones** would you like to try? / I like the
black **ones** in the window.
The **one** next to the movie theater.
b Yes, we have purple **ones** and green **ones**.
Which **ones** would you like?
c Yes. This **one** has a good map and this **one** has
lots of historical information.
I'll have the **one** with the map, please.

Phrase Bank

This Phrase Bank is organized by topics.
► The audio is on the ID Richmond Learning Platform.

Expressing opinions, agreeing and disagreeing

Unit 6
I guess bowling is usually safe.

Unit 7
I'm not sure if he's crying or sweating. What do you think?
I think if they make downloading cheaper, there will be less piracy.
I think most men enjoy action movies.
Actually, I didn't think Joe was that great.
I have to agree with Alice.
It wasn't as good as I expected.
I thought it was OK.

Unit 8
Do you think robots will replace teachers?
Oh really? I don't - I prefer to use my fingerprint.
Yeah. I hope so.
Oh, I hope not.
I don't think machines will ever feel anything.

Unit 8
I disagree.
Really? I don't think we'll change.
No, not a chance!

Unit 9
Weddings are boring 'cause they're always the same.
People usually fall in love with someone they find physically attractive.

Making guesses

Unit 8
Maybe machines will have human emotions.
Ten years from now, there will probably be house-cleaning robots.
Well, I don't think the Internet will change much.
Yeah, I doubt it. But we'll find different ways to use it.

Unit 9
He must be a celebrity.
It can't be a pear, because of the texture.
It might be an apple, because of the color.
Do you think they're German?

Unit 10
It could be about an old lady that decides to leave her home.

Making suggestions

Unit 6
Let's go clubbing.

Unit 10
She should definitely buy a raffle ticket.
She needs to eat more—she looks really thin.

Memories

Unit 6
I don't remember the last time we went to the beach.

Unit 9
The last time I was absolutely exhausted was after going clubbing.

Money

Unit 10
I have 50 dollars, but I want to save the money.
If I get another job, I can earn more money.

Talking about preferences

Unit 6
Do you feel like going out?
I'd rather stay in.
I'd prefer to stay in.
I can't stand swimming.
I'd like to go to New York.
My favorite outdoor activities are swimming and hiking.
We adore playing basketball.
Would you rather eat Italian or Mexican food?

Talking about problems

Unit 10
Lack of sleep is a problem for me.

Showing desire

Unit 8
I'd love to have a self-driving car.

Unit 10
I'd like to exercise more and eat better.

Sports

Unit 6
You have to kick the ball into the goal.
You play the game with a bat and a ball.

Phrase Bank

Movies

Unit 7

My favorite movie is *The Green Book*.
I've never seen *The Artist*.
It has a superb plot and character and it's based on a true story.
For action, how about *Spiderman: Far From Home*?
Did it have good reviews?
Would you recommend it?
Who's the main character?

Being a fan

Unit 7

I'm really into plants and I have my own garden.
I'm obsessed with Manchester United.
I'm really into sport.
I'm crazy about music.
I'm a big fan of getting involved with campaigns.

Pausing

Unit 7

Anyway, the big day arrived and I got there early.
Where was I?

Predictions

Unit 8

Am I going to marry my boyfriend?
Probably. / There's a good chance.
Definitely. / For sure. / Absolutely.
Are we ever going to travel through time?
Will we have house-cleaning robots?
Probably not. / I doubt it.
Definitely not. / Not a chance. / No way.

Giving advice and responding

Unit 9

If I were you, I'd talk to your boss.
Thanks for the tip. I hadn't thought of that.
What about calling my brother?
Why don't you go to the mall?
I'd find out how Juan feels.
Thanks for the suggestion, but I don't have time now.
You should go home and go to bed.
You're right.
You'd better start working harder.
That's a good idea.
Yeah, I guess so.

Describing people and things

Unit 10

This is my sister Jane, who lives in L.A.
This is the hotel that we stayed in.

Other useful expressions

Unit 8

Why on Earth did she decide she should wake me up early?

Word List

Unit 6

Leisure time activities
to go bowling
to go camping
to go climbing
to go clubbing
to go diving
to go fishing
to go hiking
to hang out
to work out

Verbs of movement
to climb
to fall
to fly
to get
to jump
to run
to snowboard
to swim

Compound nouns
hairbrush
lunchbox
mailbox
toothbrush

Prepositions of movement
across
along
around
down
into
out of
over
past
through
towards
under
up

Sports equipment
bat
fins
gloves
hoop
helmet
mask
net
puck
racket
snorkel
stick

Sports verbs
to catch
to hit
to kick
to shoot

Other words
harness
secure
to scream
to shake

Unit 7

Movie words
main character
to dub
to play someone
plot
review
scary
sequel
soundtrack
to star in
subtitles

Movie genres
action
adventure
animated
comedy
documentary
drama
horror
mystery
thriller

Unit 8

Technology
active contact lens
button
facial recognition device
speaker
surveillance camera
vending machine

Phrasal verbs
to get up
to plug in
to switch off
to switch on
to turn down
to turn up
to wake up

Unit 9

Marriage
bride
bridesmaid
ceremony
decorations
engagement party
gift registry
groom
guest list
honeymoon
reception
wedding invitation

Adjectives
amazed
amazing
bored
boring
confused
confusing
depressed
depressing

embarrassed
embarrassing
entertained
entertaining
excited
exciting
exhausted
exhausting
frightened
frightening
interested
interesting
irritated
irritating
relaxed
relaxing
satisfied
satisfying
scared
scary
stressed
stressful
surprised
surprising
terrified
terrifying
tired
tiring

Romance
to be attracted
to be in love with someone
to break up
to cheat
to date
to dump
to fall in love with someone
to have a crush on someone

Performers
actor
athlete
clown
comedian
dancer
gymnast
magician
musician
singer
skater

Characteristics
adaptable
charming
friendly
intelligent
irresponsible
mature

Unit 10

Causes and symptoms of stress
caring for a child
deadlines
financial problems
lack of exercise
lack of sleep
multitasking
peer pressure
poor diet
pressure to succeed

Relieving stress
to breathe deeply
to eat well
to exercise
to go clubbing
to have realistic deadlines
meditation
to plan your time
to relax
to sleep well
to spend time with friends
to take a break
to take medicine

Lifestyle changes
to drink less soda
to eat better
to eat less salt
to exercise more
to get a new job
to get more sleep
to lose weight
to organize and plan time
to spend less time online
to watch less TV
to work from home
to work less

Money verbs
to be able to afford
to cost
to earn
to pay
to save
to spend
to waste
to win

Richmond

58 St Aldates
Oxford
OX1 1ST
United Kingdom

Fourth reprint: 2024
ISBN: 978-84-668-3251-9
CP: 105610

Publishing Director: Deborah Tricker
Publisher: Luke Baxter
Media Publisher: Luke Baxter
Content Developers: Paul Seligson, Neil Wood
Managing Editor: Laura Miranda
Editor: Hilary McGlynn
Proofreaders: Angela Castro, Nicola Gooch, Diyan Leake
Design Manager: Lorna Heaslip
Cover Design: Lorna Heaslip
Design & Layout: John Fletcher Design
Photo Researchers: Victoria Gaunt, Emily Taylor (Bobtail Media)
Audio Production: John Marshall Media Inc.
ID Café **Production:** Mannic Media

We would like to thank all those who have given their kind permission to reproduce material for this book:

SB Illustrators: Leo Teixeira, Amanda Savoini, Fabiane Eugenio, Odair Faléco, Talita Guedes

WB Illustrators: Alexandre Matos, Rico, Leo Teixeira

SB Photos: ALAMY STOCK PHOTO/AF archive, Aflo Co Ltd, Andrea Spinelli, CJG – Technology, Art Directors & TRIP, Caia image, Chris Howes/Wild Places Photography, Cultura RM, David Moody, Everett Collection Inc, Hero Images Inc, Jit Lim, Justin Kase zfivez, LJSphotography, Mircea Costina, Myron Standret, Nikolaj Kondratenko, Noriko Cooper, Panther Media GmbH, Peregrine, PhotoAlto, RooM the Agency, Science Photo Library, SIRIOH Co LTD, Sueddeutsche Zeitung Photo, Tetra Images, World History Archive, Zoonar GmbH; CARTOONSTOCK/Alexei Talimonov, Mark Lynch; DESIGN GRAPHIC; DIAMEDIA/Martin Poole/Moodboard; DINNERINTHESKY.COM; GETTY IMAGES SALES SPAIN/Abel Mitjà Varela, Adam Burn, Adam Taylor, adamkaz, AFP, akinshin, apomares, alenkadr, alexey_boldin, Andrea Spinelli, andresr, Antonio_Diaz, Archive Photos Creative, Ayumi Mason, Bambu Productions, Bertrand Rindoff Petroff, Betsie Van der Meer, Bettmann Archive, BSIP/UIG, Burak Karademir, Burke/Triolo Productions, Caiaimage, Cavan Images, CEF/Tim Pannell, Chris Ryan, Creatas, CSA Images, DingaLT, doble-d, d3sign, Daniel MacDonald, Darryl Leniuk, David Sacks, Deagreez, DEA/A. DAGLI ORTI, deepblue4you, Digital Vision, Dimitrios Kambouris, DreamPictures, edurivero, E+, Elva Etienne, Elizabeth Barnes, Elisabeth Schmitt, Ekaterina Romanova, erikreis , Eugenio Marongiu, EyeEm, Ezra Bailey, FilmMagic, Fly-Jet, gaspr13, Geber86, George Clerk, Geir Pettersen, Georgette Douwma, Gerhard Egger, grinvalds, Gray Mortimore/Staff, GregorBister, Hans Ferreira, hatman12, Hero Images, Hill Street Studios, Hoxton/Sam Edwards, Highwaystarz-Photography, Holger Leue, Inmagineasia, icarmen13, imageBROKER RF, iStock, iStockphoto, Jasmin Merdan, JGI/Jamie Grill, Jim Hughes, lechatnoir, Maskot, PhotoAlto/Eric Audras, Jackal Pan, JGI/Jamie Grill , Jochem D Wijnands, John Lamb, John M Lund Photography Inc, John Parra, Johner Bildbyra AB, JohnnyGreig, John Rowley, Jon Lovette, Joseph Johnson, Joshua Rainey, Judith Collins, Julian Ward, Juice Images, Katrina Wittkamp, Katsumi Murouchi, Kevin Mazur, killerb10, Kirill_Liv, Ljupco, Klaus Vedfelt, Kryssia Campos, Lawrence Manning, Lilly Dong, lisafx, Ljupco, Luciano Lozano, Luis Alvarez, Lumina Images, Maglara, mapodile, Marc Dozier, Mark Stahl, Maskot, maxkabakov, Media photos, Melvyn Longhurst, Milkos, Mikael Vaisanen, M.M Sweet, Morsa Images, Michael Dunning, Mikael Vaisanen, m-imagephotography, Moelyn Photos, Morsa Images, MStudioImages, mustafagull, mystockicons, nadia_bormotova, natrot, nd3000, Netfalls Remy Musser, Neustockimages, nicemonkey, Nick David, Nora Sahinun, Obradovic, OJO Images RF, Onoky, Owen Franken, ozgurcankaya, PATRICK LUX, pattonmania, penguiiin, PeopleImages, Peter Carlson, Pgiam, photodisc, picturegarden, Pixalfit, pixhook, poba, Presley

Ann/Stringer, Prykhodov, RapidEye, Rasulovs, Ray Kachatorian, Roc Canals, REB Images, Religious Images/UIG, RG-vc, RichLegg, Robert Decelis Ltd, Roberto Machado Noa, Roc Canals, Roman Märzinger, rusm, Russ Rohde, RyanJLane, RyanKing999, Samir Hussein, Scott Olson, SDI Productions, Shaul Schwarz, shironosov, SimplyCreativePhotography, Sidekick, Simon Ritzmann, Siri Stafford, Smederevac, solarseven, SSPL/Science Museum, South_agency, Stephen Simpson Inc, Stone Sub, Stuart Westmorland, sturti, Sylvain Grandadam/robertharding, Steven Puetzer, stock_colors, Sylvain Sonnet, Tanya Constantine, Tara Moore, Tatiana Gerus, Tegra Stone Nuess, TheCrimsonRibbon, thongseedary, Tony Garcia, Tom Werner, The Image Bank, The Washington Post, Tom Merton, Thomas Tolstrup, Thinkstock, Tomas Rodriguez, Tim Clayton – Corbis, Tim Hall, Tinpixels, Tisk, Turgay Malikli, Ty Allison, Ukususha, Uwe Krejci, valentinrussanov, VeranikaSmirnaya, View Pictures Ltd, vm, Wavebreakmedia, Westend61, Westend62, WireImage, wonry, wuttichaijangrab, Yamada Taro, Yuri_Arcurs; SHUTTERSTOCK/ A24/Moviestore, Africa Studio, AJR_photo, Alexander Prokopenko, Allmy, Aliaksei Tarasau, Andrey_Popov, Anatoly Maslennikov, Anatoly Tiplyashin, Anna Peisl, Anttoniart, Antonio Guillem, Apple's Eyes Studio, Artur Didyk, Artur Synenko, Bakai, BoJack, baranq, bbernard, Billion Photos, Branislav Nenin, Cbenjasuwan, Constantine Pankin, Chris Ratcliffe, Color Force/Lionsgate/Kobal, Damir Khabirov, Dave Clark Digital Photo, Dean Drobot, Djomas, Elnur, flower travellin' man, Fizkes, Frantic00, Freebulclicstar, Hekla, hlphoto, Igor Marusichenko, Jonas Petrovas, Jorg Hackenmann, Julia Savchenko, Juri Pozzi, Kalamurzing, karelnoppe, Kldy, Kotin, KPG_Payless, Krilerg saragorn, Kzenon, Ifc Prods/Detour Filmproduction/Kobal, LoopAll, lukas_zb, LusiG, Macrovector, Marvel/Disney/Kobal, Maximumvector, Mega Pixel, Mindscape studio, modus_vivendi, Monkey Business Images, nicemonkey, OlegDoroshin, Pattanapol Soodto, pavila, Peter Komka/EPA-EFE, Phil Hill, PPstudio, PONG HANDSOME, PrinceOfLove, RexRover, Roxana Gonzalez, sebra, Serge Gorenko, Serg Zastavkin, shoot66, siamionau pavel, sirtravelalot, Smith1979, Stock-Asso, stockfour, Syda Productions, Tatiana Chekryzhova, Techa Boribalburipun, TeddyandMia, Terekhob Igor, TheRocky41, Thurman James/CSM, Universal/Kobal, Val lawless, Victor Kochetkov, Vitalinka, vovidzha, VStocker, Warner Bros/Kobal, Wavebreakmedia, Yakov Oskanov, Yevgenij_D, 9nong, Zimmytws; ZUMAPRESS/Whitehotpix/Chris Murphy. ARCHIVO SANTILLANA

WB Photos: ALAMY STOCK PHOTO/AGB Photo Library, CHROMORANGE/Herwig Czizek, Diego Grandi, imageBROKER, JN, Mile Atanasov, MNStudio, Montgomery Martin, Minden Pictures; CARTOONSTOCK/Carroll Zahn; GETTY IMAGES SALES SPAIN/aedkais, Ariel Skelley, Beyond foto, Brand X, BrianAJackson, Busà Photography, Caiaimage/Martin Barraud, Carol Grant, Chesky_W, Colin Anderson Productions pty ltd, Copyright Rhinoneal, Corbis, CreativeDJ, Cultura RF, Digital Vision, dmbaker, Drazen_, E+, Erik Isakson/Blend Images LLC, Erikreis, EyeEm, FotoSpeedy, FilmMagic, franckreporter, Fuse, Getty Images AsiaPac, Getty Images North America, George Pimentel, Geri Lavrov, gionnixxx, GlobalP, Hero Images, Huronphoto, Image Source, iStock Editorial, istockphoto, jcrosemann, Jeff Kravitz, Jerod Harris, Jekaterina Nikitina, Juanmonino, Jupiterimages, Jurgenfr, Karl-Friedrich Hohl, Kent Weakley, Kinemero, Michael J Cohen, Mipan, Mint Images RF, Obak, Klaus Vedfelt, oneword, ppa5, Peter Parks, Photo by Brook Rieman, Picture Press RM, Predrag Vuckovic, Roy Hsu, Sergeyryzhov, shapecharge, SolisImages, sturti, Taxi, The Image Bank, Timothy Norris, www.peopleimages.com; LUNCHEAZE; PLAINPICTURE/Jasmin Sander; SHUTTERSTOCK/Anitasstudio, Chiang Ying-Ying/AP, Dmitry Rukhlenko, egd, Gladskikh Tatiana, Hugo Felix, Inxti, Jenny Goodall/Daily Mail, kwanchai.c, Lineicons freebird, Marvel/Paramount/Kobal, Monkey Business Images, Nomad_Soul, Nina Anna, Radu Bercan, Ted Shaffrey/AP, Topseller, Zkruger; ARCHIVO SANTILLANA.

Videos: Lori Herfenist

Printed in Brazil by Forma Certa Gráfica Digital
Lote: 800.391